AND THANK YOU FOR WATCHING

Mark Austin

D0263892

Atlantic Books
London

First published in hardback in Great Britain in 2018 by Atlantic Books,
an imprint of Atlantic Books Ltd.

This paperback edition first published in Great Britain in 2019
by Atlantic Books.

1 3 5 7 9 10 8 6 4 2

A CIP catalogue record for this book is available from the British Library.

E-book ISBN: 978-1-78649-451-1
Paperback ISBN: 978-1-78649-450-4

Printed and bound in Great Britain by
Clays Ltd, Elcograf S.p.A.

Atlantic Books Ltd
Ormond House
26–27 Boswell Street
London WC1N 3JZ

To my family, especially Maddy, who has been to hell and back, and then had the courage to help others.

And to Didier Drogba
19.05.2012

CONTENTS

INTRODUCTION

THIS WAS NOT how it was meant to be. I had always wanted to play cricket for England or be a drummer in a rock 'n' roll band. So what the hell was I doing standing on parched scrubland in the South African bush with a gun to my head?

I had been marched into the field at gunpoint, ordered to look straight ahead and say nothing. If I turned around they would shoot. My mouth was as dry as the terrain around us. The men were angry, very angry, and kept screaming at me. I couldn't understand a word they were saying. I was gripped with fear, felt nauseous and thought I was probably going to die. My young producer, standing alongside me, thought we were definitely going to die. He was shaking. It was his first major foreign assignment. And there we were, side by side, facing possible death at the hands of screaming Afrikaner militiamen. In Bophuthatswana, for God's sake. A place no one had heard of. On a wretched story no one would remember in a few months' time – and, worse, would not matter in a few weeks' time. What a way to go. Wrong place, wrong time... again!

Or not, because the two most prized boasts of the foreign correspondent are 'I was there' and, even better, 'I was there first'. It is what we do. We go. We always go. It is not – in most

1

cases – through any great bravery, or a warped desire to notch up a close scrape in a South African field. It is because we want to be there, we want to witness what is happening and we want to get the story out to the world.

So, wrong place, wrong time? No. In fact, in this business the opposite applies. It is the madness of what we TV news people do. What we choose to do. I was actually in the right place at the right time. It may have turned out to have been the wrong place had that gunman pulled the trigger. But I was where I wanted to be, and yes, where I had to be if I wanted to get the story.

I say this because, if you are reading a book about the life of a foreign correspondent and travelling anchorman, it helps, I guess, to understand what motivates us. It is sometimes glamorous, often exciting and frequently fascinating. But it also can be tedious, dispiriting and routine. And yet time and again we are drawn to places like Afghanistan, Bosnia, Iraq, Syria and Sierra Leone. It is part competitive urge, part a need to be there, and part the desire to seek out the truth – or as close to it as it is possible to get.

I am not one of those war junkie correspondents who thrive on the adrenaline of conflict and witnessing bad stuff. I have known many reporters – male and female – who are in their element in war zones, who love the challenge, who relish the hardship and even find the danger quite alluring. I say this not in criticism; in fact, quite the opposite. I have undiluted admiration for the journalists who do feel that way. They are brave, courageous and resourceful. And the bottom line is this: if they did not go to the godawful places to bear witness, who would do it? Who would be there to cast a light on those dark corners of the world where conflict rages, war crimes are committed and atrocities take place? The answer: no one.

And that is just what those who perpetrate such monstrous outrages want to happen. They want to operate in obscurity, in darkness. Good war reporters don't allow that. They shine a light. The Anthony Loyds, Jeremy Bowens, Marie Colvins (God rest her soul), Christina Lambs, Kim Senguptas, and countless cameramen and women and photographers of this world should be saluted for the work they do.

However, I am not someone who welcomes the danger. I have been to many war zones, but I don't relish it, I don't feel some sort of missionary zeal to do it and I certainly don't enjoy it. The fact is, if you're daft enough to agree to go to these places, and you do it often enough, you will get into difficulties. More often than not the threat is sudden and comes from nowhere, and whether you live or die can be pure luck – which road you take, which hilltop you film from, which hotel you stay in, which local fixer you hire, and who you take advice from.

I have good friends who have been killed or seriously injured in war zones. I was with the ITN reporter Terry Lloyd the night before he and his cameraman and their fixer were killed in Iraq. That story is in this book. The BBC's John Simpson, one of the great foreign correspondents of our age, was with his camera team in northern Iraq when they were bombed by 'friendly forces' who got their coordinates wrong. He survived. Terry didn't. The lottery of war.

I survived, or at least I have so far, largely due to an innate cowardice. In fact, I've found that cowardice is a much better protection than any amount of flak jackets, helmets and armoured vehicles. Cowardice has stopped me going to many places and doing many things in war zones, and I think there are many camera crews and producers who would probably thank me for that. My cowardice has served me well.

This book is not supposed to be just about war stories or close brushes with death. I have included them because that is what I get asked about most often, but also because most intensely insecure TV reporters, particularly those who later sneak off to the comfort and sanctuary of the studio to become presenters, like it to be known that they have earned their spurs, they have seen action and they've been in the thick of it. I guess it's the feeling that you haven't made it until you've been shot at. It really is that pathetic. Honestly.

But this book is also about the other big stories I have been privileged to cover in thirty years as a foreign correspondent and presenter for ITN, and now as Washington correspondent for Sky News.

I write about the Rwandan genocide in 1994 and what it's like to report on a story where almost a million people died at the hands of machete-wielding, grenade-throwing murderers, just because of their ethnicity. Recent African history is replete with outbursts of tribal slaughter, but this was a massacre on an altogether different scale. It was not a simple tale of mutual hatred between rival ethnic groups descending into terrible violence. This was a carefully planned, meticulously carried-out genocide. 'Genocide' is an oft-misused word. Not in this context, though. A green, lush, beautiful land of rolling hills and endless valleys became a vast human abattoir. It is by far and away the most grotesque story I have ever covered. I have yet to meet a journalist who was not deeply affected by what they witnessed there. My friend, the BBC correspondent Fergal Keane, to this day has nightmares about being at the bottom of a pile of rotting corpses that are moving and touching him, 'like a mound of eels at the supermarket'.

I have always managed to compartmentalize much of the bad stuff: detach it, file it away to be forgotten about. But not Rwanda, not what I saw there. Not then, not now, not ever. In his brilliantly written book, *Season of Blood: A Rwandan Journey*, Fergal recalls: 'Although I had seen war before, had seen the face of cruelty, Rwanda belonged in a nightmare zone where my capacity to understand, much less to rationalize, was overwhelmed. This was a country of corpses and orphans and terrible absences. This was where the spirit withered.'

That is it. That is what I felt. Right there... in words I will not be able to match. But I hope nevertheless to convey some sense of what occurred in that godforsaken country.

I also hope there is much to uplift you in this book. I spent time with Nelson Mandela just before and after he became President of South Africa. What a time to be living in Johannesburg that was. Those were intoxicating days in South Africa, a roller coaster of emotion that was mercifully to lead to one of the great moments in modern African history: the inauguration of the country's first-ever black president. I will never forget standing on the lawns in front of the government buildings in Pretoria, looking up at the skies as South African military aircraft staged a flypast in tribute to Mandela. That's the same military that for decades used its machines of war to oppress the entire black population. I listened as Mandela's booming voice rang out: 'We shall build a society in which all South Africans, both black and white, will be able to walk tall, without any fear in their hearts, assured of their inalienable right to human dignity – a rainbow nation at peace with itself and the world.'

It was a magical time. And how joyous, just a couple of weeks earlier, to be up at dawn as the sun rose in the sky, to film the endless queues of people waiting patiently to cast a vote for the very first time. And how they waited. Some standing in line for hours. But they sang and chanted and cheered, knowing that this was the day that would change their lives and their children's lives forever.

Yes, 1994 was quite some year in my life. Mandela's rise, South Africa's freedom, followed by Rwanda's horror – all within a few months of each other. And it was a year made even more memorable by the birth in Johannesburg of our first daughter, Madeleine. Born in the new South Africa, a child of the rainbow nation, she has always held that country close to her heart, as we all have. The few years we spent living there were perhaps the most inspiring period of our lives – or at least they were for me.

But Maddy also features in this book in a way that I would much prefer she didn't. At the age of seventeen, she became seriously ill with the eating disorder anorexia. It nearly killed her. That it didn't was down more to good fortune than anything else. Her ordeal lasted three years, thankfully short for a sufferer of anorexia; it can last for years, even a lifetime. So this book is, on a very personal level, about what happens when your own child becomes the biggest story in your life.

I have written much about the terrible toll that it took. Angered by the lack of resources in this country to deal with anorexia, Maddy and I made a documentary about it. But here I try to describe what it is really like, trying to read the news in front of millions of people every night when your daughter is wasting away at home and you can do absolutely nothing about it. It is an awful condition to witness; it tears away at the very fabric of family life and it tears away at your heart. They were terrible days, watching my sticklike teenager – hollow-eyed, emaciated and devoid of life – just wither away without seeming to care. Why didn't I just stop working? Why didn't I just stay at home and devote all my attention to try to make her better? It's a question I have been asked many times since I first wrote about it. And in this book I try to come up with an answer.

Much of this book was written in the United States, in my apartment in Georgetown, Washington DC, from where I have observed the most extraordinary story in modern politics.

The book opens and closes with the political phenomenon that is Donald J. Trump. As I write, the true extent of the Trump challenge to American democracy and to the cherished ideals and norms of this great country is still being determined. Some – those who voted for him, primarily – would say that is no bad thing. He has upended orthodoxy, changed the Republican Party, infuriated the establishment and ripped up the foreign policy rulebook. But he has done nothing he didn't say he would do. He has been true to himself, to his campaign and to his promises. And in that, there is a core honesty to the man not often acknowledged.

But to others, he represents a crisis of political morality of considerable magnitude that is unsettling and not a little frightening. It is not the fear induced by a clever, strategic, manipulative demagogue who is out to entrench autocratic rule, overturn the rule of law and ditch well-honed democratic principles and freedoms. No, it is the fear – or for some, the excitement – inspired by the unpredictable, the chaotic, the abnormal and the dysfunctional, all of which coexist in this presidency of the bizarre.

That perfect storm is buffeting America right now. The Trump chapters thus have the benefit of being composed virtually as things happen, but such immediacy also imposes unavoidable limitations and risks. Reporting almost as it happens is imperfect for a book like this. It offers little time for proper reflection and perspective, and there will be some events that are overemphasized and others that will appear underplayed in light of new developments.

But at least with Trump there should be no issue of memory failing me. In other chapters covering events and incidents occurring two or three decades ago, that will inevitably be the case, and for that I apologize. I write of those days as I remember them, without diary or perfect recall, and I regret error if and where it appears.

If it sounds a rather harrowing read in parts, I'm afraid it is. But I hope it is also as entertaining and as much fun as this job can often be. There has been so much enjoyment and there have been so many laughs along the way. The crazy journeys, the tales of the unexpected, the mistakes, the humiliations and the great moments of sport I have been lucky enough to witness first-hand – these have all made it an enormously eventful but enjoyable career so far.

When things go wrong in television news, which they often do, we tend to take ourselves far too seriously. I know I do. We think it is the most important job in the world. We hate losing to the opposition, we hate falling short. But I've come to learn that perspective is one of the greatest qualities a journalist can possess, but one that is most often in short supply.

My wife – an A & E doctor – is far more rational. She really does work in a world that is life and death on a daily basis. She does it quietly and undramatically. And she will always throw the same words at me when I bang on about a failure or a mistake or a job badly done.

'Yes, it's important,' she will say, 'but in the end, it's only television.'

And she's right.

TRUMPTOWN

NO ONE SAW it coming. No one. No one, that is, except a rock band called Rage Against The Machine. In 2000, while shooting a video on Wall Street, they forced the New York Stock Exchange to close early. At one point in the finished video, you see an onlooker holding up a sign proclaiming 'Donald J. Trump for President'. Protest and prescience... quite some performance. In truth, it probably had more to do with the director of the video, Michael Moore.

'I think it was either Michael Moore's idea or one of his staffers,' Rage guitarist Tom Morello told a New York newspaper. 'It wasn't a warning, it was just meant to be a joke – pure humour. But it turned out to be Nostradamus-like.'

If it was Moore, a well-known leftwing filmmaker and activist, then hats off to him. But even he can't have meant it seriously. Not sixteen years before the event. Much later he did predict that Trump would be the Republican nominee for president. And he went on the following year to foresee his eventual victory. In a now-celebrated blog he said: 'This wretched, ignorant, dangerous part-time clown and full-time sociopath is going to be our next president. President Trump.

Go ahead and say the words, 'cause you'll be saying them for the next four years: "PRESIDENT TRUMP."'

And, of course, that is exactly what the world is saying: President Trump. And the world is getting used to it. *President Trump...* it trips off the tongue like you never thought it would.

Michael Moore – whose political bias against Trump is self-evident – may choke when he says those words, but he saw it on the horizon, he saw what was happening in America and elsewhere; he saw the new politics that was unfolding.

Most of the rest of us didn't. Certainly I didn't, and neither did others supposedly more in tune than me with what is happening here in the US. Not the media – at least, not the increasingly smug, complacent, centre-left-leaning, liberal progressive, mainstream media – who failed to appreciate what was happening outside their immediate metropolitan elite circles. Not the politicians, and not even the pollsters, whose job it is to know these things.

To all of them, the political events of 2016 came as a terrible shock. Brexit, Trump and the rise of the populist far right in continental Europe were unforeseen, inexplicable and alien. To them, it was as if the world had lost its senses, as if the natural order of things was thrown into tumult, as if prejudice and ignorance was running amok. It was unsettling and it challenged assumptions.

The game had changed. Out was the old politics of left and right. In was a new politics, more complex and more assertive. It was the politics of revolt.

Trump has an innate ability to identify an opportunity and exploit it. He spoke to, persuaded and eventually dazzled parts of America that felt the country was no longer theirs, and who were crying out for someone to speak up on their behalf. Trump was that man. For all his foibles, weaknesses and character flaws, he was the one politician who seemed to care – and he played the part brilliantly.

His timing was ingenious. America was ready for him, and he was ready for America. He had also become a big name. It helped that he had starred in a primetime reality show, *The Apprentice*, for fourteen seasons, and had given hundreds of interviews. CNN worked out that he had spent more time in front of a camera than even the Hollywood movie actor Ronald Reagan.

So, Trump mastered the media, then manipulated it for his own purposes and ultimately turned it into enemy number one. It was all very clever, insightful and perfectly legitimate as a political calculation, and highlights the great strength of Donald Trump.

Less legitimate – in fact, downright cynical – was his courting of a subset of American voters who remain consumed by racial prejudice. These are not only white supremacists, but also a substantial block of the white working class who fear immigration and harbour resentment against the black and Latin American minorities in America.

How did he do it? Well, partly by questioning the birthplace of America's first black president, Barack Obama. 'I'm starting to think that he was not born here,' he said. There was not a shred of evidence to support Trump's claims, but it gained traction with a racist minority that he decided were his potential voters. It was deeply cynical, hugely offensive to many, but also highly effective.

And just as effective was his promise to build the wall along the border with Mexico. He played on the fears of many white working people about the growth of immigration. Across the Midwest rust belt of America, in towns where steel and coal jobs were being decimated and livelihoods ruined, he spread the message that immigrants were the problem: *You don't have your jobs because of immigrants.* It wasn't true. Their jobs were gone. No one had them. But again it resonated, it hit home.

Even the *Access Hollywood* tape – in which he can be heard boasting about how he treats women, and how when you're a powerful celebrity you can do anything, even 'grab 'em by the pussy' – even that didn't stall his progress to the White House. It was extraordinary.

It was also, of course, as much a vote against Hillary Clinton as it was for Donald Trump. While Trump courted the white working class, Hillary Clinton ignored it. Part of the blame, perhaps, lies indirectly with her husband Bill. The immensely popular former president expanded the appeal of the Democratic Party, and it became the party of choice for the professional classes of America.

Lawyers, teachers and the educated classes began embracing the party of Bill Clinton in large numbers. The Democrats, for so long the natural home for blue-collar workers across America, had changed. Many in the working classes saw this transformation and resented it. It also didn't help that while Trump made several visits to the Midwest of the US, Hillary made only a few.

For all these reasons, the greatest political earthquake in the history of modern America was triggered.

At the election in 2016, Trump won 63 million votes, and tens of millions of voters continue to support him. No one believed it until it happened. He stunned America, the world – and, by his own admission to colleagues, himself.

Yes, Trump is in the White House. It's for real. And it's the single most extraordinary political story of my lifetime. So when the opportunity came to spend a year covering this phenomenon called the 'Trump presidency' for Sky News, I leapt at the chance and hotfooted it to Washington DC, where this bizarre, thrilling, crazy, intoxicating, unedifying, depressing, unpredictable drama is being played out on a daily basis.

Every day, almost every hour, seems to bring another remarkable twist or turn in the Trump story. It is a story like no other, and it raises all sorts of questions about how to report it.

Just as there are no rules for President Donald Trump – or no rules that we recognize – so the rules have changed when it comes to covering him. On my several visits to Washington pre-Trump, it always surprised me how deferential journalists were towards presidents, and senior politicians in general. But particularly presidents. There has long been a reverence among reporters for the office of the president, which has always translated to whichever individual happens to be occupying the White House. It is just the way it is. It is a marked contrast to Britain, where, if anything, the general attitude of the press towards politicians, even prime ministers, is one of scepticism, suspicion, sometimes ridicule and often outright contempt.

In America, those who go into politics are genuinely seen as serving the American people and serving the country. In

Britain, they are often seen as serving themselves, and in it for the publicity and the expenses. Broadly speaking, Britain is way too disdainful; and America has been way too respectful.

Not anymore. With Trump has come an erosion of the media's respect for the presidency. In fact, following his sustained attack on many of the country's mainstream news outlets and his tedious 'fake news' retort to anything he disagrees with, it is not so much an erosion as a complete disintegration of respect for the president. It makes for an uncomfortable and often unpleasant relationship. It is tense, demeaning and unedifying. And it is ultimately bad for democracy, and for holding the government to account.

On arriving in Washington DC, in September 2017, I had a problem: how to cover this extraordinary story and this unusual, unpredictable and nonconformist president.

I had noticed the reporting of many mainstream TV correspondents was tinged with a kind of haughty disdain for Trump, which at times turned to outright contempt. Certainly, CNN and MSNBC are openly and unapologetically critical of Trump. They really do have nothing good to say about him. I am stunned by some of the coverage from previously largely impartial media outlets.

There is no question that Trump – with his weird combover, orange complexion, habitual tweeting, glib pronouncements, and strange ways – cuts a vaguely comedic figure as president. But he is also occupying the office of the most powerful leader in the world. Everything he says and does is significant, has consequences and shouldn't be trivialized or dismissed.

As I flew across the pond, I also thought that he deserved to be treated with the same seriousness and respect as previous presidents. He had won an election, after all. The people of America had decided that Donald J. Trump was the man to represent and lead them around the world, and that was important. Free elections sometimes throw up random and awkward results, but that is the nature of democracy – and the job of a journalist, or at least a correspondent working for an impartial British television news channel, should be to report in good faith and without bias what the president does and says, what it may mean, and what the consequences are likely to be.

Anyway, who's to say this was an 'awkward' or 'random' result? As I arrived in Washington, some journalists and columnists were already reporting the Trump presidency as some sort of political 'freak show'. It is much easier to mock this president than to take him seriously, but trying to be fair is the challenge you have to set yourself every day. My view was that if enough Americans had deemed him a suitable candidate for the White House, why should I sneer?

In London, before flying out, I'd asked John Ryley, the boss of Sky News, how he thought I should go about reporting this strange phenomenon. 'You must report it as it deserves to be reported,' he said. 'And try not to lose the sense of impartiality.' He said this as if he knew it might be difficult.

So I pitched up in DC with the firm intent to give President Trump the benefit of the doubt. I wanted to find out about his followers and what motivates and drives their support for him, and I wanted to ensure I gave their views a real airing. In short, I wanted to cover President Trump as I would any other American president.

It soon became obvious that this would be impossible. The sheer unrelenting deluge of news from the Trump White House was overwhelming. Almost every week brought a new drama that would provoke a media frenzy for seventy-two hours or so, until, as sure as night follows day, it would be usurped by the next one. And it would be Trump's reaction to the media reaction to the initial drama that would keep the story rolling frenetically along.

Covering this White House is unremitting, and a bit like trying to drink from a fire hose. You can't really do it, and no one turns the fire hose off, so in the end you just stand there and get drenched. Trump is a day-to-day, moment-to-moment presence in your working life, and one's reporting of him becomes instinctive and emotionally driven in a way that I am not sure is terribly useful to the public.

'You know Trump is a pathological liar,' a senior correspondent with a top US broadcaster said to me within a few days of my arrival in Washington. 'He tells untruths and seldom gets called out for it.'

I disagree with him. I think Trump tells lies but he does generally get caught out and challenged. The fact checking site, PolitiFact, has never been busier... Early in the presidency it deemed that just 5 per cent of Trump's statements were true and 26 per cent were mostly true. But a huge 69 per cent were found to be basically porky pies – the worst rating for a president. And most papers or political magazines have tried to chronicle Trumps fibs at one time or another. The *Washington*

Post decided that Trump made 492 false or misleading claims in his first 100 days. *Politico*'s Maria Konnikova made the point that all presidents lie but that Trump 'is in a different category. The sheer frequency, spontaneity and seeming irrelevance of his lies have no precedent.'

She argues that Nixon, Reagan and Clinton were economical with the truth or lied to protect their own reputations, but 'Trump seems to lie for the pure joy of it'.

It began on day one, with his claims of the largest inauguration crowd ever. It set a pattern. He also claimed Hillary Clinton had five million illegal voters and that he had the longest list of congressional achievements since Roosevelt, even before his tax bill was passed. It was preposterous.

Elizabeth Drew, a political journalist and author who has covered six presidents, told me: 'Trump lies far more than any president ever. He lies all the time, every day. You've seen the statistics, they're stunning.'

The *New York Times* columnist, Charles M. Blow, went further: 'Trump's incessant lying is obscene. It is a collapse in morality; it is an ethical assault.'

I know what he means. The danger is that, eventually, constant lying will batter a nation and its people into submission. It becomes a kind of distorted reality, and in the end people are too exhausted to question or fight back.

Watching him up close in Washington and around the country, I am not at all sure that Donald Trump is wilfully dishonest. It seems to me that he sometimes says the first thing that comes into his head to defend his position. I am certainly not saying that Trump has even a token obedience to the truth, but sometimes he just repeats claims he's heard that suit his arguments, and other times I think he just lazily throws out figures or what he believes are facts.

The one thing about Trump is that he hates being wrong – he can't be wrong – so he has a habit of trying to persuade his audiences that he's not wrong. And sometimes that involves some creative thinking.

What he unequivocally does do, it seems to me, is sow confusion at every turn. I was sat in my Washington apartment one evening when a news alert sounded on my mobile. It was nothing major, but it was to become hugely illustrative of the way the Trump presidency was playing out.

The alert said: 'Democrat leaders say deal agreed with Trump on Dreamers, tied to border security and excluding the wall.' In short, it was about a group of several hundred thousand immigrants who had come to America illegally with their parents and who had no official papers. President Obama had afforded these so-called Dreamers some protection, but Donald Trump, playing to his core support on immigration, wanted to remove that protection. So, it was a good story if Mr Trump had changed his mind, an even better one if he was also giving up his plans to build that big wall all along the Mexican border.

The following morning, Donald Trump tweeted: 'No deal was made last night on DACA. Massive border security would have to be agreed to in exchange for consent'.

Then this: 'The WALL …will be built'.

The clear suggestion of the tweets was that the wall was part of the deal over protection of the immigrants' status. But a few hours later, he arrived in Florida on a visit and told reporter that the wall would be built but would come later.

By now, everyone having to report on this was scratching their heads. And then this presidential tweet pinged onto journalist's iPhones: 'Does anybody really want to throw out good educated and accomplished young people who have jobs, some serving in the military? Really!'

So a man whose campaign promise had been to build a wall as soon as he came to power, and to end the protection for the Dreamers, was now less than committed to both plans. Or at least he seemed to be. No one quite knew.

I was asked to go on air and talk to Kay Burley in London about the story. 'Give me a few minutes,' I said. We phoned the White House for clarity. We didn't get it. 'The president's words speak for themselves,' I was told. And that, loosely translated, means they didn't know. I am not even sure if Trump himself knew. Or whether the White House knew whether he knew...

I went on national television and tried to explain. I don't think I got away with it.

But Trump does get away with it. The very fact that he's in the White House is evidence of that. He's living proof that politicians can get away with telling voters just about anything that sounds good, no matter how unlikely or implausible it is. After all, Trump promised to cut taxes, and to his credit, he delivered; but he also promised to increase spending on infrastructure. He promised to provide healthcare to all Americans and pay off the national debt. He promised to build a wall at Mexico's expense. He promised all these things, and paid no price for the obvious inconsistency of the promises.

Now, show me a politician who doesn't spray around empty promises at election time and I'll show you a pig soaring through the sky. But the Donald took this to a new level of disingenuousness. He just said things that he thought would appeal to millions of voters, fed up with the political elite and the establishment, and the people, or at least many of them, lapped it up.

But delivering on those promises is another matter altogether. It is notoriously difficult for any American president to do half the stuff they've pledged to do during a campaign. President Obama won the White House, but fought a constant battle with both Houses of Congress, often dominated by his political opponents. He struggled.

Now, President Trump has all the advantages of a Republican president working with a Republican-controlled Congress, so it should be easier. But not so. Such is the extraordinary nature of Trump's promises that when they collide with political realities they sometimes crash and burn.

But, here's the thing about Donald Trump. However many problems or obstacles he encounters in delivering on his pledges, however many unfulfilled promises or uncovered lies, his core support seems to be unwavering. And that is largely because they believe he is really trying to deliver on his campaign pledges. And they also believe him when he says others are to blame when he can't deliver. It's the fault of the Democrats or the establishment or the system. Anyone and anything, but not Trump. Not at all.

And there is something about the way Trump relates to and connects with his supporters, something in his language and tone, that means he is able to carry it off. It is a skill that is instinctive and natural to him. It cannot be taught, and I am not sure I have seen a politician anywhere in the world who carries it off with quite the same success.

Within weeks of arriving in Washington, I realized he was an extraordinary political animal who operates like no other politician. He is a bruiser, a narcissist and an instinctive purveyor of untruths, but he is also a clever political operator. Elizabeth Drew – who knows a thing or two about presidents – believes Trump is 'shrewd but not wise'.

He knows what will appeal to his core vote and he is unafraid to pander to it, even if it means alienating supposed allies. And he has no hesitation in jeopardizing America's special relationship with the UK if it means he can score a hit with his supporters.

Shortly after I arrived for my assignment, I was awoken early by a call from London telling me there had been a terror attack on a tube train in Parsons Green, in south-west London. Only scant details were known. 'What's it got to do with me?' I asked rather petulantly.

What it had to do with me was that Donald Trump was already commenting about the attack on Twitter, his favoured form of communication. His first offering was this: 'Another attack in London by a loser terrorist. These are sick and demented people who were in the sights of Scotland Yard. Must be proactive!'

How on earth did he know the perpetrators were known to the police? How did he even know who they were? It had only just happened.

And a moment later this: 'Loser terrorists must be dealt with in a much tougher manner.'

And then, tellingly, Trump added that his own proposed ban on visitors to the US from predominantly Muslim countries should be 'far larger, tougher and more specific'.

So there he is, spouting forth about an attack in Britain, and at the same time promoting his own controversial measures and policies – even if it meant, at the same time, annoying the authorities in Britain. In Trump's world, that's fine.

Now if Trump really did know the intelligence about who the attackers were, it was a grotesque breach of protocol that undermines the relationship between the US and the UK. If he didn't, if he was just guessing – or worse, just talking tough to appeal to his voters – then that is equally unacceptable. I know for a fact that senior figures at Scotland Yard and within MI5 were furious at the unwarranted and unwelcome intervention.

But, the point is, Trump doesn't care. It suited him domestically to appear tough on terrorism. He'd upset Republicans by apparently reaching out to Democrats on the Dreamer issue and here was the opportunity to rebalance things and mollify his political base.

He'd done exactly the same thing earlier that year. In June, he had criticized London's mayor Sadiq Khan over the city's response to another terrorist attack. Again it was on Twitter, and again an unguarded post caused no end of diplomatic trouble.

How Donald Trump got his 'intelligence' information so soon after the Parsons Green bombing is also instructive of the modus operandi of Donald Trump.

Shortly before his initial fusillade of tweets that September morning, a security analyst, Jim Hanson, had appeared on Fox News, the right-wing TV station in the US that Trump watches habitually in the morning. Hanson had said: 'My fear again is that we're going to find out this is someone who is known to the police.'

A website for Mr Hanson's firm, Security Studies Group, says it focuses on 'defending the value of American power against the true threats we face', and talks about a Washington elite that has been 'unable or unwilling to address and communicate the most basic requirements of American nationhood'. So, in other words, Mr Hanson is a 'Make America Great Again' Trump supporter.

The most likely scenario is that the president was watching his mate on Fox, took what he said at face value, because why wouldn't he, and then fired off his tweets. The White House did not deny he had been watching Fox. Jim Hanson or MI6? I know which I would trust.

It was ten hours before Trump tweeted what he should have tweeted in the first place: 'Our hearts & prayers go out to the people of London'.

The whole thing summed up the Trump way of doing things. The picture is of a president who makes instinctive policy decisions on the hoof, depending on the political weather at that particular time. In my first few weeks in Washington, as hard as I tried, it was difficult to detect any consistent political philosophy underpinning the Trump presidency.

It was rather a never-ending series of adjustments or recalculations designed to satisfy or enrage whoever he felt needed satisfying or enraging. Trump is a tactician rather than a strategist. He is a dealmaker, he is transactional, and like all politicians he keeps a close eye on the opinion polls. The Trump strategy is that there is no strategy.

Elizabeth Drew put it to me like this: 'Trump makes a lot of noise and dominates the scene through sheer force of personality and lack of inhibition, feeling no need to observe the norms, which can take him into risky territory... The sheer dazzlingness of his performance makes us forget what it's about.' She calls him the 'somewhat corpulent Flying Wallenda of politics'. And she is not alone in expressing alarm at the lasting damage he may be doing to American political culture and institutions including the Republican Party.

What many people also worry about is what he is doing to America's standing in the world. Whoever the president was, whoever was leading the country – whether Republican or Democrat – there has long been an acceptance, in the West certainly, that, despite all the flaws, America is, broadly speaking, a force for good. Not simply a heavily armed policeman patrolling the globe, restraining, tackling or extinguishing threats to peace and stability; but a beacon of freedom and liberty and democracy, a country upholding an enlightened world order.

But Donald Trump seems dismissive of the notion that America should stand up for anything but itself. The 'America First' philosophy is popular in many parts of the country, but my concern is that it turns the country in on itself rather than embracing the interconnectivity of this world.

'America First does not mean America alone' is an oft-repeated mantra of the Trump administration. And yet, slowly but surely, the United States is becoming more isolated from its traditional allies. Trump's decision to withdraw from the Iran nuclear agreement is a case in point. Trump was so set on scrapping the deal – and some believe it was simply because it was Obama's signature achievement – that he had no qualms about upsetting every single Western European ally.

I witnessed the most extraordinary diplomatic love-in between Trump and French president Emmanuel Macron in Washington. It was a spring romance to lift the heart. But – and here's the point – it did not even survive the month of May. Trump's decision on Iran did for that. *Une affaire provisoire.* And Trump – who apparently knows a thing or two about affairs – didn't care. The only really special relationship seems to be between Trump and his core supporters.

Correction: he also cares about his relationship with Israel. His decision – long considered but never implemented by previous presidents – to move the US embassy in Israel from Tel Aviv to Jerusalem was again done in the face of huge opposition from European allies. But it played well with many Jewish voters, and, particularly, with a few very wealthy Jewish donors. The fact it was also followed by bloodshed and dozens of deaths among protesting Palestinians didn't seem to matter. He sent his son-in-law, Jared Kushner, to Israel for the occasion. It was also Kushner's job to resuscitate a peace process the move to Jerusalem had effectively killed off.

Successive American presidents of either party have always advocated that a democratic and unified Europe was in the best interests of the United States. But Donald Trump seems to think otherwise. He fetes nationalists set on dismantling the

European Union, for instance. He pointedly met Nigel Farage, the former leader of the UK Independence Party, before he met Prime Minister Theresa May. He cheered Brexit, and taunted Germany over their trade imbalance with the US.

Further, he called NATO 'obsolete' and complained about American obligations to an organization whose members were not all paying their way. It actually worked. Trump's threat to leave brought an immediate dividend of about $30 billion in extra revenue.

To stand alone, strong but isolated, above all others but also apart? Is that really the way forward? Trump maybe thinks so. It reminds me of a saying that has always stuck with me: 'If you want to go fast, go alone. If you want to go far, go together.'

Trump is often teased for his apparent respect for authoritarian leaders like Russia's President Putin. It was a predilection that manifested itself in the strangest of ways as he began the second year of his presidency.

He ordered the Pentagon to come up with options for a grand military parade through Washington DC. He had admired the pageantry of the Bastille Day parade on a visit to Paris, and wanted to 'outdo' the French with a display of American military might.

This from a president who had appointed several serving or former generals to key positions in his administration, and who had made many heavily political speeches and announcements in front of military audiences.

It was another break with an established norm: that the military's separation from partisan politics was to be respected by the executive. This was Trump politicizing the military, turning it into a political prop for him to use to satisfy his base and also to send out a warning to his political enemies. It was as if he were saying, 'I have supreme power because I own the military.' It was the stuff of autocratic regimes, and it unsettled many in both the military and politics.

It may simply be that Donald Trump saw a military parade as an extension of his tactic of using patriotism, and the flag as a core issue that played well for him. But it leads the military into difficult waters. At best, it makes life awkward for the generals; at worst, it tarnishes the military's integrity and compromises its independence.

As one Iraq veteran put it: 'Our service members have better things to do than march in Washington, at a time when we remain committed in Syria, Iraq and Afghanistan.'

It is sometimes difficult to know quite how the rest of the world views Trump, although there was a telling moment after one of his first major overseas trips. I was sitting in the Sky News office in DC one lunchtime, when the White House suddenly announced an address by the president that afternoon. Trump had just returned from a two-week, five-country, three-summit trip to Asia, and had received, at best, lukewarm reviews in the mainstream media. The *New York Times* – or the 'Failing New York Times' in Trump-speak – had described him as a 'bewildering figure to countries that had already viewed [him] with anxiety', and they questioned his achievements on the tour.

Trump was clearly furious. First, he posted a series of angry tweets calling the *NYT* 'naive', 'dumb' and 'failing', and then he called an astonishing press conference. It amounted to a thirty-minute paean to himself. It was self-indulgent, self-justifying and self-congratulatory: 'They treated me personally with warmth, hospitality and respect... real respect.' He said he was leading the 'Great American Comeback' and insisted America's standing in the world had never been greater.

There was no question Trump had been welcomed warmly. There were red carpets, state banquets, ceremonial welcomes and fawning speeches. The *New York Times* said President Trump made the mistake of mistaking flattery, which was doled out in spades, for respect. It was enough for Donald Trump to be able to say 'they loved me'; ergo, it was a triumph. But the truth of the trip was there was little of substance to report and little to shout about. The whole performance was extraordinary... and definitely not normal.

Trump came to power partly on a promise to change things and 'drain the swamp' of Washington politics. It was a noble intention, but he filled his cabinet with zillionaires and a few have been embroiled in allegations of spending public money in wasteful ways. Just the sort of behaviour he professed to want to eradicate.

Washington needs to change, but in attempting to do so Trump is also trampling on some of the accepted norms in American public life. And the erosion of customs and traditions is worrying many Americans. Centuries to forge; months to dismantle; years to rebuild? That is how they fear it could be.

While I was in DC I was asked many times why I didn't forget about Trump and report more on other stuff going on around America. And it's true, it was very easy just to concentrate on the incessant news emerging from the White House, to the exclusion of other important issues.

But my feeling was that to stop reporting all the Trump stuff, the day-to-day craziness of the presidency, would be to accept that it was becoming routine and normal. I felt strongly we shouldn't do that. The last thing America and the West needs during the Trump presidency is a lazy, compliant, accepting media. Holding power to account is always the responsibility of a free press.

In a way, the Trump White House has become a sort of cult of personality rather than a regular presidency. There is nothing necessarily wrong with that. In fact, his speeches can be riveting. He breaks away from the script with ad-libbed passages delivered in a language his supporters understand and relate to. It is hugely effective on occasions, it is not easy to do, and it's brave. Trump does not get enough credit for his speeches.

But just as it was Trump's character and personality that won him the office and served him well during the campaign, so it was to become less helpful to him once he was actually governing. Many of his problems stem from his character, particularly his impulsiveness.

His firing of the FBI director James Comey may have satisfied his *Apprentice*-style love of summarily dispatching people from his presence. But it was to cause him no end of trouble. Comey was leading a criminal investigation into whether Mr Trump's top advisers colluded with the Russian government to try to steer the outcome of the 2016 election.

It was bizarre timing, and raised the immediate spectre of political interference by a sitting president into an investigation by the main law enforcement agency. It was a rash move that was to have far-reaching consequences. It immediately led to Democratic calls for a special counsel to lead the Russian inquiry. And it was that investigation, led by Robert Mueller, that was to haunt Trump for months.

The inquiry became an obsession with the media, it arguably took attention away from alleged wrongdoing by the Clinton campaign involving a secret dossier on Trump and the Russians, and it drove the president to distraction. At every press conference he would scream, 'No collusion,' and repeat it several times. It was a PR disaster of the president's own making.

He also became convinced of political bias among top FBI and Department of Justice officials – some of whom he had appointed. He waged war against them, believing they deliberately precipitated the investigation into collusion with Russia by somehow joining forces with a British former MI6 officer in the pay of his enemy Hillary Clinton, who produced a secret dossier.

He even insisted that a classified memo, produced by the Republican leader of the House of Representatives' intelligence committee, be released without redactions, a move that infuriated his own intelligence chiefs.

Democratic leaders believed that Trump would use the memo – which was not all it seemed – as reason to fire Robert Mueller. That would have been political suicide for Trump, and he probably knew it. He desisted, or at least he had at the time of writing. But he was determined, at the very least, to undermine the investigation into his Russia links. It seemed to become his mission in life.

And the extent of Trump's links to Russia is the great mystery of his presidency. It is difficult to work out. There has been a good deal of speculation that his real estate empire had taken large amounts of money from oligarchs linked to the Kremlin; there were unsubstantiated rumours that he had engaged in sexual shenanigans with hookers while he was in Moscow running the Miss Universe contest; and there were unconfirmed claims that Russian intelligence had compromising material.

His reaction to the Special Counsel's indictments against thirteen Russian individuals for meddling in the 2016 elections was strange. He didn't respond to Russia's assault on America's democracy at all. He was muted and quiescent in a way that was truly bizarre. And it was seized upon by the *New York Times* columnist Thomas Friedman, who couldn't come up with a reason for Trump's reticence:

> … whatever it is, Trump is either trying so hard to hide it or is so naïve about Russia that he is ready to not only resist mounting a proper defense of our democracy, he's actually ready to undermine some of our most important institutions, the FBI and the Justice Department, to keep his compromised status hidden.
>
> That must not be tolerated. This is code red. The biggest threat to the integrity of our democracy today is in the Oval Office.

What also became clear to me, after a year of covering this president, is that there are in fact many Donald Trumps. There is Trump the dealmaker; there is Trump the base seducer, who indulges his core support at every opportunity; there is Trump the flip-flopper, the guy who listens to the last person to talk to him; and there's Trump the gunslinger, who fires off insults and abuse to anyone who offends him.

In January 2018, the many Trumps all started fighting each other and there was no clear winner. They basically started brawling on the Oval Office carpet while, outside, the government was grinding to a halt. Congress was at loggerheads over the funding bill, and at midnight on Friday 19 January, the government shut down.

The date is significant because the following day marked a year since he was sworn into office. On that anniversary, the government was shut down, there were women's marches in cities across America, and the Trumps were beating themselves up in the White House. It was not how it was meant to be.

The Trump punch-up was over the issue of the Dreamers – the children of illegal immigrant parents who the Democrats were insisting be given protected status. Republicans and Democrats in the Senate could not agree on a funding bill with Dreamer protection linked to it. Trump the dealmaker wanted to forge an agreement; Trump the base seducer wanted to stand firm and appear tough on immigration; Trump the flip-flopper couldn't make up his mind; and Trump the gunslinger just wanted to fire off tweets blaming the Democrats for the crisis.

Result: Trump sat stewing in the White House while political chaos reigned. In the end, the shutdown was short-lived and it was the Democrats who backed down, but Trump was still the target of their criticism.

The Senate minority leader, Chuck Schumer, said: 'The great dealmaking president just sat on the sidelines.' Many

Republicans also bemoaned a president who didn't seem to understand the complex issues involved, and who didn't stand up to be counted when it mattered. I think it is unfair criticism – Congress got him into the mess, and he felt Congress should get him out of it.

But the point is that the Democrats backed down, and Trump could claim victory very quickly. At this point, the gunslinger Trump kicked in and he taunted the Democrats, not something that would make a deal any easier. It was as if winning the political battle was more important than the issue itself. I am not sure he actually cared about the Dreamers.

The whole spectacle of the government shutting down as both parties squabbled over highly partisan policies was pretty unedifying. It was a good example of why Trump's election mantra – 'Drain the Swamp' – caught the mood of many Americans. The whole situation reminded me of a line in one of Marvin Gaye's protest songs: 'Politics and hypocrites is turning us all into lunatics.'

And if the Trump circus wasn't enough, my arrival in Washington coincided with hurricane season in the United States.

I was still trying to adjust to the time difference when my mobile rang at some ungodly hour of the morning. It was Emily Purser, a Sky News producer, who uttered a sentence I will never forget. 'Mark,' she said, 'sorry to wake you at 6.30 but the office want to send us to the Bahamas.'

As a welcome to my new job, I thought that would take some beating. Unfortunately, as so often happens in this line of work, we would be flying in just as everyone else was leaving.

Hurricane Irma was on its way, having already devastated the Caribbean islands of Barbuda and St Martin. Now it was the Bahamas, and then possibly Florida in its path, and the Sky News foreign desk decided a spot of storm chasing was what I needed.

We flew to Charlotte in the Carolinas and managed to jump on one of the last flights into Nassau, capital of the Bahamas. There were ten people on the flight and we were three of them. You'll not be surprised to hear that the Bahamas isn't such an attractive holiday destination when it's in the path of a storm packing winds of 150 miles an hour.

We got there, we went live several times predicting a dooms-day scenario and we were the main story on Sky News for a few hours. The producers loved it; the people of the Bahamas braced themselves and feared the worst. Not for the first time, I felt distinctly uncomfortable that a major catastrophe – or, in this case, an imminent one – should cause such palpable excitement in newsrooms.

Anyway, mercifully for the people of the Bahamas, Hurricane Irma turned left at the last moment and virtually missed us. It slammed into Cuba instead. We were in the wrong place, with no story, and the airport was closed.

We were stuck. At the insistence of our cameraman Duncan Sharp, we checked into a hotel called the Atlantis. It was vast, gaudy and awful, and the walk to my room was ten minutes via a ghastly casino where I lost two hundred dollars at blackjack.

A week later, however, we did get hit by a different hurricane on a different island. This time it was Hurricane Maria, which smashed into Puerto Rico as a Category 5 storm with winds of

155 miles per hour. I had never experienced anything like it. From a balcony at the Sheraton hotel in San Juan, we filmed its ferocity and the destruction it caused. We ventured out once it eased slightly to a Category 4, but I was knocked over, bruising my ribs, and we abandoned any notion of courage under nature's fire.

The following day, we headed out to the worst-hit areas and filmed the devastation, which was considerable. Vast areas of one of the poorest American territories were destroyed. Homes, businesses and hospitals were damaged, and 90 per cent of the island was left without power. The electric grid was so badly hit that the authorities predicted some parts of the island would be without electricity for six months or more.

I recount this story because it is more instructive of Donald J. Trump than it is of a hurricane called Maria.

Trump's response was slow and his disengagement was obvious. As the real extent of the damage and suffering became clear, he was more concerned with picking a fight with NFL stars who were kneeling during the national anthem to protest police brutality against African Americans. He showed scant interest in the ordeal of 3.3 million people in the American territory of Puerto Rico.

Eventually, the mayor of the Puerto Rican capital San Juan, Carmen Yulín Cruz, was pleading for help on American network television. 'We are dying,' she told President Trump.

Trump responded not with sympathy, understanding and increased aid and resources for the island, but instead with a blistering attack on the beleaguered mayor and her people. Typically, of course, it was delivered on Twitter: 'Such poor leadership ability by the Mayor of San Juan, and others in Puerto Rico, who are not able to get their workers to help. They want everything done for them.'

This is typical Trump. When under fire, fire back with interest. He simply cannot accept criticism, act on it or ignore it, and move on. He has to bring a shotgun to a fist fight and use it. It may satisfy his bristling pride and ego, but in this case it seemed massively counterproductive. His response brought a marginally negative story to the front burner and turned it into a partisan political scrap. Most Puerto Ricans identify with the Democrats, not the Republicans.

There may have been other examples of American presidents demeaning and humiliating public officials trying to cope with a disaster... but I can't think of one.

And what about 'they want everything done for them'? This is the bit that is either unwittingly or deliberately borderline racist – it doesn't really matter which. It is red meat for his core support, America's disillusioned white working class who voted for him in such numbers. This is the bit that says Puerto Ricans are lazy, looking for handouts and expecting something for nothing.

And that wasn't all. The next tweet in this Saturday morning sequence told us even more about Trump. It read: 'The Mayor of San Juan, who was very complimentary only a few days ago, has now been told by the Democrats that you must be nasty to Trump.'

Nasty to Trump... there you have it. You have a major humanitarian crisis on your doorstep, you have millions of people without power, drinking water, enough food or medical supplies, and yet the president perceives this unfolding drama as being about him. He is unable to view it through any other prism.

This is astonishing stuff from an American president. In a few impetuous tweets, you have the Trump character laid bare. But you also have a glimpse of the political operator at work. He is somehow turning what should be a vote-losing, badly handled disaster into an event that plays well with his base. I don't know how he does it, but he does it. Time and time again.

Trump is hard to admire. His manner is offhand and often childishly antagonistic, his style of diplomacy is brash and one-dimensional. He is dealing with both North Korea and Iran in precisely the same way: threaten to unleash the world's most powerful military, impose tough sanctions, and wait for them to cave in. Indeed, it's as if the same swaggering brinkmanship that served him so well in the shady, thug-dominated world of Atlantic City casinos and New York real estate is now apparent in his dealings on the international stage. His crude, back-alley scrapping with Kim Jong-un suggested we were rushing headlong towards nuclear disaster, led by two narcissistic schoolyard bullies. But it brought North Korea to the table. It's impossible to predict how it will work out, but maybe Trump is on to something. Maybe it really is that simple when dealing with dictators, Iranian spiritual leaders and China's communist autocrats. It's a risk, though. Fine if it works, less ideal if it doesn't. His options narrow alarmingly if it doesn't, and conflict becomes much more likely.

Trump's way of international dealing is a different way but not necessarily a wrong way. A lot of his supporters broadly agree with him, and it certainly doesn't mean he is incapable of succeeding. You may sometimes deplore the way he conducts himself, but it would be a foolish mistake to consider his methods and ideas unpopular or out of touch.

Treat him with contempt at your peril, because he revels in that and thrives on it. When Hillary Clinton referred to a section of his support as a 'basket of deplorables', she was playing into his hands. It rallied his core supporters against her, and may also have persuaded some undecided voters to go for Trump. She paid the price at the polls.

Trump is a president who does things unconventionally but he is also, in many ways, a president to be reckoned with. I'm on the political roller-coaster ride of the century... and I am loving every minute of it.

NOTES FROM A SMALL NEWSPAPER

THE FIRST LESSON I learned in my first job in journalism was that no one likes subeditors. They are, in truth, a breed apart. The 'subs' on the *Bournemouth Evening Echo* were – by and large – elderly, pipe-smoking, intimidating, eccentric figures, who occupied a rather gloomy, tobacco-smoke-filled office where reporters were seldom welcome.

Peter Tait, Jack Straight and Austin Brooks, wonderful names all, were veterans of the game I was starting out in. They were characters, but it seemed to me they derived their working pleasure from unnecessarily redrafting stories, rewriting your best paragraphs, and competing among themselves for the most cryptic or opaque headlines. And although we were grateful for the corrected mangled sentences, poor spelling, split infinitives and other grammatical howlers, they seldom, it seemed to us reporters, improved the way a story was told. Looking back, that was harsh, unfair and largely unjustified; but that's the way we reporters felt.

In 1977, however, all that changed. There was a much younger addition to the subeditors' office. He was a bearded, bespectacled fellow from Des Moines, Iowa, who had arrived in England as a backpacker, fallen in love with a British girl, eventually pitched up in Bournemouth, and landed himself a job on the *Echo*. He cut an incongruous figure in the subs room, and not only because of his American Midwest accent.

He used to do things few of his fellow subs would ever bother to do. For a start, he actually talked to junior reporters, and even deigned to venture into the reporters' office. On one occasion, the newsroom door swung open and I could see he clearly had me in his sights as he headed straight for my desk. He asked if he could pull up a chair – another first, by the way; most subeditors just told junior reporters what they were doing. No one 'asked' us anything.

I only have a vague recollection of the story he wanted to talk about; it was a court case involving a prominent local business-man accused of assaulting his wife. But I do remember it was the first time we had properly met. I also recall he had rewritten the intro and the end, and had moved the quotes about in the middle. I had to acknowledge that it was much improved by his intervention.

As he rose to return along the corridor to the subs office, he said, 'Anyway, nice to meet you, Mark. My name's Bill... Bill Bryson.'

Yes, that Bill Bryson. Before he became famous, and before he'd written about the *Bournemouth Evening Echo* in a way I can only aspire to... and hopelessly fail.

In Bryson's book of travels around Britain, *Notes from a Small Island*, his section on the subeditors' office was priceless. He describes one colleague 'so old he could barely hold a pencil', who would routinely open one of the high windows with a long pole kept for the purpose: 'It would take him an hour to get out of his chair and another hour to shuffle the few feet to the window and another hour to finagle it open and another hour to lean the pole against the wall and shuffle back to his seat.'

His recollections of Bournemouth are equally hilarious:

The parks used to be described on maps as the Upper Pleasure Gardens and Lower Pleasure Gardens, but some councillor or other force for good realized the profound and unhealthy implications of placing Lower and Pleasure in such immediate proximity and successfully lobbied to have Lower removed from the title, so you now have the Upper Pleasure Gardens and the mere Pleasure Gardens, and lexical perverts have been banished to the beaches where they must find such gratification as they can by rubbing themselves on the groynes. Anyway that's the kind of place Bournemouth is – genteel to a fault and proud of it.

How I wish I had that story when I was on the *Echo*!

The *Echo* still lives on (though it now has *Daily Echo* on the masthead), and its survival is something to cherish in an environment where many local papers have long since disappeared. I have to admit that learning my trade there was one of the great fortunes of my life.

I joined from school instead of going to university as most of my friends did. My starting pay was precisely £36.28 per week, and I will never forget my first day. My light blue Ford Cortina Mark II was more of a skip on wheels than a car, but in between bouts of infuriating unreliability, it did its job. And on Monday, 18 July 1977, that job was to get me to the art deco offices of the *Echo* by nine o'clock sharp. I was the new junior reporter, and I was utterly petrified.

I was to report to the office of the editor, Mr William Hill. A large, stooping, austere figure, he would seldom venture from his dark, wood-panelled inner sanctum. He wanted me to sit in on the morning editorial meeting and introduce me to some of the people I was to be working with. When they trooped in, what struck me was that they all seemed quite old and quite male. In fact, there was only one woman in the meeting: Sally Ford, who compiled the Echo Diary, a local gossip column of sorts, but relatively gentle, certainly not scurrilous, and, in truth, as uncontroversial and unprovocative as the paper itself. But Sally was good at it. She got out and about, knew a lot of people and took no nonsense.

I came to rather like Mr Hill, but it seemed to me his philosophy was not to do anything that would risk upsetting the readers, though quite how he knew anything about his readers was always something of a mystery to me. He never seemed to leave his office.

But he ran a tight ship, knew the sort of paper he wanted to turn out, and left you to get on with it as long you didn't make any serious howlers. And, in my eyes, any shortcomings he may have had as an editor were more than made up for by his inexplicable decision to employ me, a decision for which I will be eternally grateful.

So there I was that Monday morning listening to the news editor, Carl Whitely, a loveable Yorkshireman with the sharpest instinct for news and two talented sons who worked as reporters on the same paper.

The newsroom had a big desk in the middle for the junior reporters. The single desks around the outside, by the windows, were occupied by the senior hacks. We trainees would aspire to them; you'd made it then. All around were untidy stacks of yellowing papers, discarded cuttings, well-thumbed phone books and overflowing notebooks. Filling the air, particularly as deadline approached, was cigarette smoke and the incessant clatter of the manual typewriters; no computers in those days, or mobile phones. How on earth did we cope? But we did. The tools of the trade back then were chewed biros, appalling shorthand and a good pair of sturdy shoes. 'Put in the legwork, lad,' Carl used to say, 'and the stories will come.'

On that first Monday, after the morning meeting, I was told to report to the office of the deputy editor, Pat Palmer. It was an altogether unnerving experience. He sat at his desk, taking snuff while looking through the readers' letters piled up in front of him.

When I walked in, he looked up briefly and then returned to his letters. I stood there uncomfortably for what seemed like ages, and then he told me to take a drawing pin from the dish on his desk. On the wall behind him was a huge map which almost precisely represented the circulation area of the newspaper. He beckoned me over towards the map.

'Shut your eyes, turn around a couple of times and then stick the pin into the map, BUT KEEP YOUR EYES SHUT,' he bellowed.

Trying to ignore the overwhelming feeling that I was in the presence of a madman, I did what he asked. He peered at where my pin had landed.

'Ah, Stanpit! An interesting village. Off you go,' instructed Mr Palmer.

He wanted a double-page spread by the Wednesday. I had two days to find my notebook, find Stanpit and, most alarming of all, find a story. And not just any story. It had to sustain eight hundred words across the centre pages of the *Echo*.

'And just remember,' he said as I headed out of his office, 'there's a story in everyone and everywhere. Shut the door on your way out.'

I felt nauseous as I walked rapidly back into the newsroom, grabbed my coat and car keys and rushed out of the building with a sense of rising panic. It was already midday.

There's not a lot in Stanpit... or there wasn't in 1977. There'd been a lot more going on there in the eighteenth century, when the historic coastal village near Christchurch was teeming with shipwrecked smugglers who would fight regular battles with well-armed tax collectors. But I figured that was an old story.

I thought a drink at the village pub, The Ship In Distress, would be a good place to start, but the best thing about that pub was the name. (It's now a very pleasant gastropub, by the way.) A couple of lunchtime drinkers sat at the bar bemoaning the price of a pint, and the landlady said a local Tory councillor was having an affair with a leading light of the Townswomen's Guild. Or so she'd heard. Promising, I thought, but not really what the *Echo* was after.

I walked along to the village hall, where I remember introducing myself to a Mrs Appleby who was unloading paper plates, cups and serviettes from the boot of her car. I asked whether she knew of any good local stories. 'Oh yes,' she said.

'My grandson is five today and we're having a little party for him. Balloons and everything. Come and take some photographs, perhaps?'

I moved on despondently. Soon it was 5 p.m. and I had nothing to speak of – or, more importantly, to write about. I was in trouble. My career was no more than eight hours old, and it was dying a very sad death on a coastal road in Dorset.

I climbed a turnstile and walked for a while alongside Stanpit Marsh, an area of astonishing natural beauty and a haven for birds and other wildlife.

Then it happened. A woman walking her dog, a smile, a quick 'good evening' and then, 'Sorry to ask this, but have you signed the petition?' It's a question I will never forget. Five simple words: 'Have you signed the petition?' A sentence that made my heart sing. A sentence that saved my job.

'No, what petition?' I asked.

'My petition. I'm so fed up the council are allowing development on the marsh. It's the beginning of the end and I think it's an absolute disgrace.'

Within fifteen minutes I had the story. The following morning, I called the council and discovered they had indeed given planning permission for some new homes, and it would involve reclaiming a small part of the marshes. A few more calls, a few more angry quotes and the eight-hundred-word, double-page spread was taking shape. I had my story, and my first byline under the headline which I never quite understood:

STAMPIT STANPIT

My career as a journalist was up and running… Well, sort of. For the next few weeks, all I was entrusted with was rewriting readers' wedding reports.

Every Tuesday morning I would be handed a huge pile of these reports, with accompanying photographs, and had to find something different to say about each of them. Not easy when they were all the same…

'More than 100 friends and family attended the wedding on Saturday of Mr David Smythe and Ms Eleanor Crabtree at All Saints Church, Moordown. The beautiful bride, given away by her father, Roger, looked stunning in a layered lace dress with taffeta and satin. The sumptuous reception was held at The Dog and Pheasant in Winton… etc, etc…' You get the drift.

I did a dozen a week, not because it was news, but because the families of the betrothed paid a fee to have the reports in the paper and the *Echo* needed every penny it could get to survive.

I rewrote accounts of dream wedding after dream wedding as best as I possibly could, if only to progress to reporting the meetings of the Bournemouth Philatelic Society…

The key to local newspaper reporting, it seemed to me, was to find a good local row or controversy that could run for days. The knack was to create the row yourself. Find the issue, make the calls to the right people who you know will be upset and – *bingo!* – a controversy in the making.

One of my first, and perhaps the best, was the 'Cormorant Beak Bounty Scandal'.

A friend had told me that the Wessex Water Authority were offering £1 a beak in an attempt to cull the cormorants who were blamed for killing local trout, salmon and other fish. Dozens of the birds were being shot every month.

I tipped off the Dorset branch of the Royal Society for the Protection of Birds, who were predictably 'outraged by the wholesale slaughter of the cormorants' and called for an end to the 'horrific' practice.

My story began: 'Bournemouth bird lovers were horrified today by the revelation that scores of cormorants are being killed and mutilated for money...'

Then I went to the fishermen who were carrying out the cull, and they explained how the cormorants were pests that threatened local fishing stocks.

On day two, another page lead began: 'A Mudeford fisherman today sprang to the defence of the cormorant beak bounty...'

Local newspaper journalism in a nutshell.

In many ways the daily trawl around council meetings, magistrates' courts and the general stuff of life was, and remains, the rawest form of journalism. Getting out, knocking on doors, a chat over a cup of tea at the cop shop, a natter with the landlord of the local pub... that was the way local reporting worked. It was journalism at ground level, and it played a vital role in local communities. And, along the way, I learned so much about the trade – and quite a few of its tricks, too.

For years I had read the *Bournemouth Evening Echo* as a teenager and longed to be a reporter. It seemed to me a dream job. In those days, newspapers were still a thriving industry. I had read so many front-page stories carrying the byline of Pat Hogan or Roy Yeomans, the paper's top reporters, and now I was sitting in the same office as them, watching them, learning from them. They would do the police, fire and ambulance calls each morning, which often produced the biggest stories of the day.

Pat and Roy always competed ferociously for the front-page lead, but what they wanted most of all was the story that could be sold on to the national, Fleet Street papers. They were always on the phone trying to flog their stories, usually to the *Daily Mail* or the *Daily Express*.

Roy, the chief reporter, was the master of the art of selling stories to the national press. He was a real operator. I remember once getting a story about dead rats being thrown onto the stage of the local concert hall during a punk rock concert. A friend was there and phoned me.

It was some sort of weird prank by followers of the band Radio Stars. I told Roy I was writing it up for the following day's paper, and he said he'd like to see a copy of it when it was finished. In the meantime, he'd also phoned his mate who ran the concert venue and who'd confirmed to him that there had been an incident, but also volunteered the additional information that one member of his staff had reported that it was actually dead puppies that were hurled onto the stage.

By six o'clock that evening Roy had nicked my story, changed it from dead rats to dead puppies, got a quote from the local RSPCA office and sold four hundred words to the *Express*. Some other papers also ran it the following morning, with a predictable tabloid sense of outrage. I think he made £120 in all for that... around three times my weekly wage.

Then, at that morning's editorial conference, there was the obvious questions to me about why my story had appeared in the national press before it had a showing in the *Echo*. I had to say I had no idea.

Of course, my story would now have to appear with the new 'information' and with the headline:

'Claims Dead Puppies Thrown on a Bournemouth Stage'.

I was less than certain it was true, but didn't want to upset Roy or ruin a good story. Later clarification determined that what had actually been thrown were certainly not dead puppies, and not even dead rats, but rather offal in a plastic bag covered in fake blood.

Still, by then Roy had coined it and moved on to his next earner: a local woman's cat had been rescued from the high branches of a tree by the fire brigade, and then killed when the fire engine reversed over it leaving the premises. Another few quid in his pocket...

In truth, Roy was a seriously good reporter who made his career in local journalism in a way it is very hard to do now. He also taught me a great deal about the trade of newspaper journalism: how to flesh out the barest scrap of information or merest detail. And he made and cultivated his contacts with huge enthusiasm. He wined and lunched councillors, police officers and local businessmen. They liked him, and tended to repay him with information and stories.

How did I end up at the *Echo* at the age of just nineteen? It was a difficult decision. Most of my mates were off to university, but I was desperate to be a reporter. I just decided that was what I wanted to do. I wanted to be a foreign correspondent but I needed to start somewhere, so I thought local newspapers would be as good a place as any.

My father, Mike, was clear in his advice: 'If you've decided what you want to do, you're better getting on and doing it than spending three years at university.'

Although my mother, Jane, had been a teacher of infant children, mine was not a particularly academic upbringing. My father left school at fourteen and began work as a commercial artist, eventually joining Pontin's, the holiday camp firm, where he worked his way up to become Fred Pontin's right-hand man. He had done well without going to university. He thought I could and should do the same. Neither my sister, Sarah, nor my brother, Nick, went to university. We all chose a path and set off down it.

Incidentally, all three of my children have gone to university. Or at least my son, Jack, had a crack at it before succumbing to the temptations of professional football and coaching. It just seems the accepted thing to do now, but I am not convinced it is right. Ever since Tony Blair set an arbitrary target that 50 per cent of young people should attend university, we seem to have a glut of graduates with average degrees facing a dearth of graduate jobs. More youngsters would be better off being guided towards more vocational courses. There is no shame in it, and it should be encouraged. If actual courses can be tied even loosely to actual jobs offered by actual employers, then no one loses. But the current system is skewed in another way too, as many academically gifted children in state schools are missing out on university because of poor teaching and a lack of ambition at school and at home.

But, as I say, forty years ago things were very different. There were decent jobs in journalism for an eighteen-year-old with A levels. I took my father's advice, scrapped plans to do English at Exeter, and enrolled in a nine-month course run by the National Council for the Training of Journalists in Portsmouth. It was a course that covered shorthand, law, public administration and writing, and after narrowly surviving scurrilous accusations that I had cheated in my hundred-words-per-minute shorthand exam, I passed and that led to the job on the *Echo*.

Within three years of joining the *Echo*, I moved to the BBC in London and never looked back. After a few months learning about foreign news and how to write radio scripts at the BBC World Service in Bush House, I managed to wangle a six-month contract at BBC Television News as a scriptwriter for the newsreaders on the lunchtime and the early evening news.

The switch from newspapers and radio was not easy. For a start, the style of writing is totally different. In television you have to imagine the spoken word, and you need to be spare and concise and stick to time. Three words a second is the golden rule, and in those days there were not many links that were longer than thirty seconds.

A 'link' is the introduction to a recorded videotape report compiled by a correspondent. And aged twenty-four, it was my job to write them for the likes of Jan Leeming and Sue Lawley. It was quite daunting but also quite enjoyable. Both women were very professional but also great fun. I have to confess to a crush on Sue. She was sassy, sexy and smart, and I was in awe of her.

Newsroom rumours swirled of some sort of romance; speculation that was, unfortunately, hopelessly wide of the mark. But never let the facts get in the way of a good story.

Then some reptile in the office tipped off *Private Eye*.

A piece appeared in the Grovel column suggesting I was having an affair with Sue. I was flattered, she was furious. Sue wanted to sue. Charming, I thought. She was even more angry when the story was picked up by the *Express*...

Things then took a bizarre turn, with another appearance in the next edition of *Private Eye*:

Grovel's exclusive about newscasterette Sue Lawley, 37, being romanced by Corporation minion Mark Austin, 24, caused some surprise among the friends of Alan Tomlinson, a flamboyant BBC World Service producer given to wearing tight-fitting trousers and silk shirts.

The Adonis-like Austin also used to work at the World Service and became so friendly with Tomlinson, 34, that the two shared a flat and were inseparable. However, the friendship ended when Alan departed Bush House in mysterious circumstances. He now lives in Honduras.

Now, 'Adonis-like' I can probably live with. But 'minion' really irked. And as for the suggestion of a relationship with Alan, it was laughable, not least because he was seeing an awful lot of a certain Bianca Jagger at the time. Hence, I suspect, his 'mysterious' departure to central America.

We were good mates, shared a huge flat overlooking the river in Putney, and had some cracking parties to which he often wore those tight-fitting trousers. I'm not sure he possessed a silk shirt.

Now I wanted to sue. But, eventually, Sue and I both saw the funny side of the whole thing. At least I think she did; Jan Leeming was certainly amused.

In truth, it was the most exciting thing that happened in that job. The problem was I didn't really want to do it. I wanted to be a television reporter and a foreign correspondent, I had no doubt about that. So I came up with a plan. Although it nearly always pays to work really hard at being good at something, sometimes it can also pay to try your damnedest to be bad at something, or at least extremely mediocre.

My admittedly high-risk strategy was to be a second-rate scriptwriter, while all the time trying to persuade anyone who would listen that my real strengths lay as a reporter. In fact, it was so high-risk that one programme editor, a fearsome Yorkshireman called Derek Maude, became so fed up with me that he was on the verge of getting me kicked out.

Derek, a legendary figure at BBC News in the 1980s, wore a patch on his right eye, and a senior correspondent at the time, Michael Cole, offered what seemed like very good advice to a young scriptwriter in his first week at the BBC. He said that Derek had a very clear idea of where everyone should sit in his editorial meetings. The place for new young writers like me was slightly behind him on the right side, where he was spared 'the chore of having to see you'.

Odd, I thought, but I was delighted such a revered figure as Cole seemed to have my back. I duly pulled up a chair on what was quite literally Derek's blind side.

Of course, far from being his preference, it was the one thing that infuriated him. He absolutely *had* to be able to see everyone in front of him. It was his one hard and fast rule: *be visible*.

'Austin,' he said, 'where are you? Get in fookin' front of me where I can see you.'

It was not a great start to my relationship with Derek, a key man in the BBC newsroom.

Actually, sitting on his blind side was not the only thing that angered Derek. Overwriting was his other bête noir. He hated verbosity in news scripts, and had two sayings that stuck with me: 'Son, the greatest story in the world was told in two words: Jesus wept' and 'Don't use ten words when one will do. It's what you leave out that fookin' counts'.

Part of my strategy was therefore to throw in unnecessary adjectives at any opportunity, just to annoy him and to prove that I wasn't cut out for scriptwriting.

Derek was a programme editor of wonderful news judgement and made clear decisions, unlike many editors. In the fast-moving news business, sometimes you just have to make a decision about stories and running orders and get on with it. Too many programme editors, it seems to me, vacillate and change their minds and seek advice from too many people. Derek wasn't one of them. He made his decision, and that was that. To be fair, it is such a subjective business that quite often you can make a perfectly sensible argument for leading with one story over another. The decision is the important thing.

And the best decision he ever made was to tell me that I wasn't going to make it as a newsroom writer, and to get out on the road where 'I could make a nuisance of myself and be useful at the same time'. It was music to my ears.

Not only did he tell me that, but he also told the news editor at the time, John Exelby, a wonderful man with a wicked sense of humour and an unrivalled news sense. We got on well, shared a love of cricket, and I grew to like and respect him enormously. Before I knew it, at the age of twenty-five, I was a national reporter for BBC TV News.

Everyone needs their lucky break, and mine came because a very successful BBC News correspondent and presenter, Chris Morris, had a dinner date he didn't want to miss. It was late on a Friday afternoon, and word was coming in of a robbery at a jeweller's in St James's in central London.

I was a very inexperienced junior reporter at the time, but because I was on my own and everyone else was assigned, I was sent to the scene. I thought I would be news-gathering with the cameraman until a more senior reporter could get there. It was a big armed robbery, with staff held up at gunpoint by men in balaclavas and more than two million pounds' worth of jewellery stolen. I did a couple of interviews with eyewitnesses and a senior police officer at the scene, and then my pager went off. It was Chris Morris asking me what I'd got and telling me he probably wouldn't get there.

I was asked to do the report for the *Nine O'Clock News* and couldn't believe my luck. I did a piece to camera and headed back to edit my first story for the BBC's flagship programme.

Chris Morris later told me he could have easily got to St James's, but thought I deserved a chance on the main programme. It was a great gesture and one I will never forget. I felt I was on my way in television news.

By far the biggest story I covered during my time as young reporter at BBC News was the miners' strike of 1984–5. It lasted a year and was the most bitter and violent industrial dispute in living memory, without parallel perhaps anywhere in the industrialized world. On one side, thousands of workers, fighting for their jobs, futures and families and led by the radical unionist Arthur Scargill. On the other, a Conservative government led by Margaret Thatcher, determined to crush the strike and prepared to use the police force to do it.

It was characterized by violent confrontations between flying pickets and police, and it was hugely unpleasant to cover.

It is the hatred I remember. The raw, visceral hatred on display every day. It was my first experience of a protracted industrial dispute, and I wasn't at all prepared for what I was witnessing, what it was doing to the people caught up in it, on both sides, and what it was doing to the country.

It would become our daily routine or a ritual: we would wake before dawn, more often than not in some drab, soulless hotel close to the mining villages where from house after house would emerge the men intent on defending their livelihoods.

We would drive through dark streets to the gates of the pit or the coking plant or the power station, wherever the pickets were targeting on any particular day. By first light, all the players in this hideously choreographed but all too real confrontation would be in place. The pickets, the police and the press.

And, eventually, the still-willing workers would arrive, by car and coach. Either scabs or brave heroes, depending on your point of view. Needless to say, the striking miners hated them. Cries of 'Judas' and 'scum' filled the cold morning air, missiles flew, miners charged and police beat them back.

The strikers hated us, too. Particularly the BBC, which, for some reason, they viewed as merely an extension of the Thatcher government. 'BBC – British Bullshit Corporation,' they yelled at us. ITN got similar treatment: 'Here they come, Lies at Ten' was the greeting they got from the miners.

My job was not only to report, but also to keep an eye out for missiles, half bricks or bottles, which would often come flying at the camera whenever we tried to film. One morning, at the entrance of a threatened pit near Rotherham, I saw something hurled towards the cameraman. I shouted a warning, he ducked and the projectile hit me square on the shoulder. It wasn't a brick or a bottle, and was mercifully soft. It turned out to be a plastic bag full of liquid which burst on impact. It was warm, and steam rose from my soaked overcoat. Then the smell hit me. It was urine. A cheer went up. 'Take that, you lying BBC bastard,' shouted one of the strikers.

I wanted to talk to them, to tell them that they had got it wrong, that we sympathized with their plight and were not on Thatcher's or anyone else's side. But there was no point. The narrative was set in their minds and nothing could shift it now.

It went like this... Thatcher wanted to destroy the mining communities in a politically motivated attack on the working class. The police were Thatcher's 'boot boys', doing the dirty work of the state. And the media, specifically the BBC, had the job of portraying the miners as the bad guys.

It was the way the strikers saw it, or most of them. And it was desperately sad. But the daily violence became the story, and, consequently, the barrier to the real reporting of the human stories of suffering that the closure of the pits was causing.

I often used to wonder about the tactics of Arthur Scargill. Confrontation and illegal picketing were always going to lead to violence that would in turn play into the hands of the government. I thought they would have done far better to give the media stories of the decimation of traditional mining communities. Stories of families struggling to survive in the face of heartless government decision-making would have influenced public opinion more than endless pictures of violent picketing.

But the battle lines were drawn and the dispute took on a momentum of its own. It reached a terrifying and violent climax at a coking plant in a place near Sheffield called Orgreave.

I remember the day like it was yesterday: 18 June 1984. A warm day, and perhaps the defining day of the dispute. In the fields around the entrance to the plant, thousands of miners were confronted by six thousand police, many in riot gear, some on horses, and all, it seemed to me at the time, determined to exact brutal revenge if the bricks started flying in their direction.

Inevitably they did, as the lorries the miners wanted to prevent leaving exited the plant under police protection.

Then it began. First a barrage of missiles, a flurry of fists and lots of pushing and shoving. The police ranks separated and the horses charged through, followed by baton-wielding riot police on foot. The fighting lasted for hours. Hundreds were injured, and I remain astonished to this day that no one was killed.

It ended in a terrible and bloody defeat for the strikers, a beating that was to herald the eventual capitulation of the miners in what became a rout for Mrs Thatcher.

But while she may well have claimed victory it was nothing of the sort, unless you consider the deterioration of communities where drugs, drink, depression and divorce would take hold at great personal cost for thousands of British families some sort of victory.

I went back to Orgreave to present a programme just after Mrs Thatcher's death a few years ago. You will not be surprised to hear that the hatred for her remains. Maybe it will for generations. It is the scar that refuses to heal.

What I was too young and too inexperienced to realize at the time was that it was a watershed dispute, and that industrial relations in Britain would never be the same again.

The following year, I had the sort of career conversation of which dreams are made. John Exelby asked me if I fancied becoming a BBC Television News sports correspondent, which also involved presenting the sports news on the main BBC1 Saturday night bulletin. In those days it was an incredible job because the BBC had most of the big sports contracts, and the TV news correspondent would get automatic access to all the big events. I would spend my life attending Wimbledon, Lord's, the British Open and Twickenham. I would go on England cricket tours and to the Olympics for weeks on end. In short, Exelby was offering to pay me for what I loved doing... watching top-level sport.

I said yes.

A SPORTING LIFE

F OR THE NEXT seven years, I was doing little other than travelling the world watching sport. It really doesn't get much better than that. Olympics, World Cups, Wimbledons, Royal Ascots, Open Championships, Grand Nationals, England cricket tours to the Caribbean and Australia. I did the lot. And loved every minute of it.

It was not only hugely fun, it also helped me realize my real dream of becoming a foreign correspondent. Many times I would be sent abroad to cover a sporting event, only to find myself at the centre of a big news story.

After a couple of years in the job, I was poached by ITN to be their sports correspondent. It was a tough decision to leave the BBC, but ITN offered to double my salary and gave me a verbal undertaking that I would get a foreign correspondent job when one came up. I agonized for a couple of weeks. Part of me was excited at the prospect of joining a smaller, more risk-taking, adventurous news organization. But I also worried about leaving the biggest broadcaster in Britain and all the possibilities it offered.

I decided to take the plunge, and was taken aback by the BBC's attitude. They were very hard-nosed about it. My boss,

Chris Cramer, famous for being stuck in the Iranian embassy during the siege in 1980, basically told me to empty my desk and bugger off there and then. It was Cramer's style. ITN was the enemy and I was defecting. He seemed to take it personally, but I didn't blame him.

The extraordinary thing is that I didn't set foot in the ITN newsroom on Wells Street in central London for more than three and a half months. Instead, I was ordered to Heathrow for a flight to Australia to cover the America's Cup sailing and the England cricket tour. They also sent one of their top foreign desk producers, Mike Nolan. We touched down in Sydney, checked into the wonderful Sebel Townhouse Hotel, and didn't stop working and travelling all over Australia. It was astonishing – the stories just kept coming.

We had to cover the Spycatcher trial, where the British government sent over senior diplomats to give evidence to prevent the publication of a former MI5 officer's memoirs in Australia. The spy, Peter Wright, was represented by a cocky but very bright young Aussie lawyer called Malcom Turnbull.

Turnbull ran rings around the witnesses struggling to make Mrs Thatcher's case for a ban. They included the cabinet secretary, Sir Robert Armstrong, who was challenged by Turnbull about an apparent 'lie' in a letter. It was a famous exchange.

Sir Robert said: 'It is a misleading impression in that respect, it does not contain a lie, I don't think.'

Turnbull: 'And what is the difference between a misleading impression and a lie?'

Armstrong: 'A lie is a straight untruth.'

Turnbull: 'What is a misleading impression – a sort of bent untruth?'

Armstrong: 'As one person said, it is perhaps being economical with the truth.'

That phrase haunted Armstrong; it became a huge story and we were in the middle of it. The British government lost, Turnbull later became Prime Minister of Australia, and the trial enabled me to get on air, not as a sports correspondent, but as a foreign correspondent. Mike Nolan and I did more than a hundred stories in three months. We were based in Sydney so long that the Sebel Townhouse made us 'resident guests'.

We weren't the only ones. The other resident guests at the Sebel that Australian summer included Phil Collins and Elton John. Elton had the penthouse suite, and when he wasn't performing he was watching the Test cricket.

England had a great tour, and actually won the Ashes in a memorable match in Melbourne. We were allowed to film the celebrations in the dressing room, and as the champagne was spraying and the beer was being downed, in walked Elton plus entourage with more crates of champagne.

That night, the England boys had a huge party. Ian Botham – who had become a good mate – invited me along. There are not many parties where Elton John is the DJ for the evening. It was quite some celebration.

Botham likes a party. He came to my fiftieth, by helicopter, and landed in a friend's paddock. He's a good man with a big heart and the constitution of an ox. You go drinking with him at your peril.

The job of sports correspondent was not only a guaranteed ticket for the greatest sports events you could imagine, but also a ticket that got you behind the scenes, in with the players, into the inner sanctum of sport.

It was all an utter privilege. But why? Why sport?

I'll tell you why. Because it matters.

Sport holds us in thrall, it transcends the humdrum and the routine, it lifts the spirit and crushes the soul, it breaks down barriers and ignores national boundaries. It is inspiring and deflating, exciting and tedious, uplifting and depressing, and most of all... it is important. As important as a Shakespeare play or a Mozart symphony.

My sporting hero at that time was David Gower. Strange in a way, because sporting heroes are normally formed in child-hood. Gower is my contemporary. But from the moment I saw him bat, I thought, 'That is how I would like to bat, that is how players should bat.' He didn't actually get that many runs in that game at Bournemouth's Dean Park in August 1975, but those he did get were pretty stylish. He batted with what seemed to be effortless grace. I am sure it was not effortless, but that was the impression. Leicestershire's Gower got 20 or so that day; Hampshire's Barry Richards got a century. Richards was already a great, but it was the teenage Gower that caught the eye.

Now, they say never meet your heroes because you'll be dis-appointed. I not only met him, but I pissed him off wretchedly, nearly cost him the England captaincy, and it is a wonder that we're now – reasonably speaking – mates.

Within three years of that day in Bournemouth, he was playing for England and was becoming a star. He famously dispatched his first ball in Test cricket for four. The thing about Gower is that I have seldom seen a cricket ball hit with such power and yet with such a lightness of touch. It is called timing. It is the essence of batting, and Gower had it in spades.

There is no question that Gower qualifies as a great batsman. He scored 8231 runs in Test cricket at an average of 44.25. The thing everybody says about him is that he could and should have been even better. With that talent, he should have worked harder and more runs would have followed.

But that is to miss the point about Gower. Simon Barnes caught the essence of it, as he so often does, in his book on sporting heroes. 'People said Gower would be better if he put his mind to it,' writes Barnes. 'It seemed to me that Gower's basic strength was that he didn't put his mind to it. Rather he gave himself up to his gift.'

I actually think Barnes is half right. It seemed to me that Gower worked harder and tried harder than he appeared to. He certainly cared more than he allowed people to know. At least *I* think so. You're never quite sure with Gower.

What is sure is that his record as captain of England was not so great. But his reign was at least highly entertaining, for which, as a reporter at the time, I was exceptionally grateful.

While still with the BBC, in early 1986, I was lucky enough to be covering the England tour to the West Indies. It was my first overseas cricket tour, and Gower was the England captain. He was under considerable pressure, having predicted the West Indians would be 'quaking in their boots'.

It was a typical Gower throwaway comment, made after crushing the Australians in the summer, and one, if he's honest, he probably regrets. The truth is, it inspired the West Indies' fast bowlers to produce the most consistently dangerous bowling ever seen – and Gower and England paid the price.

Sadly, the first Test match at Sabina Park in Jamaica was untelevised. There was no Sky Sports live coverage in those days, and I was supposed to be there with a single cameraman to record events for posterity. Unfortunately, the West Indies Board of Control asked us and ITN for £300,000 to produce news coverage and a few longer pieces for *Sportsnight* and *Grandstand*. It was outrageous, and we refused to pay. Consequently, we missed what has been described as the 'scariest Test England ever played'.

It's the last England Test match of which there is no footage whatsoever. Or none that I have seen. And from all accounts, it is probably just as well. It was brutal. A dodgy wicket, a hostile crowd and even more hostile bowling. There was no respite from the bouncer onslaught led by a fearsome character called Patrick Patterson. He was not one of the very best West Indian bowlers, but he was certainly, on that tour, one of the most lethal.

The correspondent for *The Times*, who had seen a bit of cricket in his time, wrote that he thought someone would be killed. One England batsman, Mike Gatting, had already gone to hospital. He was hideously injured when a ball from Malcolm Marshall in a one-day game skidded off the pitch and smashed into Gatting's nose. Marshall apparently found a piece of bone lodged in the leather of the cricket ball.

Needless to say, England were well beaten in the first Test. It was a slaughter in the Caribbean sunshine, and in many ways set the tone for the entire series. And Gower and his team were under as much pressure off the field as on it. It was the height of the tabloid wars, and Ian Botham was newspaper fodder.

Into this unhappy camp, I arrived for the second Test.

Things didn't get any better. The cricket was one defeat after another, and myself and ITN's sports correspondent, Jeremy Thompson, spent as much time covering the off-field shenanigans.

Gower was accused of not caring about practice and was criticized for going off sailing instead. Ian Botham was making headlines for allegedly taking dope – and breaking a bed in Barbados during a 'love romp with a model' – and the narrative became about an ill-fated tour where the wheels were coming off.

When the Botham story broke in the *News of the World*, I was called early one morning and told to get his reaction. Jeremy Thompson was asked to do the same. I spent an age outside Botham's hotel room being told he would be making a statement and to hang on.

I waited more than an hour before his lawyer emerged, closely followed by Thompson and his camera crew. 'All done mate, not sure he's doing another interview.' Fortunately, he did, but he was in a terrible mood and basically just slagged off journalists. It was that sort of tour.

In a way it was wonderful for us, a different story every day, but it was a nightmare for the players who saw no respite from the battering, on or off the field. And relations with Gower, who felt under siege, were not easy.

At one press conference early on in the tour, Gower was actually asked whether he was having an affair with the wicketkeeper Paul Downton's wife – he wasn't. It tied into reports that Gower's relationship with his long-term girlfriend was on the rocks.

Tabloid reporters were suddenly everywhere. Gower later wrote: 'Every non-native face on the islands was a potential booby trap, and not even the cricket correspondents could recognize every one of the scandal-seeking merchants.'

The atmosphere between press and players was ghastly.

During one interview, Gower rather impatiently asked me if the BBC was here to cover the cricket or the 'off-field distractions'. I told him I would cover both and he cut short the interview.

It didn't help that, in Trinidad at the time, a calypso song by Gypsy with the lyrics 'Captain, this ship is sinking' was playing everywhere. Unfortunately for Gower, it became the soundtrack to the tour and also the soundtrack for a BBC Sport piece I put together as things fell apart. He was not impressed, though he seemed to understand it made good telly, and my relations with Gower and the team suffered.

At the end of this turbulent tour, Jeremy Thompson and I decided to throw a beach party for players from both teams and the press guys. We thought it was the least we should do. Everybody got stuck into the rum punch and it was a long night. Gower was in no mood to party, he was fed up with the whole trip, and later described it as the lowest point of his international cricket career. It was pretty disastrous, but I can't imagine any other Test team would have fared much better against the most fearsome pace attack in the world.

But here's the point about Gower. What often goes unacknowledged in relation to that tour is that he was, by some distance, England's most successful batsman. In the last four tests, he made scores of 66, 47, 66, 23, 10, 22, 90 and 21.

Gower's languor conceals real guts and serious courage in

the face of such dangerous and intimidating bowling. It was failure, but it was an immensely brave failure, and that will do for me. He lost his job the following summer.

But if Gower was unimpressed with me in the West Indies, he was furious with me a couple of years later.

In 1989, he regained the Test captaincy for a home series against Australia. Once again, it didn't go well. England were 2–0 down by the time of the fourth Test at Old Trafford. I was covering the game with the ITN cricket camera team – Derek Seymour, the cameraman, and Alan Florence, a soundman, who had also started doing a bit of camerawork at square leg, side-on to the pitch, to give us a few more picture options. The BBC wouldn't in those days give us access to their outside broadcast coverage.

On the Saturday, England were in the field and under the cosh. Australia were piling on the runs and Gower's team were staring at another defeat. At the end of the day's play, I was editing our material and putting a report together for the main evening news. Halfway through the edit, Alan Florence appeared and offered us his tape from square leg. 'There is something you might be interested in,' he said. 'David Gower flicked a V-sign at some fans who were barracking him. I got the shot but I don't know what it's like.'

We had a look at it. It was a pretty good shot, and I thought it showed the pressure that the England captain was under. Also, it had not appeared on the BBC coverage, so they seem to have missed it.

I thought about whether to use it, whether it was fair on Gower. I decided that if he did it in the middle of a Test match with cameras everywhere, he must have expected it to get picked up. Anyway, use it I did. Not in any sensational way, just as a shot in the middle of the piece.

A few minutes later, David Norrie, the cricket correspondent for the *News of the World* appeared. He had heard we had the shot and was asking to see it. Norrie was a mate, so I agreed.

'That's our back-page splash, right there,' said Norrie.

Our piece aired at ten o'clock that night and I didn't think any more of it. We headed off for dinner and a few drinks. The following morning, my hotel room phone rang. It was the England captain. He was furious. Beyond angry. There was a lot of swearing. He said something about Ted Dexter, the chairman of selectors, phoning him the previous night about the incident. Gower wanted me to come to his hotel later that day – which, being Sunday, was a rest day.

I went to meet him and he was still fuming. Dexter had wanted him to apologize and he'd refused. He thought it was wrong to use the picture, it was making far too much of a trivial incident and it was pure mischief-making.

I felt bad. After all, this man, though I didn't tell him, was my cricketing hero. I mumbled something like, 'Well, what did you expect,' and he made it pretty clear he wanted me out. I left.

On the way back to my hotel it occurred to me that, with Gower refusing to apologize, I may have cost him the captaincy. I thought it was pretty clear that Gower was again fearing for his job.

I may well have contributed to that fear coming true. He was sacked at the end of the series, which England lost, 4–0.

Gower and I have since become friends. We've never really

discussed the V-sign affair. I think he forgives me. But I'm not entirely sure.

I have covered six Olympic Games and I have loved them all. Seoul because it was my first one; Barcelona because of the majesty of the city; Athens because, despite the chaos, it was the birthplace of the Games; Beijing for Usain Bolt; and London 2012 because it was in the city of my birth.

But my favourite Games of all, so far, has to be Sydney in 2000. It was an uplifting festival of sport, outstandingly organized in a breathtaking city that welcomed the world with a warmth and a spirit that has not been surpassed.

And I also witnessed one of the most memorable Olympic moments of my lifetime: the women's 400-metre final, won by the Australian runner Cathy Freeman.

A few years before those Games, I had reported on Australia's Stolen Generations – Aboriginal children stolen from their parents and placed with white families. It was state-sanctioned racism that caused enormous suffering and pain. Cathy Freeman's grandmother was one of the stolen infants.

So I was aware of the long journey that Freeman and her Aboriginal people had made, from appallingly persecuted natives to citizens battling for equality and fair treatment. And I was aware how much Australia wanted Freeman – the country's foremost Aboriginal athlete – to symbolize the Sydney Olympics. They wanted her to be an icon of national unity; to symbolize reconciliation between black and white.

It is why she was chosen to light the flame at the magnificent opening ceremony. She carried the torch *and* the hopes and expectations of an entire nation. It was an extraordinary amount of pressure placed on an athlete about to run the most important race of her life.

So the final of the women's 400 metres on Monday, 25 September 2000, was no ordinary event.

Freeman took to the track in the Australian team uniform of green and gold. But on her feet were track shoes of yellow, red and black. Yellow for the sun, red for the land and black for Australia's indigenous people, the Aborigines.

I will never forget the noise. It sounded as if the whole country were roaring as one. Deafening. And then they were away. It was difficult to take your eyes off Freeman in that stadium. She was in lane six, wearing a kind of space-age hooded bodysuit, and she was flying. In the lead at 200 metres but then she slips back. Is the pressure too much? Britain's Katharine Merry is ahead of her, or so it seems. Maybe this is the story, a British gold... I know Katharine and I am sure she won't mind me saying that I hoped it wouldn't be. I can't believe I'm writing that. But that is how I felt watching this race.

Freeman wasn't finished. She came back and powered clear. As she crossed the line, the look on her face was just remarkable. No real joy, just a shake of her head and she's on her haunches. A penny for her thoughts. Everything she has worked towards has just become real. She is an Olympic champion. And more importantly perhaps, she has fulfilled her obligation to Australia. An unfair obligation, but an obligation all the same.

She rises to her feet and the pressure seems to drain away. She smiles and heads off on her lap of honour. In her hand, both an Australian flag and an Aboriginal one.

I can't think of an athlete who has run a race so weighed down by the burden of expectation. But she ran and she won, and Australia should love her for that.

But if the Olympic Games made a hero out Freeman, they made a villain out of Ben Johnson...

I was drunk. There is really no way to pretend otherwise. There were too many people there with long memories, and every reason to put me right if I deny it. They were drunk too, but they'll still remember, just like I do. Because, in the end, it was one of the most sobering experiences of my life on the sporting road.

It was the night before a rest day for athletes in the middle of the 1988 Olympics in Seoul, and ITV were throwing a party. A big one. We took over a nightclub in the city centre, invited the world, and the world came. The boss lost his credit card during the evening (apparently) and one of the cameramen proffered his. The bill came to over ten thousand pounds; it was that sort of night. We were having a good Games, with several exclusives, big interviews and great access to the medallists.

But when it happened, we were not prepared for one of the biggest sport stories of the century.

I didn't believe it when I first heard it. It was about three in the morning when the phone rang in my room in the athletes' village. It was the foreign desk in London, and through the alcohol-induced fog, I could tell they were in a state of some considerable agitation. 'Ben Johnson's been done for drugs, we need a piece and a live in two hours' time.'

'I assume this is some sort of joke,' I remember saying.

It wasn't. Within minutes, the editor of *News at Ten*, Nick Pollard, was on the phone. 'Mark, I need this done quickly. I'm going to lead on it.'

These were my first Olympics. I was twenty-nine years old, the biggest sports story of the twentieth century was breaking, and I was in no shape whatsoever to do it.

Three days earlier, I had stood overlooking the 100 metres finishing line and witnessed what I thought was the single most amazing piece of sporting theatre I had ever seen. It was a perfect duel. Lewis v Johnson, head to head in front of 100,000 people in the stadium and a billion or so watching on television around the world.

Carl Lewis had beaten Johnson in the LA Olympics four years earlier. But since then, Johnson had set a new world record of 9.83 seconds. Then in early 1988 he injured a hamstring and struggled to recover. It was touch and go whether he would make the much-anticipated showdown with Lewis.

That he did was, with hindsight, probably due to recovery-enhancing drugs. But he was there all right, bulked up like a well-muscled boxer and with burning ambition in his eyes.

The starting gun, the roar, the almost-subliminal spectacle. The red vest of Johnson, the agonized face of Lewis, the dip for the tape, the outstretched arm and the index finger pointing at the sky. It was an unforgettable moment – and a moment was all it was. But it is there, ingrained in my memory.

Everybody looked from Johnson to the trackside clock. And up it came... 9.79 seconds, a new world record. We all knew we had been watching something special; now we knew we had been watching history.

Johnson was the fastest man in the world... ever. What a race! What a man! What a day!

But three days later, as I hauled myself out of a bed I would not see for another twenty-hour hours, I knew the whole event had been a sham. And so began the most dramatic day of my sports reporting career.

The man who was to save my skin in the next couple of hours – our picture editor, Bill Frost – met me outside as, miraculously, a taxi drew up and tipped out another well-refreshed journalist returning from the bars of Itaewon.

It was Mike Collett, a good friend and then the correspondent for the agency UPI. 'My God, where are you off to?' he said. Mike obviously hadn't a clue what was happening. 'Haven't you heard?' I said rather cruelly. 'Ben Johnson's been done for drugs.'

With that, we raced to the ITN office and edit suite. As I drank bottles of water, gathered what thoughts I could muster and tried desperately to sober up, Bill was calmly putting together the pictures he knew I would need. He didn't wait for my words. He just laid the pictures as he saw fit. It was the best way to get it done. I needed all the help I could get.

I will never forget the opening. The starting gun fired, the deafening crowd noise and then my words: 'Three days ago the world watched Ben Johnson become the fastest man on earth... tonight we learnt it was all a fraud.'

The video report wasn't the problem. The problem was the live report straight afterwards. The news presenter, the legend-ary Sir Alastair Burnet, had agreed the question with me. It was to be something about 'late developments in Seoul tonight, Mark Austin can bring us up to date... Mark...?'

That would leave things pretty open for me to say what I could put together coherently.

In the event, it was nothing like that. What Sir Alistair said was: 'Early hours of the morning in Seoul as you can see… Mark Austin is there. Mark, exactly how many athletes are on drugs?'

Now there are two things about that question. One, when he said 'early hours of the morning… as you can see', the only thing they could see was my face (in a studio). So I must have looked like it was the early hours of the morning. Charming.

Two, 'exactly how many athletes are on drugs?' was not the expected or the easiest question. It is what is known in the business as a 'hospital pass'.

I must have worn a look of astonishment, followed by fear, followed by agony. I mumbled something about it being very difficult to tell and then resorted to the answer I had prepared. I got through it, and no one has ever mentioned that I looked or sounded the worse for wear. But I knew I should not have been broadcasting.

It was the only time I have ever broadcasted worse for wear. And I will never do it again.

The next hours were frantic, with Johnson's chaotic departure from Seoul airport, an extraordinary press conference by the International Olympic Committee, and the realization that sport, or certainly athletics, would never be the same again.

It was further proof, if ever it were needed, of sport's power to change things… and the following year, events within football proved it again.

*

As a sports correspondent, you don't expect to turn up at a football ground to find scores of bodies lying on the floor of a gymnasium that has become a makeshift mortuary.

But that was my experience in 1989 at Hillsborough. It was a story that was, in the most tragic way imaginable, to sum up everything that was wrong with English football in the eighties. Poor policing, inadequate and dangerous terracing, and fans fenced in like animals.

I arrived at Hillsborough in the early evening. The terraces were clear of people. All that were left were mangled crush bars, torn fencing, clothing and shoes scattered across the concrete steps. Men's shoes, women's shoes, children's shoes. How many of the people who had been wearing them were dead? Just because they went to a football match. Just because a wretched football ground had been transformed into a cage; a death trap.

Yes, such appalling conditions were the culmination of a decade of violence and unsocial behaviour by a minority of football fans across the country. But they were also the result of years of neglect by the footballing authorities. One of the richest sports provided the direst facilities for spectators. These were dark days for English football.

It formed a grim backdrop for the 1990 World Cup in Italy. The English team were written off as no-hopers, and the Italian authorities were braced for trouble from English fans.

So it was with some trepidation that I flew into Rome to begin reporting on what we firmly believed would be a short-lived tournament for England. We even justified renting a top-notch, budget-busting BMW 7 Series for the long road journeys, by convincing ourselves England wouldn't last beyond the group stage.

After a 1–1 draw with the Republic of Ireland in the first group game, our prediction was on course. But another draw with the Dutch and a win over Egypt meant England somehow topped the group. We extended the 7 Series rental for a few more days and headed to Bologna. A David Platt volley put England through to the quarter-finals, and we had to start planning our explanation to the bean counters in London.

Off to Naples for the quarter-final against Cameroon. By now we were winging it. No hotels were booked because no one had thought England would progress so far.

I managed to get one, but there was a hitch. When we turned up they denied knowing anything about the booking. They asked for my name several times. And several times I told them: 'Mark Austin... A-U-S-T-I-N... Austin.'

Nothing, and the hotel was now full. I was not pleased but they were adamant. 'Do you have the spelling as O-S-T-I-N?' I asked. Nothing.

And then, as we trudged towards the door to leave. 'We have a booking tonight for a Mr Stin,' said the receptionist. 'Marco Stin?'

'Well, that's probably me,' I said. It was. They had my number against it and my credit card. The crew called me Marco for the rest of the trip.

Needless to say, Cameroon were swept aside, setting up a semi-final in Turin with West Germany.

It was to be no ordinary football match. It was a game that transcended football. In short, it was a game that changed English football in ways that would have been unimaginable months earlier.

To us, camped in our edit van outside the Stadio delle Alpi, it seemed like a very important (and hugely unexpected) football match. The biggest since the World Cup final in 1966. It was, however, far more significant than that.

The country was behind England like they had not been for decades. And not just soccer fans. Lots of people – different people, of all classes – suddenly got interested in football. Watching the games became a family affair. Back in the UK, it was all-consuming. Flags, horns blowing, parties, houses painted in red, white and blue, and Luciano Pavarotti's 'Nessun Dorma' – the official World Cup song – sounding from a million homes.

The game itself was extraordinary. England played like a team possessed. Gary Lineker, in particular, was outstanding. It was 0–0 at half time, but England were on top.

For the second half, I nipped from the edit van into the ground. The action was not to be missed, even though we had to do a huge edit for *News at Ten* in London.

But on the hour, a disastrous piece of luck for England. A fluke of a free kick, a massive deflection, and the ball looped over Peter Shilton and into the net. 1–0 to West Germany.

Back to the van, to put together a piece on the inevitable German win. But after eighty-one minutes, a clinical finish from Lineker levelled the score. 1-1, and nine minutes left. My God, England were tantalizingly close to a World Cup final.

All square after ninety minutes. Extra time came and went with near-misses, heart-stopping moments and Gazza's famous tears.

And then... penalties. Lineker scores, Beardsley scores, Platt scores. And then Pearce has his saved. Germany have scored all theirs.

It is down to Chris Waddle. He smashes it over the bar and falls, crestfallen, to his knees. England are out. They don't deserve to be. But they're out.

It must have been horrendous to watch in the stadium and at home. In a cramped edit van, with the pressure of getting the story put together with the clock ticking away and editors in London screaming at me to have it ready for the top of the programme, it was very different.

I was so engrossed in the process, the drama sailed over me much as Waddle's penalty flew high into the stands.

I was there but I missed it, that's the only way I can describe it. I tell everyone I was there to witness it. But in my heart I really wasn't. I was in a van in a state of exasperation and tension, trying to get my job done.

England lost, but strangely English football won. People realized this was a sport that could unify the country. It was a sport that could exhilarate people. It was a sport that you could be proud of. The team weren't quite as bad as we thought. And in Bobby Robson, we had a manager so thoroughly decent that it seemed the national game might be worth fighting for and salvaging from the doldrums.

Other things helped. A report came out that radically changed the way football clubs treated their fans, all-seater stadiums became the norm, and through the nineties, hooligan-ism was hugely reduced – and, of course, Gazza had showed everyone that it was OK to cry. It was quite a tournament. Marco Stin and the BMW only just survived.

If Italia '90 had consequences beyond what would have been imagined, then the Rugby World Cup in South Africa five years later had an even more dramatic effect.

It is often said that sport and politics should never mix. That's utter nonsense. Sometimes sport can help shape a country's politics. And there is no better example of that than in South Africa. First of all, the international sports boycott of that country was one of the most important catalysts for change. Rugby in particular was an essential part of the identity of the apartheid regime's support base, and denying the country the ability to compete on an international stage was too painful for many in South Africa.

It was, of course, not the reason the country changed so dramatically in the early nineties. That was mainly down to the belated realization among the white leadership that the violent suppression of an overwhelming majority was not only repugnant but also no longer acceptable, practicable or tenable. But the sports boycott hastened that realization, no question about that.

And that wasn't the end of it. Once the decision had been taken to move to a democratic system of government, sport – and again rugby in particular – played a role of enormous significance.

One sportsman, one shirt and one event were largely respon-sible. The sportsman was Francois Pienaar, the shirt belonged to him, and the event was the Rugby World Cup final in Johannesburg on the afternoon of 24 June 1995.

I was there, in a seat high in Ellis Park Stadium, which afforded me a privileged view of an event that transcended sport and proved to be an occasion so transformative and emotional that even Hollywood – with all the saccharine romanticism it could throw at it – failed to do it justice.

Nelson Mandela had been president for a year, but South Africa was far from the united rainbow nation he had envisaged. The image of Mandela as a leader of a terrorist organization intent on destroying the power and privilege of the white population still endured for many Afrikaners. Indeed, the potential for white armed resistance to undermine the relatively peaceful transition had not completely receded.

Mandela knew he had work to do. And in the Rugby World Cup he saw the perfect opportunity. But he needed an accomplice.

He identified one in the captain of the South African team, Francois Pienaar, a son of apartheid for whom separatist white attitudes had shaped his thinking when he was growing up.

'I remember when I heard Nelson Mandela's name mentioned at barbecues or dinner parties, the word "terrorist" or "bad man" was an umbilical cord almost to his name,' he once said in an interview with the *Observer* newspaper.

Anyhow, just a month after becoming president, Mandela invited Pienaar for tea at his office in Pretoria, and set in train a process that was to pay huge dividends the following year. Mandela won over Pienaar in the way he won over most people. Pienaar was putty in the president's hands.

Less easy was the other part of Mandela's grand strategy... how to persuade the country's black population to embrace a sport they all viewed as a much-hated symbol of the apartheid regime.

For them it was very simple. Soccer was the sport of the black townships. Rugby was the sport of the oppressor. And a token 'coloured' or mixed-race player in the Springbok line-up was not going to change that. In fact, the likelihood was that it would serve only to reinforce the belief.

The president at first got short shrift at the mere suggestion that blacks should support the Springboks. But somehow, over some months, things changed. He was helped by the willingness of the South African players to learn the words of the new African part of the national anthem, 'Nkosi Sikelel' iAfrika' ('God Bless Africa'), and by their realization that they had a huge role to play in helping Mandela unite the country. He also persuaded the *Sowetan*, the English language newspaper set up to promote the liberation struggle, to back the team, and to urge its readers to set aside suspicion and hatred.

By the time of the final at Ellis Park, Mandela's work was almost complete. There was just one other thing. Minutes before kick-off, he walked out onto the pitch to shake the players' hands, wearing the green Springbok shirt given to him by Pienaar. It was a gesture of enormous political bravery and great vision. It was met with a strange silence, as 60,000 overwhelmingly white rugby fans reacted with disbelief. It would soon give way to something quite extraordinary.

A few Afrikaner flags that had been hoisted were rapidly furled, a section of the crowd started chanting 'Nelson, Nelson,

Nelson...!', and soon the entire stadium was belting it out in unison.

It was the most astonishing moment. Around me, my wife was in tears, Jeremy Thompson's wife Lynn was in tears, and soon so was I. That much was predictable. What was less expected was that entire rows of burly, unsentimental, Afrikaner rugby diehards were also crying, or fighting desperately hard not to.

Mandela had pulled it off; he'd won over the hardest audience imaginable, and hundreds of millions of people around the world had watched him do it.

At the end of the game, he reappeared to hand over the trophy to his captain and chief collaborator, Francois Pienaar.

'Francois, thank you very much for what you have done for our country,' he said.

'No, Mr President. Thank you for what you have done for our country.'

There were celebrations that night both in the white suburbs and the townships. And that – trust me – is a rarity.

I can't remember the score; suffice to say South Africa beat New Zealand. It is not the game that mattered in the end; it was everything that went on around it. Sport and politics... sometimes it really is the perfect mix.

The reason I was in South Africa for this historic game was that, just over a year earlier, I had become ITN's Africa Correspondent based in Johannesburg. One man – Nelson Mandela – was to become a big part of my professional life.

MANDELA

NELSON MANDELA PUSHED open the heavy steel door and ushered me in to the cell that was his home for nearly two decades.

'You first, Mark,' he said. 'After all, I have seen it plenty of times before.'

I walked in ahead of him. It was tiny, barely eight feet wide and seven feet long, with a thin mattress, a hard pillow, a small table and a slop bucket in the corner. Above us was a window with six vertical bars, through which a tall man like Mandela could peer out at the prison courtyard.

'My God, it's small,' I said. 'How on earth—'

He cut me off. 'You get used to it, you know.' He told me there was barely enough room to lie down to sleep. Then he laughed. 'But it is my fault. I shouldn't be so tall.'

It was typical Mandela. Dry, funny, self-deprecating, and illustrative of his total lack of bitterness and recrimination.

Mandela had invited me and a camera team to accompany him on a trip back to the prison on Robben Island where he had been incarcerated. And there we were. Mandela and I standing in his cell, chatting away. Just the two of us. I remember thinking to myself how lucky I was. That there are not many jobs like this.

'Don't you hate the men who did this to you?' I asked him.

'No, no,' he said. 'I despised the system, not my jailers.'

Mandela – or Prisoner 46664 (the 466th prisoner to arrive in 1964) – told me that when he and his Africa National Congress comrades landed on Robben Island, a warder's first words were: 'This is the island. Here you will die.'

It could have happened like that. It was a gruelling place and a harsh regime. They were forced to crush stones with a hammer to make gravel, and were made to work in a blindingly bright limestone quarry without sunglasses or shade, day in day out.

Mandela not only survived, but the imposing figure standing next to me in that tiny cell in 1994 was now the first black president of South Africa.

To have met Mandela and to have witnessed his role in the transformation of South Africa is one of the great privileges of my lifetime. I was fortunate enough to have interviewed him on many occasions, and I spoke with him privately on many more. Mandela was kind and thoughtful, always seemed to remember your name, and on one occasion saved my professional skin.

When he'd been in office for almost a year, the Queen arrived in South Africa on a state visit. After a reception at Durban City Hall, he took his royal guest on a short walkabout to meet the crowds. My cameraman Andy Rex and I were stuck on the wrong side of the security barriers, and to my horror I noticed the BBC's royal correspondent Jennie Bond doing a quick interview with a smiling Mandela as they walked along.

This was not at all ideal. How on earth had she got so close to Mandela and the Queen? That was not supposed to happen. I felt a growing sense of panic. I now needed to get an interview of my own, or there would be hell to pay. But how?

It seemed impossible. Andy and I were not even close to them. There was a crowd, five deep, in front of us. We weren't even remotely in his line of sight, and we were barely within earshot. The crowds were cheering and a military band was playing. As they neared the area where we were stood helplessly, I decided to wave my arms manically and yelled 'Mr President!' at the top of my voice. Nothing, not even a glance in our direction.

By now, Mandela was in earnest conversation with Her Majesty (that's the Queen, not Jennie Bond... The BBC reporter had disappeared with what she no doubt considered to be a well-earned scoop). I pushed my way to the front of the crowd, apologizing as I went, eventually reaching the security ropes. Mandela was about twenty yards away. I resumed the frantic waving and shouting, and finally, mercifully, I caught his eye. I think he must have thought I had temporarily lost my mind. He showed enough concern to come slightly closer and I bellowed a request for a 'few quick words on this momentous day'. He stopped, realized my predicament and beckoned us through the throng of security men.

'What the BBC shall have,' he said, 'you shall have.' Short interview secured. Career saved.

I returned to the other side of the security cordon before I realized I had been a few feet from the Queen and had failed to ask her a single question. But that was Mandela for you. Charismatic, warm and, when he wanted to be, considerate.

I relay these personal memories of Mandela because they genuinely do tell you something about the man that he was. They are small moments, trivial details. But even so, they can be every bit as instructive as the grand gestures on the big stage that everyone knows about.

Put simply, Mandela's ability to put people at ease, to open his heart, even to his enemies, and to make people feel good about themselves was key to the way South Africa was to turn out.

I firmly believe it was the nature of the man that made the new South Africa possible. Without Mandela, without his generosity of spirit and without that precious ability to persuade the country's black population to set aside all the perfectly natural instincts for vengeance and retribution, the miracle would not have happened when it did or how it did. I am absolutely certain of that.

But it was a close-run thing. When I first arrived in South Africa, a few months before the election, things were very grim indeed. And about to get worse.

I had covered conflicts before, most recently in Bosnia in 1992, but never had I arrived to work, live and set up home with my family in a country where violence and chaos had become the norm. But that was South Africa in early 1994. And in particular, it was Johannesburg in 1994, the city my wife Catherine and one-year-old son Jack would be living in. More than once I questioned what I was doing taking them there.

On our arrival, the turmoil was not immediately obvious. Our flight landed at Jan Smuts Airport – yes, this was still a South Africa that lauded the architects of apartheid. We moved

Terrible haircut, great phone, awful pose. A publicity picture circa 1988, aged 29.

Covering the Open Golf for ITN in 1990. Graham Phillips, cameraman, and Peter Staunton, producer, in the driving seat.

Rwanda, 1994, the most horrific story I have covered.

Reporting the Mandela inauguration, May 1994.

One of the great moments. A post-interview team picture in 1994 with President Nelson Mandela, cameraman Andy Rex, soundman Gugu Radebe and producer James Britten.

Mandela would often smile and always looked you in the eye when talking to you. He also knew the importance of the message and the media.

Mozambique floods, March 2000. Helping a winchman lift flood victims into a South African Defence Force Chinook helicopter.

A proud moment. Andy Rex and I pick up an Emmy in New York for our Mozambique floods coverage.

May 2000, in Freetown, Sierra Leone, when British forces arrived to save the capital from attack.

Presenting the ITV *Evening News* from Kuwait just days before the start of the Iraq War, 17 March 2003. Mike Inglis is the cameraman.

Writing scripts for the ITV *Evening News* in a disused house in the Iraqi desert, 25 March 2003.

Our studio in the desert during the Iraq war, 26 March 2003.

Our convoy comes to a halt on a mined road en route to Basra, Iraq, 6 April 2003. Our mobile satellite dish can be seen second from the back. In the distance sabotaged oil facilities burn.

Inside Iraq, 8 April 2003. Preparing for another live broadcast.

My friend and colleague Terry Lloyd is seen making his last televised news report from the Iraqi border on 21 March 2003. A day later he was killed.

In Basra, Iraq, 10 April 2003. A great team for a tough assignment. *Left to right*: Nick Edwards, me, Mike Inglis, Alan Bugby, Ted Denton, Derl McCrudden and Steve Gore-Smith.

effortlessly through arrivals, hopped into a large four-wheel-drive Land Cruiser and moved comfortably through light traffic until the motorway gave way to the wide, tree-lined avenues of the northern suburbs. This was where people like us – white, affluent and privileged – lived in large houses with extensive gardens, expansive lawns and large blue swimming pools, all neatly nestled behind high security walls, electric gates and barbed wire. Our house, in Dunkeld, was enormous. Six bedrooms for the three of us, and a housemaid and a gardener who both lived on the premises. Welcome to the world of a foreign correspondent in Africa.

What became immediately apparent is what I already knew. There are in fact two South Africas. I say 'are' and not 'were', because to all intents and purposes, nearly a quarter of a century on from the end of apartheid, there are still two South Africas.

But in early 1994 the difference between them was slightly (yes, only slightly) more pronounced. One South Africa is relatively small and largely white. The other, much bigger and largely black. The first is comfortable, mainly peaceful, relatively prosperous, with modern infrastructure and developed communications. The second is not. It is hideously poor, grossly underdeveloped, with overcrowding, hunger, destitution and violence. And in the early nineties, there was violence like you would not imagine. There were several murders a day, both political and criminal. There was necklacing, where a tyre is put around the neck of the victim and then petrol is poured into it and set alight. There were rapes, robberies, and machete attacks on tribal and political rivals. The police were not only ineffectual, but were often accused of fomenting the violence to give the appearance of chaos. How can these black people run the country if this is what is going on? That was the question the violence was intended to raise in the minds of people inside and outside the country. It was cynical in the extreme.

This South Africa was made up of tribal homelands and townships dotted across the landscape, close enough to the nice, privileged areas to serve the needs of their wealthy inhabitants. But far enough so those inhabitants didn't have to smell the sewers, or hear the gunfire or the cries of women being raped at knifepoint by gangs of drunken men.

When I arrived in the country, the townships, particularly those to the east of Johannesburg, were engulfed in chaos and murder. The struggle against apartheid was reaching a bloody and dramatic denouement. Nelson Mandela had been released from prison a few years earlier, his African National Congress (ANC) party was no longer a banned organization and South Africa was edging towards the first-ever truly democratic elections. Mandela and the then president, F.W. de Klerk, were deep in negotiations over when and how the transition would happen.

But things were not going well. White extremists and Zulu militants were both threatening to boycott the elections, secede from the new South Africa and plunge the country into civil war. Every day it seemed the news became increasingly bleak. The white right-wingers were blowing up electricity substations and pylons, but by far the worst violence was in the townships, where gun battles and massacres were an all-too-common feature of the intense political rivalry between the ANC and supporters of the Inkatha Freedom Party, led by Chief Mangosuthu Buthelezi.

Inkatha began life as a non-political organization designed to preserve Zulu culture and traditions, and initially operated with the full blessing of the ANC. Gradually, however, Buthelezi moved away from the ANC and closer politically to the largely white National Party, who saw an opportunity to fund and arm the group on the premise that 'my enemy's enemy is my friend'. Buthelezi soon made some form of Zulu secession his obsession, and slowly built up a network of fighters and warlords in Natal. The stage was set for a prolonged and deadly war, which would be brutally exploited by elements in the white police force.

Any opportunity to fuel the fighting in the townships was seized upon by the police, and it has long been assumed that rogue units effectively operated as death squads, going on random killing sprees to inflame the conflict that was already costing dozens of lives every day.

But the violence was principally 'black on black', as it became known, and it was not just political in nature. Much of it was criminal, the result of feuds, attempted robberies and street fights. The root cause of most of the murders or serious injuries was, in fact, alcohol. I remember a night spent filming in Soweto's vast Baragwanath Hospital, where from around midnight the casualties poured in. The vast majority were men with head, neck or back injuries who were wheeled in unconscious and drunk. Quite a lot had gunshot wounds. One Belgian doctor working in the emergency ward told me that he had heard that AK-47 assault rifles could be bought for around twenty dollars. You could organize a 'hit' for around thirty dollars more. Guns, drink and lives were all cheap in Soweto.

But, in a sense, even this 'non-political' violence had its roots in the politics of South Africa. Decades of oppression and neglect under the apartheid regime had led to poverty, illiteracy and unemployment, all of which contributed to high levels of alcohol and drug use that, in turn, fuelled the high levels of violent crime. It was no surprise to me that the murder rate in South Africa in 1993–94 was the highest it had ever been.

There was a war on. It was just that white South Africans and white visitors were largely immune to it and protected from it. And the worse it got, of course, the more the apartheid government leaders insisted that such chaos disqualified the black majority from any pretence of being able to run the country. Nelson Mandela knew this and knew he had to stop it. But how?

This was the South Africa in which I arrived. A country on the verge of implosion. The peaceful transition to black rule and the emergence of the new rainbow nation envisaged by Mandela looked a distant prospect, despite the continuing negotiations. It was an extraordinary time to be there.

The violence between ANC fighters and Zulu warriors had become so extreme that it was difficult to cover. It was often too dangerous to enter some townships, but sometimes terrible atrocities took place that demanded our attention and coverage.

One weekend, a Zulu gang of two hundred men, armed with AK-47s, machete-like pangas and wooden clubs called knobkerries, left a migrant workers' hostel in Tembisa township and went on the rampage, stopping cars, setting fire to them with occupants inside and gunning down entire families in their homes. By dawn on Sunday, thirty people from the ANC-supporting area of Tembisa were dead, including a five-month-old baby, executed in his bedroom with his parents. By the afternoon, the violence had spread to Thokoza township about twenty miles away. Sixteen more people died there, mainly Zulus from another hostel who were killed in a revenge attack by ANC supporters.

I was asked to go to Tembisa on Monday morning and compile a report on the violence – and, in particular, the issue of Zulu migrant workers living in the midst of largely ANC-supporting townships. Things seemed reasonably calm in Tembisa, and so we drove in.

My sound man Gugu, a big, huggable bear of a man from Soweto, did something I had never seen him do before. He put a handgun under the seat of the car before we set off. He didn't know I'd noticed, and I pretended not to. I am utterly opposed to reporters arming ourselves in almost any situation. I think it turns us into combatants rather than neutral observers. But I could understand why he did it. Such was the atmosphere for black South Africans at the time. I felt sad but kept quiet.

At the sprawling hostel compound we found barely any Zulus willing to talk. But one man told us it had all begun when a young Zulu selling milk from his bike was cornered by township vigilantes. He was accused of being a spy, and was beaten, hacked and then necklaced. 'He was a harmless kid,' we were told, and that was why the massacre took place.

It was all so familiar and typical of what was happening. The violence was beginning to follow a classic pattern, only it was becoming more frequent, almost routine. And it was all connected to the prospect of the looming elections.

I was very pessimistic about how things would turn out. The talks were stalling, Mandela and de Klerk were at loggerheads and the townships were in flames. On top of all this, many white South Africans and expat Europeans who had made their lives in the country were now talking openly about leaving. Mandela knew that an exodus of white talent and business know-how would deal a severe blow to the economy, wreck hopes for his rainbow nation and send out a terrible message to the world. A year earlier, it was an impassioned speech from Mandela that had prevented a panicked exodus of whites.

On the afternoon of 10 April 1993, Chris Hani, one of the most charismatic leaders of the anti-apartheid movement, was shot dead outside his home. He had huge popularity and support among young ANC voters in the townships. A firebrand in the style of Che Guevara, he would often appear at rallies in combat fatigues, making rousing speeches that would delight the young radicals who swarmed to hear him. The militant wing of the ANC clearly viewed Hani as a possible successor to Mandela, and a future president in a democratic South Africa. He was that popular.

It soon became clear that his attacker was Janusz Waluś, a neo-Nazi Polish immigrant. Waluś shot him once in the stomach and several times in the head.

The timing was significant. Hani was a key player in the fragile negotiations taking place following the release of Mandela, which the ANC hoped would lead to the first-ever free and fair elections in the country. At that time, the talks appeared to be on the verge of a major breakthrough. Waluś and the white extremists who had put him up to the murder didn't want that to happen. Later, at a Truth and Reconciliation Commission hearing in 1997, Waluś admitted that he'd intended to try to provoke a race war, derail the political process and halt any progress towards elections and the inevitable end of white minority rule.

Many senior figures in South Africa seriously believed it could be the moment that tipped the country into all-out civil war. 'I fear for our country,' said Archbishop Desmond Tutu. 'Chris Hani, more than anyone else, had the credibility among the young to rein in the radicals.'

It would prove to be Mandela's greatest test in the run-up to the election.

There was an upsurge in violence, and within hours more than seventy people had been killed. There was an immediate sense of foreboding after it became clear that it was a white man who had killed Hani. Until then, apart from the desperate crime rate, the privileged white population had largely been isolated from the murderous and worsening violence taking place in the townships all around Johannesburg.

Immediately after the killing, Mandela had gone on television to deliver an address to a nervous, fearful and divided nation.

'Tonight, I am reaching out to everyone in South Africa, black and white, from the very depths of my being,' he said. 'A white man, full of prejudice and hate, came to our country and committed a deed so foul that our whole nation now teeters on the brink of disaster.

'The cold-blooded murder of Chris Hani has sent shock waves throughout the country and the world. Our grief and anger is tearing us apart. What has happened is a national tragedy that has touched millions of people, across the political and colour divide.'

And then he said this:

Now is the time for all South Africans to stand together against those who, from any quarter, wish to destroy what Chris Hani gave his life for – the freedom of all of us. Now is the time for our white compatriots, from whom messages of condolence continue to pour in, to reach out with an understanding of the grievous loss to our nation... Now is the time for the police to act with sensitivity and restraint, to be real community policemen and women who serve the population as a whole. There must be no further loss of life at this tragic time. This is a watershed moment for all of us... We must not let the men who worship war, and who lust after blood, precipitate actions that will plunge our country into another Angola.

Now, it would have been easy for Mandela to pander to the angry young militants who supported Hani, in order to cement a constituency that wasn't naturally on his side. It would have been easy to call off the talks and paint the apartheid leaders as masters of the dark arts, seeking to destroy the move to democracy. It would have been popular and there was almost certainly an element of truth to it.

But he didn't. Mandela saw the immediate danger of all-out civil war and realized that was exactly what Waluś had been out to achieve. And he realized that the only way forward for South Africa was through reconciliation and peaceful change.

It is no coincidence that less than two months after the killing of Hani, negotiations between the ANC and the white government led to an agreement setting the date for South Africa's first-ever free election – 27 April 1994. It would be the date when apartheid would finally collapse and the country would get its first black president.

One other point about the Hani killing and its aftermath was the almost-immediate arrest of Waluś for the shooting. It was a white Afrikaner woman, a neighbour of Hani's, who called the police and identified the killer. In the tense atmosphere of South Africa at the time, that mattered.

Mandela had prevented an immediate descent into civil war. But he knew he now had a fight on his hands on three fronts. He had to keep the talks with the apartheid leaders on track. He urgently had to quell the conflict raging in the townships. And he also had to mollify those white right-wingers plotting to undermine the entire transition.

That particular threat was dealt with for him, in a way he could never have imagined.

It all unfolded in Bophuthatswana, a place I had never heard of before I arrived in South Africa. There, in March 1994, the world got a glimpse of the violent chaos that could ensue if things went badly wrong at the elections in South Africa, now just a month away.

Bophuthatswana was one of apartheid's great cons. It was a nominally independent black homeland within South Africa, created by the white regime in Pretoria to present to the world the impression of a free country. They spent millions of dollars on a kind of toytown capital, Mmabatho, complete with an 'independent' government and even its own president, Lucas Mangope.

But when the apartheid regime collapsed, so too did the illusion that was Bophuthatswana. Mangope – a puppet of Pretoria – refused to countenance his people taking part in the elections and demonstrations flared.

Unable to control the protests, Mangope inexplicably appealed for help from a group of white right-wingers led by a former army general, Constand Viljoen. Viljoen immediately sent men from his Volksfront militia to protect key installations. But the mission was hijacked by hundreds of khaki-clad fanatics from other white extremist paramilitaries, who took to the streets in pickups and battered old Mercedes cars and unleashed utter mayhem, firing randomly at innocent black shoppers and bystanders. It provoked fury among the locals, who ran amok, smashing up shops and businesses and looting whatever they could. Local Bophuthatswana troops only added to the carnage by shooting wildly in a forlorn bid to restore order.

Into this chaos flew our charter plane from Johannesburg, dropping us at the airfield on the outskirts of Mmabatho. We picked up the car we'd arranged and were heading towards the city, when a convoy of white racists approached. They were members of Eugène Terre'Blanche's Afrikaner Weerstandsbeweging (AWB). I asked my cameraman Andy Rex to start filming. He was reluctant, but grabbed the camera and filmed the oncoming militia from inside our vehicle.

Unfortunately, they very quickly saw what we were doing and didn't like it at all.

The lead pickup truck drew up alongside our car and several armed men jumped out. They were screaming at us in Afrikaans, and I got out of the car to try to placate them. It quickly became obvious that was not going to happen. They were furious and out of control. The tall, bearded figure who was apparently in charge pointed his pistol at me and barked orders I simply could not understand. He became more and more irate, and I thought he was going to shoot. 'For fuck's sake,' I said, 'put the gun away.'

'Fuck? Fuck?' he screamed. It was obviously the only word he recognized, and he was furious. At that point, my young producer James Brittain also got out of the car to try to calm the guy down. That didn't work either. They grabbed both of us and pointed to the field at the side of the road. In broken English, one of the racist lunatics told us to walk down the embankment into the field and get down on our knees. Two of them were now pointing guns at us.

We did as they asked and it was utterly terrifying. They told us not to turn around. We should just stare ahead.

So there we were on our knees in a dusty field in some godforsaken place no one had ever heard of, and even less cared about. Not for the first time, I wondered why on earth I put myself in these positions. James was shaking with worry. 'They're going to kill us, aren't they?' he said.

'Bloody hope not,' was all I could manage as reassurance.

I really wasn't confident they wouldn't. No story is worth dying for, but this one *certainly* wasn't. It felt like we were there for an hour; in truth, it was only a matter of minutes. Behind us, out of sight, they were emptying our car of flak jackets and camera kit. They took it all. Then we heard their trucks move off, followed closely by the sound of laughter. It was Andy's unmistakable Zimbabwean cackle. 'Hey, you two. You can come back now. They've gone.' And then more chuckling. He may have seen the funny side. James and I certainly didn't.

For James, it was one of his first assignments with us. Until joining ITN he'd been working on the local paper in Johannesburg. The blood had drained from his face, he was still shaking and he didn't speak for an hour. I, on the other hand, couldn't stop talking. It's odd how people react so differently to the same experience. We did, however, share one emotion: huge relief.

But we were still in a spot of trouble. The story was happening a few miles down the road right now, and we had no means of filming it. We made our way to the hotel where most of the media were camped, and hoped to be able to beg, steal or borrow enough equipment to get a story out.

On the streets, events had taken a highly significant turn. The South African Defence Force had moved into Mmabatho and started chasing the white right-wingers out of town. In one much-publicized incident, three wounded white racists were found slumped by their blue Mercedes pleading for help. A Bophuthatswana police patrol stopped at the scene and a constable, Ontlametse Menyatsoe, went over to speak to one of the men, an AWB colonel, Alwyn Wolfaardt. Menyatsoe asked him if he was a member of the AWB. When Wolfaardt confirmed that he was, the police officer lifted up his rifle and shot all three men dead at point-blank range, in full view of the cameras. 'Who do you think you are?' he shouted angrily at them. 'What are you doing in my country?'

It proved to be a stunning and seminal moment in the creation of the new South Africa, and quickly became a big story. Somehow, we managed to buy footage from a freelance cameraman who had captured the killings, then borrowed some equipment and sent a story to London.

The picture of the shooting was an image that symbolized the defeat of the white right, the feebleness of their pathetic last stand and the vacuity of their cause. And it went around the world. It was also the moment the threat to the elections posed by the racists receded into the distance. In the wake of the humiliating fiasco, Constand Viljoen quit as head of the right-wing coalition. The extremists were in disarray. Mandela's job of neutralizing the threat had effectively been done for him.

The outcome of the crisis also showed the loyalty and effectiveness of the South African Defence Force. White and black troops acting together for the good of the new South Africa. It was a reassuring sight for many who welcomed the transformation taking place in the country.

For many reasons, I will not forget Bophuthatswana in a hurry. Andy Rex still laughs about the day I had a gun pointing at my head. Curiously, I don't.

But our trip was marked by sadness on a personal level, too. John Harrison, the BBC's correspondent in South Africa at the time, was killed in a car accident near the capital as he and his camera team were driving to a TV station to send back a report for BBC News. It was a dreadful shock to all of us.

He had become a mate as much as a rival. At the wake at his family home in Johannesburg, the phone rang and the caller asked to speak to John's widow. It was Nelson Mandela; a measure of the man who would become president, and of the reporter himself.

A month before polling day, the Zulu Inkatha Freedom Party was still vowing to boycott the elections. They were staging protest marches in Durban and right across their Natal heartland. But on Monday 28 March, they planned a big demonstration in Johannesburg. Andy Rex and I weren't particularly bothered about yet another political march, and Andy actually suggested we played golf instead. I decided we would put the clubs in the car, but we would also go to the march to take some pictures to use should we decide to do a story later in the day. Suffice to say, we never got anywhere near the golf course.

It was a noisy and colourful march. Thousands of Zulu warriors in traditional dress, armed with knobkerries and spears, dancing and chanting their way through central Johannesburg. Andy was busy filming the scene when suddenly gunshots rang out. Pistol fire at first, but then, within a minute or two, the sustained rapid clatter of AK-47s. It was loud and close, and marchers ran in different directions; some fell close by to us, others drew their own weapons and started firing themselves.

I dived for cover under an armoured police vehicle. Andy was leaning against the wall of an office building filming the gunfire and the chaos in front of him. He claims he looked everywhere for me to do a piece to camera while the firing was taking place, but says he gave up when he saw me huddled nervously under the vehicle. I wasn't the bravest.

When I emerged, during a lull in the shooting, bodies were everywhere. We saw several dead and many, many more injured. The pavements of Johannesburg ran with blood that Monday morning.

Most of the shooting came from ANC security men guarding the organization's headquarters, Shell House, on Jeppe Street. Nineteen died there, and many others were shot dead in surrounding streets. It became known as the Shell House massacre, and reflected the still-rising tensions between Mandela's ANC and Buthelezi's IFP. The ANC claimed its guards had acted defensively and were protecting its property and staff. A subsequent judicial inquiry found absolutely no evidence for this and concluded that such a justification had been 'fabricated after the event'. It was hugely critical of the ANC guards. Later, Mandela admitted that he had given orders to protect the HQ and its staff, even if it meant having to shoot to kill.

The blame game was just getting underway, but the fact was that, just weeks before the election, dozens of people were lying dead on the streets of downtown Johannesburg. It did not augur well. In my report that night, I said that it was quite possible that Zulu fighters would now seek not only to boycott the elections but also to disrupt them with a campaign of threats and intimidation. I was convinced the desire for vengeance would be overwhelming. It is what normally happened, and we were now perilously close to the elections.

Around this time, I went to Cape Town to interview Archbishop Desmond Tutu. I wanted to know how the country's popular spiritual leader with the infectious, screeching laugh and unbridled optimism felt about the way things were going. I pitched up at his home with my cameraman Andy Rex and he seemed delighted to see us. He always greeted me with a fist bump and a wonderful smile, and I felt uplifted and special. It was as if we were great friends, and even though we were not, it made me feel good.

As usual, he was in a hurry. We set up the camera and we sat down to do the interview. And then came the crushing moment. 'Now, how are you, Michael?' he asked. As I crashed forlornly back to earth, I pretended not to notice. Interestingly, a few years later the BBC correspondent Allan Little mentioned to me that he had met Tutu on numerous occasions, and almost every time they saw each other, the archbishop failed to recognize him.

I had no doubts the interview would make a good story, but I was quietly hoping he would see some optimism for the future. I was beginning to feel a real affinity for the place, and I felt I had no small emotional investment in the country. I wanted him to tell me everything would be fine and that my family and I had nothing to worry about. As it was, I left disappointed and worried.

Even the optimistic Desmond Tutu, who saw hope and possibility in the most desperate times, could not see a way out of the current darkness. 'I have to say I am full of foreboding. It is as if a light has been extinguished. I am not sure even Madiba [the commonly used nickname for Mandela] can make this work.'

But for once Tutu was wrong, Mandela did make it work.

Just as South Africa feared the violence would intensify still further, what actually intensified was the talking. President F.W. de Klerk worked hard to bring Chief Buthelezi back into the fold, and urged the two sides to talk at a senior level. In the days before the election there were bombings and deaths, but the most significant event took place on 19 April... a week before the elections.

We were summoned to a news conference in Pretoria held by Chief Buthelezi, Nelson Mandela and President de Klerk. They emerged smiling and joking, and it was clear something was up.

In a last-minute turnaround that immeasurably increased hopes for a peaceful birth of democracy, the Zulu leader announced he was calling off the threatened boycott. At the same time, in Natal, the king of South Africa's eight million Zulus, Goodwill Zwelithini, was endorsing the decision and called on his subjects to take part in the voting.

It was never really clear why Buthelezi made the U-turn, other than, perhaps, a fear that he would become a political outcast in a successful new South Africa. Anyway, the main point was that the decision sent a wave of elation through a country that was fearful its transition from pariah state to rainbow nation would be scuppered by political violence. The miracle was happening before our eyes.

And so the day arrived... the day the new South Africa was born. And what a day it was. A day of sunshine, of optimism and hope. A day of long, snaking queues of people waiting patiently to exercise a right so many other people around the world take for granted. They stood in line for hours in the burning sun. And they didn't complain, because this was the day they had yearned for and fought for and looked forward to for decades. It was the first truly democratic election in South Africa, where the black majority could vote for the very first time.

We were out at dawn to film in Soweto township. I didn't want to miss a moment of a day it was a privilege to witness and record. We filmed the queues, we filmed a hundred thumbprints being applied joyously to ballot papers, we filmed the looks on the faces of the voters as they emerged from polling booths and we filmed their words. Those of one woman, a grandmother of seventy-one, I remember particularly well. 'I have waited for this day all my life,' she said. 'I can now die happily because I know my children and my grandchildren will be able to decide who runs this country. The days of oppression are over. The days of freedom have arrived.'

It was almost as if she had rehearsed it. She may have done, but somehow I doubt it. It just came from the heart. It spilled out with such unalloyed joyousness. She almost sang the words for our camera.

The result was not in doubt. Twenty million people voted; nearly 63 per cent voted for the leader of the African National Congress, Nelson Mandela.

The scenes on the day of his inauguration in Pretoria were breathtaking. South African Defence Force jets – part of the apparatus of apartheid era repression – led a flypast in honour of the new president who was once a prisoner. It was a jaw-dropping and momentous moment.

But the euphoria post-election did not last long. While the political violence subsided, criminal violence seemed, if anything, to worsen. Many white professionals were beginning to fear that things were becoming simply too dangerous... my wife among them.

For her, things came to a head in October 1995. A young Hong Kong Chinese doctor, Stephen Pon, was shot and seriously wounded by gunmen in the car park of the Johannesburg hospital. They made off with his BMW. Casualty staff heard the shots and rushed outside. Surgeons worked on Pon for ten hours but it was hopeless. They couldn't save him.

For many doctors and nurses Pon's death was a breaking point. If a doctor doing his duty in a public hospital was not safe, then nobody was safe. There were memorial services, protest marches and the hospital's trauma unit closed for a day.

Catherine, then herself working as a doctor at Baragwanath hospital in Soweto, decided she wanted to leave. It wasn't worth the risk. The violence was widespread, indiscriminate and growing.

And things weren't made any easier by an incident at the house when we had been woken by noises in the garden. The lights had come on outside and I'd seen dark figures prowling around the grounds. We did what we were told to do in these circumstances, and closed and locked the heavy steel door to the bedroom area. I don't mind admitting it was terrifying.

In the event, it turned out to be armed guys from the private security company we subscribed to. They returned the next morning to explain they had heard gunshots, and had found the gunman in the garage of a neighbouring house trying to steal a car that he'd already loaded with garden equipment. Again, it was unsettling.

After considerable agonizing Catherine decided to stay... a decision reinforced by a remarkable encounter with Nelson Mandela that she will never forget.

She had noticed posters on trees and municipal buildings in our area announcing a meeting for local doctors and nurses who were even remotely thinking of leaving the country.

The African National Congress leadership was worried. They knew an exodus of the well-trained white doctors could be disastrous for the future of the country.

Catherine went along to the meeting in a nearby church hall. A hundred or so other medics turned up and listened to the pleas of a local ANC politician. He was unconvincing. Then there was a commotion. The doors opened and in came a group of black women, singing, ululating and cheering. And behind them, walking slowly but deliberately towards the small stage, was an elderly, silver-haired, tall but slightly stooping figure. Emerging from the throng, it was unmistakably Nelson Mandela. My wife couldn't believe what she was seeing. He walked past her and smiled.

Mandela climbed carefully onto the small stage at the front of the hall and pleaded with the stunned, largely white audience not to give up on South Africa. He asked how he could build a new country without them. He said they were fundamental to the success of the rainbow nation he was trying to create. He said he could not succeed if they left. They were the key to the miracle happening. He needed their help.

He reached out with an emotional, powerful speech that reduced many of those listening to tears, including my wife. It was an extraordinary thing to do… It did not make him popular with many more radical colleagues, but he felt it was necessary.

You would imagine that a man emerging from twenty-seven years in prison would be consumed with anger, bitterness and a thirst for revenge. But Mandela preached reconciliation, forgiveness and tolerance, and went out of his way to make a white population – wracked with fear and suspicion – feel that they were not only wanted, but also needed.

It was another example of the remarkable character of Mandela. He was a politician like no other. But then, in so many ways, he transcended politics. He was often called a living saint. Mandela was no saint. He had personal foibles like everyone does, he helped oversee a deadly terrorist war against the racist apartheid regime, made opportunistic alliances with controversial leaders and never claimed to be anything more than human.

He made mistakes, and, in some ways, came up short as a leader himself. He admitted he failed to tackle the spread of HIV, even as terrifyingly large numbers of South Africans became infected. It took him a long while to accept that Soviet-style economics didn't work, though he was willing to switch and open up South Africa's state-run industries. How he would despair now at the unemployment, poverty and neglect that still blights the lives of millions of impoverished blacks.

Some South Africans also believe that Mandela sold out too readily in the negotiated settlement. He won political freedom for the black majority, but not economic freedom. They felt the dominance of the 'white ruling class' was not sufficiently challenged and dismantled.

I am not so sure. Mandela's overriding concern as the transition approached was to ensure that as many key people as possible in education, health, business, infrastructure, science and technology stayed in South Africa to help rebuild and reshape the nation. Many of those people were white. To have overstretched in tearing away all aspects of white privilege would have made it less likely those key people would remain. If there appeared to be a backlash, many would have gone. And that would not have been good for the economy, or the country. He knew that.

One failing, in my view, is that he did not ensure the succession was in the best interests of South Africa. Thabo Mbeki was not the man to follow Mandela. I always thought the current president, Cyril Ramaphosa, would have made a more natural successor. Ramaphosa came to the presidency too late, in my view.

And one other point about Mandela. Questions, I am sure, will one day be asked about what he knew of the activities of Winnie Mandela, his second wife and the great love of his life. She died in 2018, still celebrated in the townships, but also under a cloud of suspicion over kidnappings and unexplained deaths in Soweto.

So, no saint. Archbishop Desmond Tutu cackled out loud when I suggested it once. But when the time came, Mandela was a visionary leader who saw what was needed to make a miracle happen. And it was a miracle. South Africa's transition looked doomed many, many times in the years running up to the election. Even in the months before, from my close-up view, I often felt a low-intensity, prolonged civil war was more likely than peaceful change.

That I was wrong was down in large part to Mandela. He was a man of immense humanity and a politician who knew when to walk away. He realized that, after one term in office, he was into his eighties and his energy was decreasing. There are very few leaders in Africa who have shown this self-awareness. But perhaps Mandela was being politically smart as well.

The euphoria after the elections would only last so long. It was inevitable, given the scale of the challenge, that disappointment and dissatisfaction would set in and the ANC leadership would come under pressure. Maybe Mandela wanted to avoid all that.

After 1999, apart from occasional appearances or interventions, he slowly but very deliberately vacated the stage. The ANC did all it could to exploit his celebrity and star power, but in the months before his death he was reclusive and politically largely silent.

During the soccer World Cup in South Africa in 2010, I interviewed his wife Graça Machel. She said he was frail and tired and disengaged, but otherwise fine. In truth, by then he was struggling to remember much or recognize even famous guests.

She also told me he was disappointed by the lack of progress in improving the lives of the black majority: 'He knew it would take time, but he worries that people who voted back in 1994 for a better life are still not seeing things improve enough.'

He was right. Millions of blacks were still living without electricity or a constant supply of clean water. They had the vote and their freedom and they could elect their chosen leaders, but their daily lives remained a desperately hard slog. Political apartheid had become an economic apartheid, with a rising middle class of wealthy blacks who belonged to a political and business elite where corruption was rife.

In the end, South Africa was resigned to his imminent passing. But when it came in December 2013, it still shook the country to its core. Death in old age does not amount to a 'tragedy', I guess, but that is still how it was greeted when it happened. Millions grew up with him as either an out-of-reach, mysterious but all-pervasive backdrop to their lives, or, after his release, a constant and reassuring presence.

I was about to go on air with *News at Ten* when it was confirmed that he had passed away. We were ready with a structure for the programme, which was extended to an hour while we were on air.

My co-presenter Julie Etchingham was incredibly gracious that evening. It was her turn to lead the programme, but in the minutes leading up to ten o'clock she saw me busily typing away on my desktop computer. She knew I was putting together the main introduction to the programme and she was aware it was a story I knew well and which was close to my heart. 'You lead tonight,' she said. 'This is your story.' Not many presenters would do that.

And in a way, I did feel it was my story. I spent three years very close to it, at an emotional time. My first daughter Madeleine was born in Johannesburg in the year Mandela became president. So it was with a heavy heart and even perhaps a tear in my eye that I delivered the news that night. The hour went very quickly. There is so much to say about Mandela.

The next day I flew out to Johannesburg, and for the following week we broadcast the news each night from Soweto. There were days of mourning, but it also became a celebration of a man who had become like a much-loved grandfather to his country. His loss was keenly felt.

Suddenly, even though Mandela had not been president for

well over a decade, it was as if the country had been robbed of its founding father, its guiding hand – and its sense of self seemed damaged. This young, fragile, vulnerable democracy now stood alone.

The *Guardian* writer David Smith made an interesting observation just after Mandela's death. He wrote: 'Mandela was truly loved in a way that can seem quaint in the post-heroic age of politics. Buildings, bridges, streets and squares were named after him in life, commonplace in a dictatorship but remarkable in a democracy.'

It was certainly remarkable, the way Mandela was loved around the world.

His passing was a real test of President Zuma, who was already under pressure for allowing a sense of drift to take over the country. Unemployment and inequality still plagued South Africa. And Zuma's personal reputation was suffering terribly from allegations of corruption, racketeering, fraud and incompetence. The previous year it had emerged that he'd spent almost £15 million on upgrading his residence in Nkandla in KwaZulu-Natal province. His eventual ousting was long overdue.

There were fears Mandela's death would lead to violence; some, more fanciful, reports circulated that black radicals were waiting for him to die before embarking on an orgy of vengeance against the white population... a sort of post-apartheid and post-Mandela ethnic cleansing. It proved to be no more than rumour and urban myth. There was no such reaction.

South Africa and the world are incalculably poorer for his passing. It would be a betrayal of his sacrifice if those who follow him do not do more to right the wrongs of apartheid.

The country remains one of the most unequal societies on the planet, where tin shacks lie in the shadow of multimillion-pound mansions. I'm afraid that, soon, casting all the blame on apartheid will no longer suffice.

But South Africa has much to celebrate. It successfully ended an iniquitous and brutal form of government, without the disastrous civil war or mass chaos that afflicted so many other African countries transitioning from colonial to democratic control. That is quite something.

The challenge now for Mandela's successors is to tackle corruption and create economic and political conditions that will spread wealth throughout the population. South Africa has the chance to provide a shining example to the rest of Africa and the world. I hope it can pull it off. Nelson Mandela deserves to stop turning in his grave.

To witness the elections in South Africa was quite simply one of the most uplifting experiences of my lifetime. Little did I realize that just weeks later, in a different part of Africa, I would be cast into a world of unique grimness. A world of darkness and grotesque violence, where man's inhumanity to man was impossible to comprehend. A world where pure evil had taken hold.

I was flying into Rwanda, where genocide was taking place and no one was doing anything to stop it.

RWANDA

I F THE ELECTION of Nelson Mandela was the most inspiring story I ever covered, there is no question about which was the most depressing. Once – sometimes twice – in the life of a foreign correspondent, you will get sent to a place to cover a story that you will never be able to forget. Rwanda was that story for me, and for many others.

I have covered wars where human depravity beggars belief, where brutality and violence subsume any sense of human value or morality or dignity. But never, ever, have I reported on such blind savagery as that which befell Rwanda when the Hutu majority turned on the Tutsi population in week after week of tribal slaughter. The numbers are startling: nearly a million people – men, women and children – slaughtered in 100 days. But such bald statistics, horrific though they undoubtedly are, do little to convey what happened there. Numbers can't do it. As I write this, I am not sure whether words can either. I just hope they can, because I want you to know what took place and why.

As a correspondent in far-flung places I could normally separate what I was witnessing from my 'normal life'. I could mentally check out when I left. It was a useful trait to have, and in a way I was quite proud of it. But there was no filing away anything from Rwanda. There was no compartmentalizing. There was certainly no forgetting. It lived with me for years, and still lives with me now. Not only the appalling sights I saw, but the things people told me about what they saw. And then there's the smell. You could never really escape the smell of death. Of corpses rotting away in the African sun. At the side of the street, in forests and fields and people's homes. And, yes, in churches. Let me tell you first about the church.

The killing had lasted nearly two months when it subsided enough for us to get into the capital Kigali, at this time in the hands of the Tutsi army, the Rwandan Patriotic Front (RPF).

On our second evening in the city, I encountered a Canadian aid worker called Jim who was drinking whiskey in the hotel bar. 'It's bourbon,' he told me. 'They get it on the black market. It numbs the senses and right now I need it.'

It turned out Jim was working on logistics for the Canadian Red Cross. But he was trained as a child psychologist, which he'd realized was going to come in useful in the coming weeks and months. He told me he had just spent the day in a place called Ntarama. 'I have never seen anything like it,' he said. 'There were bodies all over the place, mutilated bodies, skeletons and skulls. And the church was attacked. Can you believe they attacked people in a church?'

'What did you see at the church?' I asked.

'I didn't go, I was just told about it. Why would I want to go and see that?'

I made a mental note of the place name, and thought that perhaps we should go the following morning. Jim told me he had spent the day at a makeshift hospital near Ntarama where he'd found several children. Most of them were badly injured, he told me, and all of them were terribly traumatized. 'They had the expressionless, vacant look of children who had seen horrific things. I can't help but think these youngsters will be scarred physically for a very long time, and mentally forever.'

He had another bourbon and changed the subject. I had a beer. Soon afterwards, I said goodnight to Jim and went to bed. I knew where we were heading in the morning, and so I identified Ntarama on my map and drifted off to sleep full of foreboding. At first light, we headed south.

My cameraman Andy Rex is a bull of a man and a former soldier in the Rhodesian Army. He had done and seen most things in television news. Little fazed him, and certainly not the sight of dead bodies. On the journey he was his usual talkative, mickey-taking self. He was a great exponent of the art of black humour, a common trait among newspeople. It is a diversion from the reality of what confronts us, pure and simple.

Forty-five minutes later, as we neared Ntarama, we saw people walking in the opposite direction carrying their belongings or pushing wheelbarrows or bicycles laden with household goods. First a few, then more and more – clusters of people making their way wearily, silently down the road, away from the place we were heading. We saw one woman carrying huge bundles of firewood, another weighed down with water containers. Two other women were carrying tables on their heads. Some sat at the roadside, exhausted and resting or breastfeeding babies.

It turned out these were Tutsi families who had somehow survived the killing, and now, a few days later, with the RPF in control, they felt it was safe to emerge from their hiding places and head to Kigali. Or anywhere they could find sanctuary. Anywhere that wasn't Ntarama.

They had been in hiding for weeks.

Our driver, Frank, eventually stopped to ask the way to the church. The man he spoke to recoiled when asked. He was shaking and muttering as he pointed to a track, on the right, about three hundred yards up ahead. We drove slowly towards the track, turned right, and climbed up a gentle slope into a forested area. We came across two boys wheeling bicycles. Frank and I got out of the car to speak to them. They answered his questions in low, faltering voices. They spoke in the local indigenous language, Kinyarwanda. They spoke slowly... a few words at a time. There were long gaps. One of the boys, his name was Habimana, was trying to say something but it was not coming out, it was barely audible muttering. In the end, our driver sat him down and asked him to say everything again. I said I wanted to get moving; the church was, after all, now in view, just a few hundred yards away. But Frank gestured to me to be quiet, and he edged closer to Habimana. Frank listened intently and I became impatient. Eventually, Frank stood up.

'What is he saying?' I asked.

'He says he has lost almost everyone in his family... his mother and brother and two cousins are dead inside the church. His father disappeared when they all took sanctuary in the church and he has not seen him since,' said Frank.

We walked to the car and drove up to the church. The first thing that occurred to me was how plain the church was. A rectangular brick building with a corrugated tin roof. If we hadn't been told it was a church, we wouldn't have known it was one. The second thing that hit us was the smell. The pungent, sickening sweetness of it was overpowering. I will never forget it.

I retched several times before we had even reached the building. I used the tucked-in part of my shirt to cover my nose and I tried to stop breathing. I couldn't handle it. I noticed Andy had a small towel with which he covered his nose as he approached the doors of the church. They were locked shut. We found an arched window at one end of the church building. I looked through it and saw wooden pews scattered haphazardly across the church. They were covered in brightly coloured cloth, like shawls and dresses, and my first instinct was that the bodies had been removed or there were not that many. But as Andy filmed, he saw the bodies, decapitated heads and severed limbs. Most were decomposing rapidly. Some were already skeletons and skulls.

I could not look for long. I turned away and walked quickly towards a wooded area where I thought I was going to be sick. I wasn't. But then I noticed more bodies in the forest. A child here, a woman's body – or rather a clothed skeleton – lying face down in the dirt there. I shouted to Andy. But he was filming now through a hole in the brickwork presumably caused by the Hutu gang attacking the church. Andy noticed burn marks inside the church, and we saw rusting grenades on the floor. Andy came over to where I was and filmed more of the scene. More mutilated bodies. More ghastliness. I had never seen anything like it. Nor had Andy. Not much renders him speechless, but this did. We walked back to the car without saying a word.

Frank told us that a local he had found wandering around said there was a makeshift hospital where some of those who survived had been taken. We drove slowly and silently. The hospital had been set up in a building belonging to the local prefecture. We went inside, and the first person I met was a Belgian professor of medicine, Alain Verhaagen, who was working for a Dutch charity. He spoke excellent English, welcomed us and our camera, and took us into a treatment room where patients, mainly children, lay – some with terrible injuries.

It dawned on me that this was the place Jim, my Canadian child psychologist friend, had told me about. Alain said he knew him and he was needed here in the coming weeks. For now, he told me, they needed antibiotics and bandages and equipment to clean out wounds. Although the area was in the hands of the RPF and Tutsi soldiers were protecting the hospital, some attacks were continuing in the area.

He showed us one child, maybe no more than six years old, a huge machete wound in his head. It was like a melon with a slice removed. It was difficult to believe someone could do this to a six-year-old. But someone had. Just as someone had hacked the arm off another child, the foot off another, and four fingers off the hand of a baby. Why that? What would it achieve? It was all so utterly sickening and mindless.

I thought most of what we would film would probably be too harrowing to be shown on TV. Andy knew that, and shot it in such a way that the viewer would be spared the true horror of what we were witnessing. It annoyed me that we had to do that. If ever the world needed to be confronted with the reality of an awful event, surely this was it. But better to censor it in the filming or the edit and get it shown than to send in a piece with all the gruesome truth which would then be dropped.

Alain was clear about what he thought was happening. 'I am convinced they wanted to wipe out the children. They wanted to kill off a generation of Tutsis. So many were slaughtered. And they were easy prey because they didn't know how to run or hide. They just clung to their parents and were clubbed or hacked to death with them.'

He pointed to the hand of the baby with the missing fingers.

'But sometimes, as you see, the children survived with terrible injuries. Maybe they just did it to destroy the people. They do it so that children grow up with terrible injury. They want the Tutsis to be dead or broken, shattered people, and this is how they think they can do that.'

He introduced us to a group of children, most of whom had bandages around their heads. A twelve-year-old girl told Frank how she had spent seven days staying absolutely still under a pile of corpses, including the bodies of her parents and sister. It defied belief, but was almost certainly true.

There were many such stories emerging of how people had survived. A nurse at the hospital told us that she had been in the church when the massacre happened. 'They came with grenades and machetes,' she said, 'so I just ran out of the church and kept running. I knew I had left my family behind. But I ran and ran until I reached the papyrus trees and the marshland, and I just stayed there for five weeks.

'We kept taking it in turns to go out for food, whatever we could get. But most of the time we just hid in the reeds and the marshes. They never came for us. One woman gave birth in the swamp.'

We had filmed more than enough for a substantial piece on *News at Ten*. So we made our way back to Kigali. It was a quiet journey. It wasn't a case of coming to terms with what we had seen. That was not going to happen. Not for a while, if ever. What we had witnessed were the consequences of acts that were beyond evil, and in a way also beyond any rational explanation.

My fellow correspondent Fergal Keane, of the BBC, wrote of Rwanda that it 'frequently rendered me inarticulate'. There is no shame in that. I had never struggled for words to accompany our pictures before, and have never done so since. But Rwanda was different. How many times can you use the word 'evil'? Find me replacements, find me anything that would do.

It was a desperate piece to edit. Looking at the footage from the church in particular, it was difficult to see how much we could actually broadcast. But Andy had shot it cleverly, so that enough material was available to give the viewer a sense of what had happened there. Still, it was hard to compute that such horrific violence could befall people who had sought sanctuary in a church.

Rwanda was supposed to be one of the most Catholic countries in Africa. Something like 60 per cent of the people believed in the teaching and dictates of the Holy See. So churches were all over the place, dominating the countryside as they once did in medieval Europe. But the sanctity of God's houses offered no protection; it was not respected by those bent on delivering death. The story of the Rwandan genocide is, in part, written in blood on the walls and the floors of churches and chapels across the land.

The genocide had started while the attention of the world's media was firmly focused on the tumultuous but ultimately historic events in South Africa. I was in Johannesburg when I first heard vague reports of the president of Rwanda, Juvénal Habyarimana, being killed in a plane crash in Kigali. I don't mind admitting that I took little notice, and had no idea at all about the likely fallout.

Even when reports started filtering through about massacres across the country, it didn't compel news desks to shift resources from South Africa to Rwanda. After all, outbursts of violence and bloodletting in central Africa were nothing new. Soon, however, pictures started emerging of the slaughter. Distant shots of machete-wielding gangs attacking people in the street, and bodies just left lying by the roadside.

Gradually, it was becoming clear that this was not just another eruption of ancient tribal hatreds in which both sides – Hutu and Tutsi – were suffering terrible losses. All too late it was dawning on politicians and diplomats that this was the calculated and organized mass murder of an entire population.

And so the world started to take an interest, and reporters started trying to find a safe way to get in and cover the massacres. It was not easy, and those who did make it in, including my ITN colleague James Mates, were forced to hole up with the small and largely ineffective United Nations force that was hunkered down in Kigali. It was too dangerous to go out. The massacres intensified and the word 'genocide' began to be heard.

The real truth about the extent of the organization only emerged later. This was far more sinister and far more planned than anyone had imagined. It was meticulously masterminded by a group of educated Hutu extremists who formed their own militia – the Interahamwe – and who feared that plans for power-sharing with the minority Tutsis would have disastrous consequences for the Hutus.

They drew up a plan to brainwash the ill-educated peasants who made up a large part of the Hutu population, and produced a set of orders that encouraged the slaughter of Tutsis in their communes and villages.

It was chilling how efficiently it was all coordinated; all done, remember, before the Internet or social media or even mobile phones were in common use. The word was spread instead by state radio, which broadcasted vile edicts and little else, day after day. Hutu-owned newspapers and magazines were also recruited to spout hatred and propaganda and promote violence against the Tutsis.

But the most virulently anti-Tutsi outlet in Rwanda at that time was the private radio station Radio Télévision Libre des Mille Collines. It was established almost a year before the genocide, and immediately opposed any peace talks between the government of President Juvénal Habyarimana and the Tutsi rebels of the Rwandan Patriotic Front. After the president's plane was shot down, it began calling for a campaign of killing to wipe out the *inyenzi* or 'cockroaches'. It even broadcast lists of specific people to be killed, and gave instructions as to where the people were hiding.

It stayed on air for weeks during the killing, and even when we arrived in June, when much of the violence was over, it was still broadcasting stuff like this:

Today is Sunday, 19th June 1994, and it's 4.22 p.m. Kigali time in the studios of RTLM. Notice to all cockroaches listening now: Rwanda belongs to those who really defend it. And you, cockroaches, are not real Rwandans. Everybody is up in arms to defeat cockroaches. From our military officers, the young people, adults, men and women. So you understand, cockroaches, you have no way out.

It's our good luck that cockroaches are so few in this country. These people are a dirty race. We have to exterminate them. We must get rid of them. This is the only solution.

These cockroaches, where did they all go? Surely we have exterminated them. Let us sing; let us rejoice, friends. Cockroaches have been exterminated. Let us rejoice, friends. God is never wrong.

Like pretty much everything else in Rwanda at the time, it was sickening. I felt it was astonishing that months into the genocide no one could take the station off the air or jam the broadcasts. It wasn't until Tutsi forces advanced through the country in late '94 and the people behind Radio Milles Collines fled to what was then Zaire that the broadcasts were stopped.

There is no doubt they played a key role in the genocide, and nearly ten years later the International Criminal Tribunal for Rwanda jailed two of the senior figures behind the radio station, Jean-Bosco Barayagwiza and Ferdinand Nahimana.

Barayagwiza, who was chairman of the station in 1994, was sentenced to thirty-five years in prison for charges including conspiracy to commit genocide. He died in prison in Cotonou, Benin, after developing Hepatitis C. His family complained that he was denied adequate treatment while he was being held. My heart bleeds for him.

I mentioned that the people behind Radio Milles Collines fled first to Zaire. Hundreds of thousands of other Hutus, whether complicit in the genocide or not, did the same. The final edict to the people by the butchers running the radio station in Kigali was to either get out and follow the leaders into exile or face death at the hands of the army of the Rwandan Patriotic Front. Hundreds of thousands of Hutus ignored promises of reconciliation from the RPF and fled across the border. But they were swapping the killing fields of Rwanda for chaos and a looming humanitarian disaster in Zaire.

The problem was that the mass exodus seemed to catch the aid agencies by surprise. Many of the refugees ended up making camp as best they could on a vast expanse of volcanic rock near a place called Goma. There was little food or water and no sanitation.

Within weeks it was a proper crisis, and we made our way to Goma at the end of July '94. By the time we arrived, cholera and dysentery had begun striking down the refugees. It was difficult to resist the thought that this was, in some way, some sort of divine retribution playing out here.

The people who had carried out the killing were now faced with death themselves. It was a desperate, pitiful scene. Starving families, with nothing but the clothes they were wearing, were trying to survive in the dust by the roadside or alongside piles of excrement in the sweltering, barren fields of red-hot rock. Andy looked at me. 'They're going to die here in their thousands,' he said. 'And they will die quickly, particularly the kids.'

He was right. They did start dying. Hundreds a day, right in front of us. I have been to places where you see people about to die, and I have been to places, many of them, where people are already dead. But never before or since have I been in a place as people were dying. We would literally be filming a child in its mother's arms when it would take its last breath. We would film young children looking acutely sick, we would include them in that night's report, only to hear the following morning that they had passed away.

As evening drew in on our first day there, I remember driving along the road to the hotel where we were fortunate enough to have rooms. On one side were people walking – new arrivals carrying pathetically few possessions and wondering by now what on earth they had fled to. If this was sanctuary... the hell of Rwanda may be preferable, they must have been thinking. And on the other side of the road, in the dust, body after body after body. Some newly left there, wrapped in sheeting. Others uncovered, bloated and beginning to smell. Who, I wondered, would collect these bodies? And what would happen if they were simply left there in the baking sun?

No one did collect them. They remained where they lay, and every day the body count rose. People moved among the dead as if they were not there. The roads were thronged with people. Women were lighting fires to cook whatever food they had, the smell wafting across the landscape, concealing the stench of the bodies. Young men held radios to their ears, hoping for the latest news from inside their country. Everywhere, too, were Hutu government soldiers, many still carrying AK-47s. They were demobilized but their weapons still gave them a power in the rapidly expanding camps, which they increasingly used to benefit themselves and satisfy their needs, whether that be water, food or women. Over the coming months, the aid agencies that would eventually arrive documented many cases of sexual assault and rape. As we drove away that first day, there was an air of menace about the place. The men, particularly the soldiers, didn't like being filmed and they certainly didn't trust us.

But they were also desperate and wanted to know what we had in the back of the car. They would peer through the windows at us, and try to stop the car and open the doors. Things grew tense. Some men in uniform started banging on the side of our vehicle, gesturing for us to stop. It was nerve-racking and intimidating. Drive too slowly and they would try to get into the vehicle. Drive too fast and you could easily kill or seriously injure someone, and that could spark a riot from which we would be lucky to emerge alive.

It took forever to drive out of the place, but we eventually made it back to our hotel – or what passed for a hotel – in Goma town. My room smelled of stale smoke, there were stains all over the carpet, and the sheets on the single bed seemed to be coated in a damp, sticky film. But at least I had a bed and a roof over my head, and we had food and bottled water. That evening, over what he insisted was a donkey burger, my cameraman Eugene Campbell made the point that we should be careful what we put in the car for the following day's trip out to the camps. We knew we had to go again; it was now a massive international news story. And he was right.

Normally we would carry supplies we had brought with us – cases of bottled water, canned tuna, cereal bars and bananas – knowing we would be out for the whole day with no access to provisions. But there were a number of issues that Eugene raised. How could we carry that stuff without it being seen by the refugees? How could we eat or drink anything in front of them without sparking a riot? And how would we avoid getting the vehicle itself stolen? They had seen us filming earlier that day, and they'd seen the 4 x 4 and all our equipment. We would be ripe for the picking. In the event, we decided to take one bottle of water each and stash some cereal bars in the glove compartment of the vehicle.

We left at around 7.30 a.m. and headed towards the same area we had been the previous day. Thousands of people were already on the road, streaming towards what were now becoming large makeshift camps. Also on the road were two white Land Cruisers bearing the logo of the International Red Cross. I have to admit we were pleased to see them. We dropped in behind them and drove into the camp area together. We parked up on the edge of the expanse of volcanic rock that was now impossible to see for the sheer number of people. We estimated about a hundred thousand more people had arrived since we had left. The numbers were staggering... and still no food or tents or bottled water in sight.

From one of the Land Cruisers emerged Nina Winquist, a young, blonde, effervescent Swede who looked around, sighed heavily and threw up her hands in despair.

'We have set up a temporary hospital over there,' she said. 'And food aid is on its way, but the numbers, the numbers... this is already a catastrophe on a huge scale.'

She was, of course, right. We made our way towards a white tent in the distance. It was easy to spot because there were no other tents there except for the one belonging to Médecins Sans Frontières.

At the Red Cross tent, Eugene immediately began filming. Desperately sick patients lay inside and outside the tent. And everywhere were children. Some on drips, and many, many more waiting for them. Among them, a Red Cross nurse from Britain, Sally Brown, was doing the best she could but was clearly overwhelmed.

'This one will die, that one will die, this one might pull through, but most of them won't,' she told us. Everywhere Eugene pointed the camera was a picture of utter despair and misery.

In the corner of the tent, a woman was dying before our eyes. You could just tell. The noise of her breathing, suddenly guttural and impaired, was accompanied by jerky movements. Sally could do nothing, she had to concentrate on those who could be saved. All she could do was lift from the woman's arms the young boy who was clinging to her through her death throes. The boy himself was very unwell, suffering chronic diarrhoea and dysentery. He can't have been more than two years old. *Two years old.* I don't know why, but for some reason I took him from Sally's arms into mine. He was no weight at all. And – again for no particular reason – I thought of home and my own son, who was about to turn two years old. There was Jack, secure in a loving home with everything he could possibly need, in a reasonably safe country. And there was this lad, who had just seen his mum die in a tent pitched on a wasteland of volcanic dust, where there was precious little food, water or help.

'His dad died in Rwanda,' said Sally. We filmed him – what else could we do? A Rwandan orphan, the first of many. The first of thousands. He made it onto *News at Ten* that night. A day later, he died. Perhaps it was for the best. That is obviously a terrible thing to say. But it is how I felt in that place on that day.

We left the tent and set up the camera outside to interview Nina. While we waited for her, I felt something tugging at the bottom of my trousers. I looked down, and a middle-aged man was trying to haul himself across the ground towards the tent. I lent down to help him, and as I did so he simply rolled over and died. Eugene and I looked at each other. 'This really is hell on earth,' I said.

'He was probably a machete man,' said Eugene. 'I bet he killed plenty in Rwanda.' Eugene was almost certainly right. The scary truth was that there were probably thousands of murderers in the sprawling camps all around us.

It was a question I put to Nina in the interview we eventually got around to. Should they be caring for people who took part in a genocide?

She had no hesitation. 'When a person is in need of help, you don't make moral judgements about whether to give them help or not,' she said.

We had our story. It was desperate, again. What a wretched place, what a wretched world... and what a wretched job I did. That's what I thought as I drove back to the hotel. Was to film these people the best I could do? Really? Shouldn't we be helping them survive? Shouldn't we be helping the Red Cross? I mean, really... Film them? Is that it?

It is a thought I have wrangled with in many parts of the world and on many occasions. I think the best answer I have is that if our pictures and my words are seen and heard around the world, then maybe money and help will follow. It is an argument that usually eases my conscience, but somehow it didn't then. Not in Rwanda or Goma. I think that such was the horror we witnessed in both places that the usual journalistic instinct to get the story out there withered away when confronted with what we were seeing. You may have thought that the reporter's instinct would be all the more acute with a big story, but with Rwanda it wasn't. One moment I just wanted to remove it from my mind, to edit it out. The next, I wrestled with whether, as human beings, we should be doing more to aid them.

The brilliant writer and Africa specialist, Richard Dowden, began one of his reports from Rwanda like this: 'I do not want to tell you what I saw today...' That is how I sometimes felt, reporting from Rwanda and Goma.

Andy, and later Eugene, kept me on course. They kept telling me it was big and it was important and to strike now because the usual 'disaster fatigue' would soon set in back home. A day later, I began to think they were right when I got a call from the foreign desk in London asking if we could do a piece on the plight of the Rwandan gorilla... I managed to delay that for a week or so, but it was instructive in how some people felt about the story and the constant harrowing pictures of African suffering.

I wondered what the viewers made of it. Were they as horrified as us? Would they watch or turn away? Would they be asking: 'Why are you showing me all this?'

More to the point, I wondered what my wife would feel seeing the pictures. How would she feel about me witnessing it all first-hand? And then I remembered that as a trauma doctor in South Africa she was seeing appalling things every day and having to treat dreadful injuries inflicted by man on man.

I have watched many a politician fly into the scenes of humanitarian disasters, say a few pious words, look suitably shaken, and depart making promises and pledging help. But never have I seen any politician look as genuinely horrified as Lynda Chalker, the minister for overseas aid, when she visited the Rwandan refugees in Goma. She arrived by car, surrounded by desperate refugees who had no idea who she was. When she got out, she saw our cameras and said how awful it all was. She then saw a truck coming towards us along the road. 'But it is good to see aid coming in,' she said. 'We need more trucks like this.'

I noticed then that the driver and his colleague in the passenger seat both wore face masks. I realized it was not full of food, but full of corpses. And as it passed we all saw how full it was. The bodies were piled to the roof of the truck. Two or three guys, also in face masks, were standing on the open trailer door, clinging to the back of the lorry. They were off to the most recently dug mass grave, and soon they would be back for more.

Baroness Chalker lifted a white handkerchief to her face to smother the smell. It wasn't just the bodies in the truck; many others lay wrapped by the roadside within yards of where we stood. We were used to it by now, and would walk past bodies and barely notice them. But she wasn't. She was traumatized by what she was seeing. She looked pale and drawn, and I thought at one point she was going to be sick. I wouldn't have been surprised.

'This is much worse, much more ferocious than anything I have experienced,' she told me. The minster was taken to a medical aid tent, where a nurse was giving a young woman a drink from a cup. Next to her lay a young boy holding a small cuddly toy. 'How is he?' asked Mrs Chalker. 'Doing very well,' came the reply. 'He was found alive in among the bodies at a mass grave.' We filmed him, and he became known as the boy who came back from the dead. There weren't many of those in Goma.

Baroness Chalker, clearly shaken, returned to her car, drove to her plane and headed out of Africa.

The truth is that Britain, America and the rest of the world failed Rwanda. It was a grotesque betrayal of a country and its people.

The Rwandan Patriotic Front, under Paul Kagame, now rules Rwanda with an authoritarian hand. The genocide was his excuse for some draconian laws and behaviour by the government, but I guess when you've been through what that place has been through, it is understandable.

Twenty years after the genocide, I went back to Rwanda to see how the country was progressing. I decided to return to the church at Ntarama, and what I found was largely representative of the way the country is dealing with the genocide.

The church has not been demolished; on the contrary, it has been refurbished. However, it is no longer a church but rather a memorial to mass murder – a physical commemoration of the events of 1994 and those who died. There are tall gates at the entrance, and a large white sign with the words EGLISE NTARAMA in black, and underneath, in red: SITE DU GENOCIDE: ± 5000 PERSONS.

I walked up to the building, which hadn't changed much on the outside. It remained a brick construction but was now covered by a large metal awning to protect it from the weather. Inside was what can only be described as a macabre but incredibly poignant scene. When you enter the main door, immediately on your right are four large shelves running the width of the building. On the bottom shelf are bones; leg bones, arm bones, all sorts of bones. And on the shelves above are skulls... hundreds of them, neatly arranged in rows and all facing you, mainly adult-size but there are several that belonged to children. On closer inspection, some are cracked, others caved in. It's a startling reminder of the numbers who died, and also of the violent way they met their death. I did not expect it. It was shocking and difficult to look at.

And all around me, hanging on the walls and from the ceiling, were the clothes that Andy and I had filmed strewn across the pews two decades before. I walked slowly down the centre of the church, with the restored wooden pews either side of me. And at the other end, where the altar once was, now stood more shelving, made of scaffolding and large sheets of plasterboard. And on them, examples of the weaponry used to carry out the slaughter. Machetes, large knives, pangas and wooden clubs with nails in. It was horrific to behold, and my immediate thought was why would the people here – many of whom belonged to the families of those killed and maimed – want such a reminder of the atrocity on full public view like this?

Then, in the doorway of the church, stood Immaculate Mukanyaraya, a tall, slim, imposing figure of a woman in her early fifties. With her was her twenty-year-old daughter Zinni. I had arranged to meet them at the memorial, although Immaculate only agreed as long as they didn't have to stay long and on the proviso that if she didn't feel up to it on the day, she could simply not turn up. But here they were, stepping nervously, cautiously, into the building they had not entered for twenty years. Immaculate had sought sanctuary in Ntarama church on the night of the killing. So too did her husband, her son, five brothers, four sisters and nine cousins. Only two of them survived. Herself and her son. Or three, counting Zinni, her unborn child.

'We heard the militiamen coming with their machetes and their axes,' she told me. 'And when they threw a grenade at the church, I thought we can't stay here. I swept up the children and we just ran out of the church and into the forest. And then we kept on running.'

Like many others, they ran down a nearby hillside and hid in the swamp below. She says they stayed there for about a month and it was there that she gave birth to her daughter. They survived due to a couple of men hiding with them who would venture out every few days and come back with food and water. 'We were terrified, all day, every day,' she said.

In the church, twenty years on, she moved slowly and looked around without saying a word to us or to her daughter. For several minutes, she just stood and looked. Then she started looking at the skulls, lifting them and examining them closely. 'I wonder which one belongs to my husband,' she said.

Immaculate told me she was glad the memorial is there, because it is important never to forget what happened. 'Could you ever forgive?' I asked her.

She looked at the shelves and then looked down. And after a minute or so, she said she had already begun to forgive. 'We have to, or we will never move on.'

Then she told me that the government had asked her to work on a local project with the wives of the perpetrators of the massacre. They were together twice a week making gift soaps that were sold in the local town.

And nearby we found an even more extraordinary experiment underway. In a village in the district of Bugesera, an Anglican bishop, John Rucyahana, was trying to realize his dream of reconciliation. When we arrived, we were met at the entrance to the village by a dance troupe singing a welcome song. But this was no ordinary village dance group. The dancers were from families of both perpetrators and victims during the genocide. And side by side in the audience were Thacien and Droselle. He was guilty of her husband's murder and yet now they live as neighbours. She tells me she forgives him because he confessed his crime and served time in prison.

The bishop says his 'reconciliation villages' dotted around Rwanda are working and helping the country recover. He introduces us to Abdul and Chantelle. Abdul was part of a

Hutu militia that slaughtered members of Chantelle's family, and now they too live in neighbouring homes. I ask Chantelle whether she is happy to live next to Abdul. 'After the genocide, I could not have lived near anyone who did the killing,' she told me. 'But now there are no problems. He takes my cow out to grass, our children play, and we live peacefully.'

Abdul admitted killing Tutsis and was given a presidential pardon after agreeing to take part in the reconciliation programme.

Among those I spoke to while I was there, there is a definite will to see the programme succeed, but the truth is you only have to scratch beneath the surface to realize Rwanda remains a country of suspicion and fear. How could it be otherwise?

President Kagame remains popular within Rwanda but faces criticism from outside, due to the fact that he's using the legacy of the genocide to impose a Tutsi-dominated authoritarian regime. His retort is to say he will take no lessons on human rights from Western countries who failed to intervene to stop the killing in 1994.

It seems to me that the best hope for Rwanda lies with the two-thirds of the population who are under twenty-five. In schools they are now encouraged to reject the categorization of Hutu and Tutsi, and instead find common cause in building a new Rwanda.

Economic empowerment will help too, and over the last few years the economy has been growing by an average of around 8 per cent and a million Rwandans have been lifted out of poverty.

Despite all that happened to her, Immaculate Mukanyaraya

is part of the process. Working in that soap-making cooperative with the wives of convicted killers, she says she can forgive but will never forget. She calls the men who did it 'animals', but says remembering the genocide with memorials and ceremonies is the best way to ensure it doesn't happen again.

Rwanda is a beautiful country scarred by atrocity, and at its moment of greatest need it was abandoned by the world. The very least it deserves is a future.

QUITE OFTEN WHEN a big story breaks, the biggest challenge of the whole process is not the writing, interviewing or filming. It is physically getting to where the story is.

That is the big difference between print journalism and television reporting. If necessary, newspaper reporters can get pretty much everything they need on the phone or by email. They just need the words, and the descriptive stuff from the scene they can often put together from witness accounts. In television, you have to be there. You need to be on the scene, in the midst of it all... and you have to be filmed doing it.

Being there is the name of the game, the most important thing. If you are not there, you are nothing. It is the foreign correspondent's worst nightmare to be stranded while the opposition is in the thick of it, broadcasting from location – and, quite often, pointing out on air that they're 'the only British broadcasters' reporting from wherever. Not being there is journalistic purgatory.

But getting there is often awkward, uncomfortable, trouble-some or downright dangerous. I have done some crazy things in the name of 'getting there'. I have flown in helicopters clearly unfit for service (in Sierra Leone); I have ridden on horseback down mountainsides (in Afghanistan); I have driven through minefields (unknowingly in Iraq); I have taken boats that leaked (in Indonesia); and I have ridden on the back of a motorbike controlled, or rather not controlled, by a mad twenty-year-old high on drugs (during riots, also in Indonesia). I have also been carried aloft, across a raging river (well, a rushing stream), by six men and a woman (in India).

It is true that occasionally the opposite applies. I have been lucky enough to fly on private jets, on Concorde, in first class; I have travelled on luxury trains, in plush limos, on super-yachts and even the Aga Khan's private helicopter. But those journeys are the exception, not the rule. More often than not it is uncomfortable, unpleasant and hair-raising.

One of the most treacherous journeys I have ever undertaken was not in some war zone, but rather while covering a sporting event. I never thought I was going to die on a road trip quite as much as I did during the Cricket World Cup in India in 1987.

In those days we had to film the games ourselves with our own cameras and do the best we could. We were blessed at ITN with one of the best cricket cameramen in the business, Derek Seymour. He was a former war cameraman who had pretty much seen and done everything, but even he wasn't prepared for the road journey by minibus from Bombay to Pune. It was a distance of about 100 miles but involved travelling along one of the most notoriously dangerous roads in India. With luck, we were told, we should make it in about four or five hours.

We had to get there for the following day's game between England and Sri Lanka, and the first mistake we made was to delay our departure to do an interview in Bombay. The one piece of advice we had been given was not to make the journey in darkness. So what did we do? We left at dusk.

Well, to be honest, that wasn't actually the first mistake we made. No, the first mistake was allowing Sanjay to drive us. Sanjay seemed a sound enough guy. Plenty of smiles and that shaking of the head Indians do when they mean 'yes, OK', if not much English. 'No problem' was about the extent of it. We were to hear a lot of that. But he was quite possibly the worst driver I have ever had the misfortune of encountering. The minibus company had briefed him on our destination, the Nehru Stadium in Pune, where we hoped to drop off our heavy equipment for the match coverage.

Weaving through the Bombay traffic, all seemed calm enough, if a little bewildering. Even in the big cities of India there seem to be no rules when it comes to driving. Not much looking in rear-view mirrors or wing mirrors goes on. Just a huge amount of horn use.

So we honked our way through the suburbs, narrowly avoiding cyclists, overladen tuk-tuks, wandering cows, dogs and pedestrians. But essentially all seemed borderline OK.

How that changed when we reached the madness of route NH 4. Sanjay suddenly turned into a man possessed by some strange driving demon. Firstly, I have to give you a sense of the road we were using. Nowadays, the Mumbai-Pune Expressway is a modern multi-lane highway; not so in 1987. Then, it was a winding single-lane mountain pass with steep inclines and equally steep drops, with no barriers to prevent cars, trucks or minibuses careering down the rocky hillside. Looking down, one could see vehicles of all descriptions, smashed-up, unreachable and abandoned. The fate of the vehicle obvious, the fate of their drivers and passengers unknown but predictable.

It was also self-evident how they ended up there. The road was full of gaudily decorated trucks bombing down the mountain with gay and reckless abandon; the drivers failing to adhere to any speed limit or lane discipline. Indeed, it was clear that which side of the road you occupied was entirely optional.

All this would just about be tolerable in daylight and sunshine. But by now we were travelling in darkness and rain. And then, of course, there was Sanjay.

He was clearly undecided whether to occupy the middle of the road and stubbornly stand his ground, relying on the oncoming vehicles to swerve around us, or to drive along the extreme edge of the road where no approaching driver would be insane enough to venture. He tried both, with mixed success.

It was absolutely terrifying, and we hadn't even really got started. Derek yelled at Sanjay to slow down. 'No problem,' came the response, with no discernible reduction in speed. In fact, the louder Derek shouted at him, the more Sanjay thought he was being told to get a move on.

The bends were the worst; you would suddenly see the lights in front of you, and I mean right in front of you, and Sanjay and the other driver would take avoiding action right at the last moment. And with every sharp turn, the heavy editing equipment mounted on the seats at the back of the minibus would crash from one side to the other. That was lethal in itself.

'No problem,' Sanjay kept repeating, as the rain intensified and I began to think this would not end well. It was one of those moments when, had mobile phones been invented, I would have been texting loved ones to say goodbye.

Then suddenly, mercifully, without warning, it was over. At least temporarily. Sanjay decided we should take a break. He stopped at a roadside restaurant called Ramakant's, a well-known resting place on this road from hell. We all ate rotis and drank beer and wondered whether we would survive. Sanjay paid a man to check the engine, top up the oil and wipe the windscreen. And then we were on our way again. 'No problem.'

By now we were entering tunnel after tunnel, some lit, some not. All absolutely petrifying. The already narrow road narrowed still further in the tunnels, and how we avoided a collision remains a mystery to this day.

The road signs were hilarious. Or they would have been, had they not filled us all with dread and foreboding: 'OVERSPEED IS A KNIFE THAT CUT A LIFE', read one. 'BE GENTLE ON MY CURVES', said another. And then, 'LIFE IS SHORT, DON'T MAKE IT SHORTER'. Why were they in English? I wondered. I didn't need to read them – Sanjay did, for God's sake. And he quite obviously couldn't. There was not a single sign saying 'No problem' on the entire stretch of road.

Then there was the sign that really did it for me: 'WATER ON ROAD DURING RAIN'. Well I never, thanks for that. Very useful.

By now Derek and our soundman, Alan, had both somehow gone to sleep. Or at least their eyes remained steadfastly shut. I, on the other hand, couldn't stop watching the road. The lights, the horns blaring, the sudden jolting swerves, the whole, wretched roller-coaster ride was somehow mesmerizing. And then Sanjay started shouting in Urdu. 'No problem' had now become 'big problem'. Yup, we had a puncture, and we limped into the next village and came to a slow, grinding halt. It was infuriating, but at the same time offered much-needed relief from the ordeal.

Eventually, tyre repaired at the roadside, we made it into Pune – never have I been so relieved to pull up at a Pearl-Continental Hotel. We unloaded our equipment and bags and bade farewell to Sanjay. 'No problem,' he said.

Duncan Jones, our picture editor who had gone on ahead to sort out camera positions and passes and other admin, had his own rather alarming experience in Pune. As he left the stadium after meeting the club secretary and scouting out a good camera position for Derek, he was surrounded by locals thrusting their autograph books and scraps of paper at him. Duncan was utterly bewildered, but decided the only thing to do was to sign them. Within minutes he was being mobbed, and police had to weigh in, beating away the throng with batons. It turns out the cricket fans thought that Duncan was the star Australian batsman, Dean Jones. Both apparently share the same initials, D.M. Jones, and that was what was written on the accreditation Duncan had hanging around his neck. It was all quite bizarre.

It was some day, and some journey. And for the record, England beat Sri Lanka by eight wickets. No problem.

If you use subterfuge to get into the most reclusive, secretive and oppressive communist state in the world, then you'd better make sure you don't get caught. Unfortunately, that is exactly what happened when my cameraman Mick Deane and I managed to get into North Korea in the early nineties. Our escape was truly extraordinary.

First, though, some background. In those days it was almost unheard of for Westerners, and certainly Western journalists, to enter North Korea, but we'd discovered a small North Korean company in Hong Kong that had begun organizing visits for carefully vetted tour groups. We'd heard they were particularly keen to allow teachers in to see their new showpiece school in the capital, Pyongyang. So we applied, posing as two secondary-school teachers, and a few weeks later, much to our surprise, we were offered visas and told to pick them up in Beijing.

Armed with a small, tourist-style video camera, we flew into Pyongyang to be met by our government contact, Mr Kim, who was to be our guide, driver, bodyguard and minder. He would be with us every hour of every day, and would see us to our hotel rooms in the evening, where a hidden camera would take over the monitoring of us. It was quite simply the most bizarre, nightmarish, Orwellian, fascinating but ultimately depressing place I have ever been to, before or since. This was in the dying days of the rule of Kim Il-sung, the so-called Great Leader, characterized by an all-pervasive personality cult, a ruthless indoctrination of the people, and the brutal elimination of any opposition whatsoever. It was a fortress-state with a million-man army, a much-feared secret security service and widespread poverty.

It was in the news at the time because, even then, there were huge fears internationally that the regime was beginning the process of building a nuclear bomb. The North Koreans were threatening to pull out of the Nuclear Non-Proliferation Treaty rather than allow the inspections demanded by the West, and the United States and South Korea were pressing for international sanctions against Pyongyang. It seemed as good a time as any to visit. And what a place it was.

We arrived at night and were taken in a government Volvo straight to the only international hotel. It was Swedish-built and at least twelve storeys high, but didn't seem to have any other guests. We were the only two people – three including our minder – in the massive dining room. There was no menu, and we were given a vegetable soup and bread and a Korean beer.

The following day, we were first driven to a station on the city's brand-new underground. We drove along vast, wide avenues with barely any traffic whatsoever. A few other official-looking cars, the odd bicyclist, but very few people. There were more street sweepers than pedestrians. Every so often, large groups of very young soldiers would march past. Everyone we saw wore buttons of Kim Il-sung on their lapels, and there were hoardings and posters and giant statues of him everywhere. At the station we descended the escalators to the sound of rousing piped music with lyrics that extolled the virtues of the Great Leader. Once down on the platform, the walls were decorated with murals depicting his military heroics. Here it was much busier, the brainwashed subjects of the Kim regime on their daily commute to government offices. They all looked cheerful, but when cameras are around I presume there is an unspoken order to smile.

We were then taken to a huge department store... full of merchandise, mainly from China, but virtually empty of people. And then the highlight of the day, according to Mr Kim

– a visit to the huge bronze statue of Kim Il-sung on Mansu Hill. Hundreds of schoolchildren had gathered there and were staring in wonderment at the seventy-foot-high monument in front of them. Their teachers were telling them what to think. I was wondering what they really thought.

It all made for good pictures and I did a piece to camera, telling Mr Kim that I wanted to record something for my own pupils back in Hong Kong. He seemed to believe me. Basically, we filmed what they wanted us to film, but we also got footage of some stuff they didn't, like the marching, singing troops. We were managing to build up some sort of picture of what life was like in the city.

That evening, just before midnight, we were taken to the main station to catch a train to the DMZ, the demilitarized zone on the border with South Korea. It was obvious to us that we were travelling at night so we would be unable to see anything of life outside the showpiece capital city. Mr Kim made sure the blinds in our carriage were pulled down for the entire journey.

The train moved very slowly and noisily through the night, and would make long stops en route. We tried to get some sleep. It was daylight when we arrived, and we found ourselves in the middle of the most militarized border region on earth. The peace treaty at the end of the Korean War was never signed, so technically a state of war still exists between North and South Korea.

On either side of the DMZ, soldiers stood all day staring at the enemy. They were surprisingly close; in places, just a few yards apart. In a prefabricated building, we were introduced to a senior North Korean soldier who, with a wall map and a huge model of the area laid out before him, pointed out the deployment of his forces on the border. We filmed the talk and got a brief chance to ask him about whether they were building the bomb. The translator and Mr Kim looked alarmed, but the soldier shook his head vigorously and laughed. 'No, no, no,' he said. I laughed too, and the tension was broken. Mr Kim, though, was becoming suspicious. Too many questions from this mathematics teacher from Hong Kong.

His suspicions grew a day later when, back in Pyongyang, we were taken to the biggest, most modern school in the city. It was truly impressive, and the pupils – model students all – were clearly well drilled in what to do and say in the presence of foreigners. They gave thanks to one man for the privilege of studying there: the Great Leader. 'A father to all of us, better in every way to our own fathers,' said one boy.

But Mr Kim had a surprise for us. He took us into a classroom where the subject being taught was mathematics. There was a translator on hand, and it suddenly dawned on me we were in trouble. The school had arranged for me to take the maths class. 'Go ahead,' said Mr Kim.

Mick realized we had a problem. He knew that not only had I never taught maths to anyone, but I had also failed to pass any maths exam ever. I am basically as innumerate as it is possible to be. I can't even count my blessings. It had, in fact, been Mick's little jest to put 'maths teacher' on our visa form. Now, suddenly, it didn't seem that funny.

I basically bluffed and fluffed my way through five minutes of basic maths before trying to turn the subject to whether they liked the school and what they wanted to do when they left. It was all pretty unconvincing, and Mr Kim was obviously unimpressed. Later that night, over vegetable soup and dumplings, he leaned forward and asked us if we 'really were teachers' or something else altogether. 'You behave,' he said, 'a bit like journalists.'

Mick laughed and said that we were asking so many questions and taking so many pictures because we wanted to make a film for our own school. But we went to bed that night thinking we had been rumbled, and were left contemplating several years in a North Korean labour camp. I, for one, was seriously concerned.

In the middle of the night, Mick came to my room and asked to speak to me in the corridor, thinking the rooms were definitely bugged. He said he thought we should leave, even though the scheduled tour had two more days to go. I agreed, but I couldn't think how we could get out without arousing yet more suspicion. We knew there was a daily flight to Beijing, but how would we get to the airport, and how would we even get booked on the flight? With no way of communicating with the outside world, we were isolated, freezing cold (it was minus 20 degrees) and very frightened.

We decided to take our chance and tell Mr Kim that we had a personal emergency and had to fly back early. When he arrived to pick us up the following morning, I spoke with him and said that we needed to leave due to a family illness. He looked flustered by what we were saying and quickly disappeared into the back office of the hotel. We feared the worst. If they found out we were journalists, we could be in very serious trouble.

Mr Kim came back and told us it was impossible to leave because the flights were full. We had no way of knowing whether that was true or not. This was before mobile phones or easy access to the Internet, so we were cut off, at the mercy of the regime – or at least of Mr Kim. Then, suddenly, he took me aside and asked to talk privately. He led me outside into the bitter cold and asked me if we were telling the truth. I had to make a rapid calculation. I reckoned he had only taken me outside so that no one could eavesdrop on the conversation. Why else? I figured he may be on our side and I was going to come clean. I was about to answer, when he abruptly told me to go get our bags. I walked back into the foyer, told Mick to pack and returned to my room to do the same.

Within minutes, we were driving at some speed to the airport. It had begun to snow heavily, the sky leaden and grey. At the airport, Mr Kim acquired our tickets, saw us through security and made to leave. Then he stopped, turned back to me, leaned into my ear and said, 'Good luck with the film... for your school.' Then he was gone.

To this day, I don't know whether Mr Kim knew what we were up to and wanted to help us or whether he suspected nothing. He was Kim the inscrutable. But we owe him.

What I do know, however, is that we were about to embark on the most crazy flight I have ever taken. Just boarding the Russian-built Ilyushin aircraft was alarming enough. The wings were covered with ice and snow, and no attempt was being made to remove it. You could sit anywhere and Mick and I managed to grab a couple of seats by the emergency exit. But all around us there was utter chaos. People were boarding overloaded with baggage, there were fights over space in the overhead lockers and the airline staff – in the bright red of the national flag – couldn't have been less interested.

Then, from the window, I saw a military vehicle heading across the tarmac, lights flashing. Three or four austere-looking soldiers in uniform jumped out and clambered up the steps to the plane. Were they coming for us? Had Mr Kim decided to report his suspicions after all?

They spoke with the pilot and stewardess before coming straight towards us, pushing people out of the way. I thought the game was up. One of the men reached for the inside pocket of his uniform and pulled out... an envelope. It was one I recognized. It was mine and it was full of $100 bills. In our rush to leave, I had left $1500 in the room safe, and the North Korean security officials were returning it. It was a remarkable moment.

We thanked them, exchanged handshakes and breathed a huge sigh of relief. The men disembarked, the door was pulled shut and the plane began taxiing with ten or so people still standing in the aisle. All the while, military music accompanied adoring images of Kim Il-sung on the seat-back screens. It was on a loop that never ended the entire flight, and each passenger was handed propaganda sheets promoting the government's achievements.

Next to us was a man standing and clutching two live chickens that were flapping and shedding feathers all over the place. A couple of seats behind us, a woman was heating water in an old battered saucepan on a sort of Calor gas stove. It was nuts.

Now, Mick Deane was not a comfortable flyer at the best of times, and this flight out of Pyongyang was certainly not the best of times. As the plane lifted into the gloomy sky, he gripped his armrests, closed his eyes and hoped for the best.

I noticed the chicken carrier was wearing a Kim button on his tunic. In those days – and indeed this is still true today – very few North Koreans could afford to fly and even fewer people were actually allowed to leave the country. So it occurred to me that the Koreans on this plane must have belonged to the elite, and if that was the elite then the mind boggles.

We were served what I took to be cabbage soup, which I politely declined. Mick didn't even open his eyes. Almost everyone on the flight was smoking. The fog from the cigarette smoke inside the plane was almost as bad as the frozen fog we'd taken off in. The ancient Russian plane shook, rattled and rolled its way to Beijing, the Kim Il-sung adulation video played relentlessly on, until finally we bounced onto the icy runway and ground to a halt. We had survived the craziest flight I've ever taken from the craziest place I've ever been to. Communist China seemed like a beacon of freedom and liberty by comparison. North Korea was that bad.

There were quite a few advantages to playing cricket for the Cathay Pacific airline team in Hong Kong. The games were fun, the upgrades flowed and just occasionally you'd discover something that could benefit your career. On one occasion in June 1991, I got a piece of information from our left-arm spin bowler that was to give me a distinct edge over my BBC rival, Brian Barron. And trust me, that didn't happen very often.

Brian was one of the most accomplished correspondents of his generation, and had seen and done it all. He was in Saigon when the Americans abandoned the city in 1975, and covered Idi Amin's overthrow in 1979. He remained grittily competitive into his fifties, which is when I came up against him as Asia correspondent. He made my life incredibly difficult, and unwittingly taught me a huge amount about being an 'operator' when on the road. But once, just once, I stole a march on him, and for that I have to thank our aforementioned spinner, Rod Eddington.

Rod, who was the top man at Cathay at the time and subsequently became chief executive of British Airways, mentioned that one of their aircraft had hit big problems flying into Manila in the Philippines. I had been toying with the idea of heading over there because there had been a number of minor eruptions of a volcano called Mount Pinatubo, just north of Manila, and scientists were predicting a big event in the coming weeks. The problem was timing. Rod said that his people had been told that a much bigger eruption was now felt to be imminent. He'd decided to make that evening's flight to Manila the last one. He told me Philippine Airlines had also suggested they would ground their flights from Hong Kong, because of the ash cloud and predicted winds. I decided then and there that cameraman Mick Deane and I should take that last Cathay flight to Manila.

It was a risk that paid off. There was a larger eruption the day after we arrived, and Manila airport was immediately closed to all air traffic. And then, twenty-four hours later, it happened. We were having dinner in the Manila Hotel when we all felt a few minor tremors. The series of small earthquakes was the prelude to one of the biggest volcanic eruptions anywhere in the world in living memory. It was also the cue for yet another perilous journey.

Mick decided we should leave immediately for Angeles City, the nearest town to the volcano. He was convinced it would be in a dreadful state given the size of the reported eruption. We phoned the driver and left within the hour. It was close to midnight. It was around ninety miles away, and it was only after about twenty miles that the problems started.

It was eerie. Suddenly, the clear night sky gave way to a thick cloud and it began raining ash. The road was covered with several inches of it, and as we wound our way along the main road to Angeles City there was another, much larger tremor that lasted well over thirty seconds. The driver stopped, turned to us and suggested we should stop a while. We told him to carry on, anxious to get to the City of Angeles.

About a mile further up the road, a mudslide suddenly came crashing down the mountain right in front of us. We skidded in sludge caused by the mud and the ash, and ground to a halt. Ahead of us, a torrent of earth, boulders and debris was lit up by the headlights. It was a horrifying spectacle. We feared we could be washed down the rocky hillside at any time. Then we heard a thunderous crash as another rockslide happened behind us. We were trapped with nowhere to go.

All we could do was sit in the minivan and hope we survived. After an hour, the torrent ahead of us subsided and we navigated a way through the debris. There were no other vehicles on the road as we ploughed on through the ash storm to within a couple of miles of the town. And then we saw the lights in the distance coming towards us. Mick got out to film what was the most extraordinary sight. Cars, farm vehicles, trailers and carts, all rammed with people and whatever possessions they could muster, made a slow, pitiful procession out of the city. Then came the people on foot. Hundreds at first, then thousands, most of them covered in white ash that gave them a ghostly appearance I will never forget. The pictures were extraordinary. Women and children trudging slowly through the ash. In this deeply Catholic country, many carried religious statues, which added to the almost biblical vision before us. The darkness, the lights, the falling ash, the desperate plight – all created a beguiling scene on our journey to Angeles city.

Mick filmed for an hour or two, and then we drove to the place they were fleeing. It was immediately obvious why. The city of angels was uninhabitable. Everywhere, buildings were on fire; homes, shops, churches, all badly damaged. And the ash kept falling. In places it was six inches deep, and yet thousands of people just sat at the roadside waiting for help and for transport to arrive. It never did; not that night, anyway.

The people of Angeles City were abandoned to their fate and at the mercy of nature. They had lived in the shadow of the mountain their entire lives, and it had turned on them in the most cruel way. Homes gone, livelihoods lost and many people killed. And we were watching the whole thing unfold. It was desperately sad to witness.

By first light, much of the area was covered in several feet of ash and mud. Square mile after square mile was inundated. Thousands were stranded in a place they no longer recognized. We realized that the only hope of getting our pictures out to the world was to give ourselves plenty of time for the journey back to Manila. We had no idea if we would even make it. The driver decided it would be best to effectively drive around the other side of the mountain and cut across the northern Philippines rather than head back the way we came. He was right, and we got back to Manila in about four hours. We were later told the road we had taken the night before was completely impassable. Another crazy night, another crazy journey and another unforgettable experience.

Decades of war, lawlessness, occupation and corruption cannot change an unalterable fact about Afghanistan: it is one of the most beautiful places on earth. There is no more alluring scene than the snow-capped mountains of the Hindu Kush, where I found myself in late 1996 seeking out Ahmad Shah Massoud, who was a formidable warrior and military commander.

To reach him, my American cameraman Jon Steele and I had to travel along the spectacular but treacherous Salang Pass. It is 13,000 feet above sea level, snow-covered for most of the year, and prone to rockfalls and avalanches. Massoud was camping out in a place called Charikar, from where he was overseeing the battle against the Taliban, who had just pushed government forces out of the capital Kabul and imposed their own strict brand of Islam. It was a memorable drive, but nothing compared to the journey we were about to make in a couple of days' time.

We found Massoud and his fellow commanders in their temporary HQ on a farm just outside Charikar. They were trying to hold back a Taliban advance from Kabul towards the Panjshir Valley, to where government forces of the Northern Alliance had retreated. Massoud had amassed tanks, heavy weapons and hundreds of fighters, and the battle was going well, if a little chaotically. Where else would you see commanders push-starting an old Russian tank?

Massoud was directing fire onto Taliban positions on the other side of the Shomali Plain, on the northern outskirts of the capital. After a few rounds were launched, Jon pointed out that it might make sense to move, on the basis that what goes out often comes back with interest. At that moment we heard the whistle, screech and thunderous explosion of an incoming shell. It landed about a hundred yards away. I hit the deck face down, Jon was still stood trying to film it, and as I tentatively got up, covered in dust, Massoud broke into uncontrollable laughter.

We spent the night editing our piece at Massoud's HQ and then sent our producer on the twenty-six-hour journey back to Pakistan in order to send the material via satellite to London. Nowadays, by the way, we would have a backpack with the equipment necessary to send the pictures from exactly where we were.

Jon and I then had a decision to make. We had wanted to get into Kabul to report on life under the Taliban. We could forget it and film another story with Massoud, we could make the long, tortuous journey back over the mountains in order to reach Kabul, or we could drive to the capital, forty-five minutes away across the deserted Shomali Plain and hope for the best. It had become a kind of no man's land as there was unrelenting crossfire, and the one road across it was in the sights of the Taliban fighters.

We asked Massoud for advice and he said he would provide a car and a driver, and added that we should cross the plain at dawn while the Taliban fighters were sleeping. It seemed like a plan. We rose at 5 a.m., washed in a nearby stream, ate canned tuna and boiled eggs for breakfast and loaded the equipment into the ramshackle vehicle that would carry us to the Intercontinental Hotel in Kabul, or to our deaths...

It seems amusing in retrospect, but at the time both Jon and I were terrified.

Our driver, Jawad, chewed tobacco, laughed a lot and drove very fast. Once out on the open plain, Jon and I scoured the mountains for any sign of Taliban positions. We couldn't see any. All seemed calm, it was a clear day. The sun was rising in the bluest of skies, birds swooped playfully and the plumes of smoke that had dotted the hillsides during the previous evening's battle had disappeared. We were very soon halfway across, and my heart was pounding a little less. It began to feel like a Sunday afternoon drive in the countryside.

And then, just as quickly, it didn't. You don't hear rockets until it's way too late. Or at least, we didn't hear the one that came spearing into the road ahead of us. Jawad swerved violently to the left, the car veered off the tarmac and he struggled to keep control. The one thing Massoud had warned us about were the landmines strewn across parts of the plain on either side of the road. In the event we missed any landmines and avoided the rocket, which had mercifully failed to explode. Jon wanted to stop and film. He was outnumbered. Jawad accelerated, chewed ever more feverishly on his tobacco and turned up the Afghan music on his car radio to full volume. I lay across the back seat wishing I was beginning a twenty-four-hour journey back through the snowy mountains of the Hindu Kush.

I also was wondering – not for the first time in my career – why on earth I had thought being a foreign correspondent was a good idea. Jon, on the other hand, found the whole incident rather amusing, his earlier terror now forgotten.

Eventually, a mile or so from Kabul, we reached a Taliban roadblock. The soldiers were suspicious but remained relaxed and smiling, and were seemingly fascinated by the large camera resting on Jon's lap. They wore *shalwar kameez* (long shirts and baggy trousers), black turbans and long beards, and carried AK-47s. They all looked like very young religious students, probably from the madrassas inside Pakistan, institutions that provided an almost limitless number of highly motivated but largely untrained foot soldiers for the cause.

They carried out a cursory search of the vehicle, looked at my passport upside down and waved us through. Jawad drove us to the Intercontinental Hotel and disappeared. He'd got us to Kabul in one piece... just. And for that I will be eternally grateful.

We spent several days in the city watching the Taliban enforce their fundamentalist interpretation of the Islamic faith. Upon taking control, they quickly introduced a number of decrees: women must not work, girls should not go to school, men must grow beards and pray five times a day, music and entertainment venues had to close and the radio could only broadcast Islamic prayer and poetry. TV shops were shut down, VCRs destroyed and tape was strewn in the trees like a decorative symbol of repression.

Strangely, they didn't mind us filming them. One group even invited us to sit down with them one afternoon at one of the palaces they had taken over as headquarters. Tea with the Taliban. They tried to outline their ideas: 'We want a pure Islamic society free from crime and corruption,' said one.

It is true that under the Taliban, crime was virtually eradicated and there was peace in the capital after years of conflict. But that peace came at a terrible price. The edicts of the Taliban were enforced without mercy. Arrests, public beatings, amputations and executions became routine. Women had basically disappeared from view. It meant that the hospitals, crammed with victims of war, were hopelessly understaffed; 80 per cent of the nurses and 40 per cent of the doctors were women, and they were no longer allowed to work.

We interviewed one doctor at her home, who spoke to us through her burka for fear of being identified: 'I can't go to my job at the hospital, I can't help my people because they say we must just sit in our houses, we can't even go outside. I feel very bad about this and I want to leave this country.'

She wasn't alone. Thousands were fleeing every day, despite the best efforts of the Taliban to halt the exodus.

Kabul was free of war, at least temporarily. But it was a place cast into the dark ages, and to Westerners like us at least, unremittingly depressing.

The Taliban's mistake was to harbour Osama bin Laden, providing sanctuary for the al-Qaeda leader and his cohorts. From caves in the Tora Bora mountains, they somehow managed to mastermind the terror operations of the organization. It was a mistake, because after the devastating attack on America on 11 September 2001, US intelligence tracked bin Laden's whereabouts, and the United States and its allies launched the invasion that toppled the Taliban.

One interesting footnote to this: a couple of days before the 9/11 atrocity, a camera crew travelled to the Panjshir Valley to interview my new friend, Ahmad Shah Massoud. Once the camera started rolling it exploded, killing Massoud and the crew, who turned out to be al-Qaeda suicide bombers. They'd wanted Massoud dead, knowing he would be a key commander for the Western allies responding to the 9/11 attack.

I was sad to hear the news of his death. I liked and, in a way, admired him. And he gave us Jawad, the driver who took us on one of the most memorable journeys of my life.

THE FLOOD

Derek Maude – the gruff Yorkshireman who was one of my first programme editors at the BBC – had a saying he would recount at every opportunity: 'Don't give me a good reporter, give me a lucky reporter.'

His long experience at BBC Television News had taught him that some reporters are lucky and some aren't. 'That's just the way it is,' he would say. I thought of him in February 2000. I was by this time Senior Correspondent at ITN. And there's no question that, at least then, I was a lucky reporter.

It didn't feel that way for several days in mid-February. I was sitting in the newsroom at ITN headquarters in London tearing my hair out. A big story was happening in southern Africa, a part of the world I knew very well, and I was not being sent. The heaviest rainfall for fifty years across South Africa, Botswana and Mozambique was causing catastrophic flooding, mainly in Mozambique, where three large rivers – the Save, the Limpopo and the Zambezi – all flow down to the sea. Millions of people were displaced, hundreds of square miles of precious arable farmland were flooded and the scenes were biblical. It hadn't escaped my attention that the BBC's Ben Brown was there and sending back reports night after night.

For some reason, it just didn't appeal to our bosses, who seemed to think it wasn't worth the effort or the money. There was always a conundrum for ITV News: which stories to cover and which to leave alone. BBC News could basically throw money and people at any major story, pretty much regardless of the cost, whereas we had a finite budget and so tough decisions had to be made all the time. As hard as I tried, I could not persuade the foreign desk to change their minds.

But still the rain fell, the flooding worsened and the BBC were now leading their *Six O'Clock News* with the unfolding drama. In the end, Nigel Dacre, the editor, stepped in and decided it should be covered. He decided to send me to join our Johannesburg cameraman Andy Rex and producer Glenda Gaitz to compile what he called a 'special report' for the slot just after the break on the *Evening News*. It was a good way of concealing the fact that it was a hopelessly late call and we should have gone earlier. But that's the way TV news works. Never admit you were wrong; just pretend it was always intended to be this way. We all do it.

Sure enough, by the time I reached Johannesburg to meet the guys and then transferred to Maputo, capital of Mozambique, the floods had actually eased and the story was losing its appeal. I will never forget arriving at the lovely Polana Serena Hotel early in the afternoon, just in time to see Ben Brown and his BBC crew heading off to the airport to fly back to London. 'Bit late?' was Ben's passing comment as we lugged our equipment into the foyer. It was not a great feeling.

I mumbled something about coming to do a feature on the aftermath and the economic cost to Mozambique. He didn't seem convinced. And neither, frankly, was I.

Somewhat deflated, we regrouped in the bar to plan what to do. The first problem was logistical. It was simply impossible to reach the worst-affected areas by land. Much of the infrastructure was damaged and many bridges were down. We needed a helicopter. Glenda decided the best bet was to bring one up from South Africa, and within a few hours we had a chopper at Maputo airport and a pilot, Mike Pingo, sitting with us having dinner at the Polana. It was to prove the best decision we made.

The floods were a cruel blow to Mozambique, one of the poorest countries in the world, which at the time was just starting to get back on its feet after a devastating fifteen-year civil war that left a million people dead and the country broken, hopelessly underdeveloped and littered with landmines. The rebel movement, the Mozambican National Resistance (or Renamo), had waged a long campaign, backed by South Africa's apartheid regime, against the ruling Marxist Frelimo government. But a peace agreement in 1992 offered the country much-needed hope and a more optimistic future. Then the floods came.

So, in 2000, it was a country without the resources or the infrastructure to withstand a catastrophe of this magnitude. We decided to do a broader story about a country's struggle through a manmade disaster and now one inflicted upon it by nature. A bit high-minded maybe, but a plan nevertheless. We went off to bed with an agreement to be up in the air by 7 a.m. Pingo toddled off with a beer to plot a route up to a place called Beira, which had been struck by the full ferocity of a slow-moving and long-lasting tropical storm, Cyclone Eline. It seemed as good a place as any to begin.

Despite the comforts of the colonial-era hotel, I didn't sleep well, and at around 5 a.m. I made my way down to reception to try to find some bottled water. It was there that I met Michele Quintaglie of the UN World Food programme, or rather heard Michele Quintaglie, on her mobile phone, gasping with horror and trying, apparently without success, to hear what someone was trying to tell her. 'When? ... No! ... Really! How bad?' she was asking. Clutching my bottle of water, I waited in shorts and T-shirt for her to end the conversation.

'Good God,' she said, trying desperately to reach a colleague on her phone. 'An entire town is underwater. Suddenly, in the middle of the night. Thousands of people are at risk right now. The Limpopo has burst its banks and inundated the place.'

It turned out that upstream in Zimbabwe they had released huge amounts of water from a dam at bursting point, with no thought for the consequences. The effect of that and another torrential storm was that the river had risen six metres in a matter of hours. It was catastrophic for the town of Chokwe. The entire population was under threat, people had already drowned in their beds in the dead of night, others were crowded on roofs, on top of vehicles, had climbed trees or were simply crammed with whatever belongings they could salvage on any area of high ground they could find. There wasn't much of it. In short, Chokwe was submerged. There was fear and panic. And there was no one to rescue them.

I immediately phoned Pingo's room, woke him up and asked him how soon we could be airborne. 'First light,' he said. 'Around forty-five minutes.' I then called Andy. By 6.30 a.m. we were lifting off. Pingo was on the radio changing the routing from Beira to Chokwe, and an hour or so later we were flying over one the most extraordinary scenes I have ever witnessed. The waters were still rising, people were desperate and stranded, and the arrival of our helicopter gave them the cruellest of false hopes. They thought we had come to rescue them. We hadn't and we couldn't.

They waved from roofs, from the tops of cars and trucks and buses and trailers, and from trees. They waved with items of bright clothing, with towels, with scarves, with anything they had. They implored us to come down and rescue them. They were obviously screaming up at us but the helicopter rotors drowned out their shouts. We couldn't hear their desperation, but we could see it. Andy remarked that it was like arriving on the set of a Hollywood disaster movie.

People were crowded onto corrugated iron roofs that looked as if they could collapse at any moment. A lone man on the roof of a straw hut pointed to his mouth and rubbed his stomach. He obviously thought we were there to drop food. We didn't have any. A woman perched high in a tree gestured to her young children gathered precariously on the lower branches. There were four or five of them. All very young. Then we noticed in the mother's arms was a baby wrapped in a blanket.

It was a harrowing scene. Andy was filming from the now-open door of the helicopter. Pingo couldn't believe there were no rescue helicopters several hours into what was by now a very serious humanitarian emergency. 'I can't see many of these people surviving this,' he said.

I couldn't either. Below us were thousands of people who went to bed last night with no sign of water whatsoever in their town. Chokwe had not been affected thus far by the flooding. Now it was fast disappearing beneath the waters. Most of the houses were completely submerged, and it was mainly the larger civic buildings that were above water. It was those roofs that supported the most people. Too many people, we thought. The structures would not withstand such weight for long.

Then, after about forty-five minutes, we heard a South African voice on the helicopter radio. Then another. And another. They were pilots heading across the border towards Chokwe, said Pingo, 'The cavalry is on its way, thank God.'

And then we saw them on the horizon. Five Chinook-style transport choppers heading straight for us. It was the South African Defence Force (SADF), and they arrived just in time. For the next hour we filmed as the pilots manoeuvred skilfully under power lines to hover over the crammed roofs. We filmed them winching people to safety. Children first, then the elderly and then women. We filmed scores of people wading through the floodwaters towards one of the helicopters that was hovering as close to the surface as possible. People rushed to clamber aboard. Pushing, shoving, splashing and waving frantically. We filmed another chopper plucking the mother and her children from the tree. This was flying of supreme judgement, extraordinary precision and great courage.

In the water were several dead animals. I saw only one human body, but it was impossible that dozens had not been swept away in the initial deluge. A pilot was manoeuvring close to the roof of a bus. Another was hovering next to a truckload of people, the wheels of the helicopter actually in the water as the people scrambled across. The chopper taking on people wading through the water was overloaded. The winchman was shouting at people still fighting to clamber aboard. He was pushing people away. The pilot was frantically gesturing to him to get people clear. He needed to get out of there, and couldn't without risking lives. Eventually, he had no choice. We filmed as he finally lifted off, the downdraught battering the people still in the water. One man was clinging to the underside of the helicopter as it swung away to dry land.

It was an incredibly dramatic scene. But then Pingo told us he too had to head off, as we were running dangerously low on fuel. We landed in the same field being used by the South African helicopters to put down the rescued. Andy and I decided to try to board one of the empty ones and film some rescues from the actual helicopter. The winchman grabbed Andy's camera and hauled us both aboard almost as the pilot was getting airborne.

I saw Pingo swing south towards Maputo to refuel. It was still only about 10 a.m. We were gathering amazing footage and I realized we were the only camera on the scene. It is a very rare thing to happen, and I don't mind admitting that even in the midst of such tragedy and desperation, I felt an exhilaration that we had a story of such visual strength to ourselves. It was exclusively ours. And it felt great. I know that will sound unfeeling and selfish and self-absorbed. But it is the truth.

Within minutes, we were back over Chokwe. This time in a helicopter with a life-saving job to do. Before we knew it, the pilot had lowered the aircraft to about twenty or thirty feet above an almost completely submerged vehicle. On its roof were three boys, struggling to hold on to the car in the downdraught. The winchman made his way down towards them. Andy filmed as he reached out to one of the boys, who grabbed his arm. He beckoned the other two boys to try to grab hold of him. It was very apparent he had one opportunity to rescue these boys and one opportunity only.

The second boy clung on to him, and then, after a precarious few seconds, so did the third. The winchman was struggling to keep hold of them as he was raised back towards the helicopter door. I was convinced one or more of the boys would plunge back into the floodwaters. When they reached level with the helicopter door, Andy put down his camera and we both helped haul the boys in. They sat there drenched, petrified, shaking... but safe. It was a wonderful moment.

The pilot had now moved on to a woman stranded on the partially collapsed roof of a straw hut. She was hanging on for dear life. Somehow the pilot hovered between two trees and managed to lower the helicopter level with the woman, who managed to scramble across. We picked up about a dozen more from another roof before we were full, and the pilot swung away and headed off. There were people left behind. They would have to wait.

The waters were still rising. It dawned on me that Andy and I were occupying precious space in the helicopter. It was an uncomfortable feeling, but I knew these images would be seen right around the world and would have an impact on viewers and on governments. I figured that alone could justify the space we were taking up. I am convinced to this day it was the right thing to do. It will become clear why later.

We returned to the field where the survivors were being

dropped off. By now a makeshift hospital had been set up in a farm building. Crew members were carrying young children to the medics. We filmed the rows of patients lying on the floor inside. A mother holding a baby attached to a drip. A young girl, seemingly all alone, wiping tears from her eyes. SADF doctors working busily and skilfully on the injured.

We had more pictures than we could ever have imagined. Dramatic footage. We could cut a twelve-minute piece, I thought, which is a very long piece for a news bulletin. And then I realized it was a Sunday. ITV News bulletins at weekends are hopelessly short; usually a maximum of around fifteen minutes. I felt deflated. We had a remarkable story to tell with immensely powerful pictures and it was all our own.

I noticed Michele Quintaglie from the World Food programme boarding one of the rescue helicopters. We jumped on with her. I wanted to do an interview while the chopper was above Chokwe.

'We desperately need more helicopters,' she said. 'Chokwe is only one town that has been inundated. There are several more and there is no one rescuing anybody in those places... Are we just going to let them die? Or are we going to help save them? The world must do more, and fast.

'The last trip I went on we pulled a baby just one month old from the arms of a man on a roof. He wanted to stay until the rest of his family could be rescued. We are finding people in very high water and they have to get out now. I am afraid hundreds will die in this area.'

She was right. In the event, more than seven hundred people perished, but not through any lack of effort or skill from the

South African pilots. It was an unbelievable display of skill, bravery and resolve in the most trying of circumstances. It was extraordinary to witness.

We had our story, and it was early afternoon. We now had to get back to Maputo to edit and send the piece to London. But where was Pingo? And how could we get hold of him? We could have the best story in the world, but if we couldn't get it back to London we might as well not have it.

I asked Andy for the satellite phone he carried in his camera bag and called the news desk. All they knew is that we had headed off at first light. They had no idea what we had got.

The programme editor couldn't believe it when I asked for ten minutes. 'The bloody programme is only thirteen minutes,' he said. 'Can you do it in four?'

I was stunned. He seemed so underwhelmed by what I was describing to him. I was furious, and decided to phone the editor, Nigel Dacre, at home. His suggestion was that we kept it until the Monday, when we could have much more time. I was totally against that idea. More cameras would surely arrive by tomorrow, and here we were now with a genuine world exclusive on a hugely dramatic story.

In the end, Nigel phoned the controller of ITV News, Steve Anderson, and told him what we had and that it was exclusive. He agreed to extend the programme by two minutes, and gave me six minutes for the piece. We reluctantly decided to keep some of the stuff back for a much longer piece on Monday's *Evening News*. We had to get cracking with the edit.

However, there was still no sign of Pingo. The flooding was now threatening the field where more than three thousand rescued people were gathered. We all had to start walking away from the oncoming deluge.

Police officers were panicking, shouting at the crowds. People began running in different directions. It was chaos. Andy filmed some more, and then he and I had to get out. There were few vehicles around but we managed to jump on the back of a water truck, which dropped us on a small patch of high land; a kind of mound that would soon be lost to the floodwaters. I began to fear the worst. How would Pingo find us? And even if he did, would he be able to land? And if he could land, would the helicopter be mobbed by people desperate to escape the flood?

I had tried several times to reach Pingo from our satellite phone, but he never answered. By now he should be almost back from Maputo. Three hours had elapsed since he left for fuel. Andy called Glenda in Maputo and tried to explain where we were for her to inform air traffic control, who could, perhaps, reach Pingo. Glenda had a map and tried to put together some coordinates to pass on. It was all speculative, we were stranded, Pingo was nowhere to be seen and I could see my world exclusive slipping away. Andy sat down, leaned against his camera bag and had a kip. Nothing much bothered him. He had an African insouciance that I envied.

By now it was 4 p.m. – 2 p.m. in London – and we had four hours to get back, edit six minutes and feed the piece to London. And there I was standing on a spit of land, with floodwaters rapidly encroaching, staring at a grey sky with no sign of Pingo.

I phoned London to say we may well not make the early evening news. After making such a fuss about the story, I felt stupid, nauseous and incredibly fed up. Then we heard the distant clatter of a helicopter and I saw a speck in the sky that was getting bigger by the minute. It must be Pingo. Would he know where we were?

As it approached it became clear it was not our helicopter. Even worse, it was another civilian helicopter with the unmistakeable figure of a man with a TV camera filming through the open door. Things were not going well.

Fortunately for us, though not for the thousands still stranded in Chokwe, the South African rescue helicopters had headed off to Maputo to refuel. It was too late to return so they wouldn't be back until first light. The cameraman had missed the real story. We still had an exclusive, if only we could get it back to London.

And then, there he was. Pingo circling above us, straining to look left and right and trying to locate us. We waved and shouted and beckoned him down. By now there was precious little space for him to land. But down he came, on we climbed and away we went. We had three and a half hours until the programme.

Pingo was showing off, flying low and fast along the deserted but spectacular beaches on the Mozambique coastline. We were back in an hour. By the time we got to the hotel I had written most of the script, Andy knew exactly which pictures he wanted in the piece and Glenda had set up the edit suite in a hotel room.

It was relatively simple. The amazing images required few words. Sometimes it is best in television news to simply let the drama unfold, with natural sound and sparing script. This was one such occasion. 'Dawn in Mozambique, and the people of

Chokwe awoke to a deluge,' was how it began, and then Andy's extraordinary images told the story. All I did was nudge it along with a few lines of voiceover.

We sent the piece off with time to spare. It made for powerful television and was to have precisely the impact I had hoped for. Before it aired, I called Michele to find out the latest situation. She told me she thought that around five hundred people had died, but many more were believed to be missing. It was turning into a terrible tragedy. A natural disaster this poor country could do without. We resolved to return at first light.

By now, it became clear that the cameraman we had seen in the other helicopter worked for the news agency Reuters, who provided their material to TV news organizations around the world who subscribed to their service. Among them the BBC. Our rivals would be getting some pictures but nothing like we had gathered, and, of course, they had no reporter there. We were well ahead on a big story. We ate and had a few beers. It felt good. But there was more to do.

Our story that Sunday evening was seen by our rivals and by government ministers. There was pressure for the UK to act. Relief agencies and rescue charities were mobilized. Downing Street asked the British High Commission in Maputo to find helicopters locally. It would take too long to fly military Chinooks in from Britain.

Reporters and camera crews would soon begin to fly in from around the world. We needed to stay ahead. ITN had decided to send in another reporter and camera team overnight. It was Robert Moore, an experienced correspondent, first-rate operator and a good friend. I was glad it was him. Meanwhile,

Glenda had decided to hire a small plane to move several drums of aviation fuel much nearer to the scene. Now it would only take minutes to refuel rather than hours. We would be able to film most of the following day. It was a master stroke.

Shortly after first light on the Monday, we were airborne with Pingo again. This time the rescue helicopters were there before us. Seven of them by now, covering a wider area than simply Chokwe. We decided to head to Xai-Xai, another town where people were stranded and dying. It emerged that in three days the Limpopo valley had experienced 75 per cent of its normal annual rainfall.

Xai-Xai, like Chokwe, was almost completely submerged. Rescues were taking place, but thousands were still stranded. We watched one helicopter lower towards the raging floodwaters, where a young boy was struggling to stay afloat. A crew member was winched down and tried to grab the boy, but the waters were carrying him off very quickly. The boy drifted away. The pilot quickly swung the helicopter around with the winchman still below. It was dangerous and difficult. The rescuer tried again, and this time, mercifully, he was able to grab the child and lift him to safety.

Rescues like this were happening all over the place. Below us, two men in a boat were pulling a fallen pine tree through the water. Only when we looked more closely did we see a man clinging to the pine. Later, a family of six were rescued; they'd been surviving on corrugated sheeting they had managed to wedge between two branches of a tree.

Pingo put us down in Xai-Xai and we transferred to a rescue boat to get more footage. It was another dramatic day.

Combined with footage from the day before, we cut nine minutes for the *Evening News*.

That night, everybody was arriving. Matt Frei of the BBC, Jon Snow of Channel 4 News, and many other 'big hitters'. Snow was gracious enough to tell me that we had beaten everybody and that our Sunday piece was 'powerful television'.

The following day was again remarkable, and because we had pre-positioned our fuel, we stole a march on our rivals. There was one very awkward moment when, as we were refuelling close to Chokwe, another helicopter set down close to us and Matt Frei jumped out. They were also low on fuel and wanted to know if they could use the drums in the field. It would save them a two-hour round trip to Maputo. I was on the verge of saying yes when Glenda intervened. 'Listen, that is *our* fuel that I arranged for *our* helicopter,' she said. 'We're not handing it out to anyone, particularly the BBC.' She was adamant, and in the cut-throat, win-at-all-costs world of television news, she was probably right.

Glenda was a prodigiously good fixer on the ground on big stories. She got things done and was effective and well organized. She was also fiercely competitive. Matt Frei was rather taken aback. He thought we were being churlish. But off he went to Maputo.

I felt bad, he was a friend. But it meant we were still ahead.

I upset another friend that day, too. Our own Robert Moore was putting together a piece on the displaced people and those in makeshift hospitals. As darkness approached he wanted to do a piece to camera on a roof in Chokwe, where scores of people were still waiting to be rescued.

He asked to borrow Pingo and the helicopter to drop him nearby. But it was getting late and we needed to get back to Maputo. We agreed that Pingo would drop Robert and his camera team, then fly us back to Maputo and return to get Robert. There was just enough daylight left.

Things were going to plan until Pingo hit some technical problem with his aircraft that required attention in Maputo. By the time it was fixed, darkness was falling and there was not enough time to get Robert. He spent the night in Chokwe, where he tells me he was eaten alive by mosquitoes and had no food or water. He also told me that at one stage he had to take refuge in a tree as snakes started appearing in the flood water. I am not sure he has ever forgiven me. To this day he thinks it was somehow my idea of a practical joke. Robert, it wasn't. But it was still highly amusing.

As we edited that evening, a call came in from London asking whether we had the pictures of the baby born in a tree. We hadn't. It turns out that a film crew from the South Africa Broadcasting Corporation travelling in one of the SADF helicopters had filmed the rescue of the baby and mother, Carolina Chirindza. She had gone into labour while clinging to the branches of a flimsy tree. Her mother-in-law held a sarong under her to catch the baby and prevent it falling into the crocodile-infested waters below. Mother and baby – named Rosita, after the infant's grandmother – were lifted away and taken to dry land, where an exhausted Carolina cradled her newborn in drenched linen. Rosita became the symbol of the floods. By now, an appeal for donations in Britain had reached £20 million. The incredible story of the baby born in the tree was to boost that still further.

Such was Rosita's celebrity that in the coming months the family was given a three-bedroom house by the local authorities. Carolina was offered a job as a cleaner by the district administrator, and slowly she was lifted out of poverty. Four and a half months after her birth, Rosita and her mother travelled to Washington DC to lobby Congress for more aid to help tens of thousands of Mozambicans affected by the catastrophe. A plaque has been erected on the mafura (mahogany) tree where she was born.

The full impact of the flooding only became clear a few weeks later. The damage was colossal. Farmland and crops were destroyed for hundreds of square miles. In 2000, nothing was grown at all over 1,500 square kilometres of some of the most productive arable land in Mozambique. Thousands of homes were destroyed, farms were ruined, clinics and schools washed away. Hundreds of people died from cholera due to filthy water, and malaria killed many others. More than 100,000 farming families lost their livelihoods. And it was not only crops that were destroyed – 20,000 head of cattle, the mainstay for some of the poorest families, were swept away in the floods or died from disease in the aftermath.

Irrigation systems all over the country were broken and the infrastructure was devastated; the main railway lines from Mozambique to South Africa, Zimbabwe and Swaziland were destroyed. And there was another, much under-reported consequence of the flooding. Much of the landmine clearance work in that part of the country was set back many years. The power of the floodwaters moved mines that had been marked for clearance. And the markings of many others disappeared, meaning the painstaking, life-saving work would have to be done all over again. The bill for damage and relief efforts of the flooding ran to well over £1 billion.

The suffering of those poor people was appalling. And yet, a few months later, Andy and I were sitting in an elegant banqueting hall in a plush New York hotel waiting to hear if we had won an Emmy award for our coverage. It has always sat uncomfortably with me that we should win awards for covering events that involve natural disasters, conflict, tragedy and death. It seems to me exploitative and unnecessary. What we do is not entertainment; it is real, it is news. We haven't created anything, as such. In Mozambique, we had merely been witness to and reported on a terrible catastrophe in which real people died and suffered enormous losses. It just didn't seem right that we should gather in black tie, eat good food, drink fine champagne and toast our 'good fortune' at being there. It all felt a bit exploitative, even fraudulent.

Anyway, win we did. And boy did we celebrate – despite my reservations. At one stage we actually left the award itself in some bar in downtown New York, before Andy's wife pointed out that it was missing. It was still there when we went back, and it has been on a shelf at home to this day.

Andy went on to win Television Technician of the Year at the Royal Television Society Journalism Awards a couple of months later, and we also won a BAFTA.

Derek Maude was right: 'Don't give me a good reporter, give me a lucky reporter.'

In Mozambique, we were lucky. Very lucky.

TERRY LLOYD

I T WAS NEVER a foregone conclusion that Terry Lloyd would go to war in Iraq in 2003. On the face of it, he was an obvious candidate. He was a very experienced, tenacious war reporter who knew the Middle East; he was comfortable covering conflicts and would not let the team down. In normal circumstances, he would have been a natural pick by the new editor of ITV News, David Mannion. What's more, Mannion was one of Terry's best mates.

But these were not normal circumstances for Terry Lloyd. Terry was recovering from a crisis in his personal life. His marriage was on the rocks, he'd been drinking heavily, and his work and family life had suffered. But at the beginning of 2003 he was on the mend and the old Terry was coming back. When it became clear that war with Saddam was almost inevitable, he threw his hat in the ring like many other reporters.

For David Mannion it was not a straightforward decision. He knew Terry was still getting over what had been a tough time. But he also thought it would be the perfect opportunity for Terry to lose himself once again in the job he loved. And he wasn't the only one. Terry was very keen to go. He always used to say, 'There's only one thing worse than going to war... and that's not going to war.' He was only half joking.

Terry was one hell of a reporter. It was he who revealed to the world Saddam Hussein's massacre of thousands of Kurds in the town of Halabja in northern Iraq in 1988. It was the first real evidence of Saddam's slaughter of his own people with poison gas during the Iran–Iraq war.

Six years later, he reported exclusively from the Balkans on the discovery of mass graves at Ovcara, which contained the remains of almost three hundred Croatian men who had been marched at gunpoint, by Serb militiamen, from the nearby hospital in Vukovar.

And in 1999, when journalists were refused entry into Kosovo, Lloyd and his cameraman, Mike Inglis, trekked for days over snow-capped mountains from Montenegro to film the Serbian advance and talk to refugees on their way out. This is part of his report on the way back along the mountain path:

At long last, we were approaching safety along the beaten track, which has become a lifeline for so many. Journeys end back at the foot of the mountain range. It's been an exhausting experience, and it can only be sheer terror which forces the young and the old, the women and the children to make that arduous and perilous trek across the mountains. Thousands have pushed the limits of human endurance already, and many more will try if they can.

It was typical Terry Lloyd – less concerned about the state of the war than of the civilians caught up in it. They were the story. And he was going to find them.

He was well-used to danger, but said he'd 'never been so

frightened' as when he was attacked by the footballer Eric Cantona on a beach in Guadeloupe. Lloyd tracked down and confronted the Manchester United star two weeks after Cantona had aimed a kung-fu kick at a Crystal Palace fan, an incident caught on live television. Terry maintained he was on the receiving end of a similar kick.

In truth, Terry took kicks aplenty in life, but he always got up, dusted himself off and went back to it. He was one of life's erratic, maverick, unpredictable – but ultimately good and warm-hearted – guys.

In 2003, he only had one thing on his mind. Getting to Iraq, to the heart of the story, and doing what he did best: putting together well-constructed, sharply written, cleverly shot news reports for ITN. David Mannion had to let him go.

Terry relished that opportunity, and it showed.

And so it was on a mid-March evening in 2003 that Terry and I met up in the restaurant of the Sheraton Hotel in Kuwait. It was the gathering place for international media awaiting the outbreak of war. It was a place of strutting reporters and camera crews, all bravado and talk, but which, if my own feelings were anything to go by, only served to conceal an inner apprehension and fearfulness about what the coming days and weeks would bring. It was a particularly tense time for Terry and me and our camera teams, because we knew that we would be operating inside Iraq on our own.

There were two types of correspondent in that war: embedded and unilateral. The embedded reporters and camera crews in Kuwait were already in place in the desert, attached to the military and awaiting the first move across the border. They would be stuck with their units for the entirety of the conflict, producing 'pooled' eyewitness reports for most of the main UK news broadcasters. It is the way the military prefers to do things, and the broadcasters have little option but to sign up to the rules and regulations imposed by the armed forces. The camera teams get fed, watered, transported and protected, but they also get censored. The military's media liaison teams closely watch everything that is being filmed, edited and transmitted, and control what you can say in your scripts. I personally don't like it, and would rather not sign up to anything that allowed a military officer to control what I broadcast. But it enables footage to emerge from the front lines that would otherwise be too difficult or too dangerous to access. It is a trade-off, but in my view an unsatisfactory one unless you are very fortunate with the senior officers and minders you are placed with.

In Kuwait, Terry and I were not embedded. We would be unilaterals: free-roaming, unrestricted and uncensored, but also largely unprotected. It was the way we both preferred it. We could make our own plans in consultation with each other, and we could head for wherever we felt the story was taking us.

Even though we were not attached to a military unit, the Ministry of Defence still insisted we were accredited as war correspondents. Terry and I had to go to another hotel in Kuwait to pick up our credentials and to get a briefing from a senior British officer, Colonel Chris Vernon, someone I had come to like and trust. But our meeting in Kuwait was a difficult one. Vernon essentially warned us to stay away from British troops. 'I don't want you anywhere near my battlefield' were his exact words. It was the clearest possible indication that they didn't want independent journalists roaming freely around the conflict zone.

The colonel made out it was a safety issue. 'We won't have the time, the men, the inclination to protect you. You'll be on your own and you should be aware of the risks of doing that,' he said. But that wasn't the whole truth.

They didn't want reporters they couldn't control anywhere near the war. They wanted to manage the message. They wanted their version of events to be the story. They wanted the reporters with them to be in uniform, part of the military operation. They wanted them, in fact, to be part of the war effort. They even gave embedded journalists the honorary rank of major.

This was nothing new; censorship in war is as old as war itself. But the stark reality of it in Iraq made me anxious. I totally understand that war reporters have to be very careful about reporting any information or event that will be of comfort or use to the enemy. Of course it should be that way. I would never, without agreement, report the disposition of forces or British losses or anything else that could help the enemy or pose a threat to British troops.

But, equally, I believe you cannot wittingly report partial truths or half truths or be used for propaganda purposes. There has to be the fullest reporting possible. It seemed to me, in Iraq, that the control demanded by the British military was well beyond what should be journalistically acceptable. Censorship may be tolerable when the war is going well, when journalists have successes to report. But when things take a turn for the worse and the difficulties really emerge, I feel you need to be able to say that – which is not a view often shared by the military. It is then that military needs and journalistic demands become hopelessly irreconciled.

I was alarmed. 'Fucking helpful, that is,' I said to Terry after the meeting.

Terry was more pragmatic. 'What do you expect him to say? They want to control us or ban us. We just have to do our job.'

He was right, and it made me more determined than ever to do that job properly. Embedded journalism was a necessary part of our coverage. But perhaps more important was our own journalism, free of censorship and restriction. Embedded reporters would not be able to tell the whole story. It was, therefore, crucial that we could. Can there be a more important role for journalists than to report without fear or favour what happens when our young men and women go to war in our name? Or, at least, in our government's name?

The colonel's attitude reinforced my belief that Terry and I had, now more than ever, a responsibility to the viewers. It may sound pompous, but that is honestly the way it felt to us.

Colonel Vernon was, however, very forthcoming and useful about the British intentions in the early days of the war. He led us to believe that British armour and troops, both the 7th Armoured Brigade, known as the Desert Rats, and the Marines, would be heading straight for the port city of Basra in southern Iraq, and also that there would be little to stand in their way.

Furthermore, intelligence from inside Basra suggested that the population there would welcome British forces with open arms, and that there would be celebrations and dancing in the streets. A sense of liberation.

The British were hopeful that upon the outbreak of war, the inhabitants of Basra would mount a popular insurrection against Saddam Hussein's forces in the city. In fact, they would encourage it, with the aim that it would trigger similar revolts in other cities in southern Iraq with a predominantly Shia population, as was the case in 1991 in the wake of the Gulf War. There was no love lost between the Shias and Saddam, who was born a Sunni and treated Shiites appallingly as a result, despite being a secular dictator.

Such a scenario would hugely assist the efforts of US–British forces to overcome resistance from loyalist militias and the regular Iraqi army, and would enable them to concentrate efforts on toppling the regime in Baghdad.

We were also told that the liberation of Basra would remove a threat to northern supply lines, help secure the southern oilfields and enable a full-scale relief and humanitarian effort to get under way pretty quickly. The British, it seemed, had it all thought out, and they were prepared to tell us.

Our meeting with Colonel Vernon confirmed one thing in Terry's mind: Basra was the place. Basra was the story. Basra was where he needed to be when the time came.

I was unsettled by the briefing; Terry was buoyed by it. On the way back to the Sheraton he had a clarity of purpose that I admired.

And that night, he seemed relaxed and confident. 'I feel good about this one, Marky,' he told me. 'You know that feeling when you have a team around you that makes you feel comfortable?'

'Yes,' I replied.

'Well, I have that feeling,' he said. But he didn't need to.

I knew exactly what he meant. I knew the strength and confidence you draw from knowing you have some of the very best people in the business right there with you. Particularly in potentially dangerous situations. We were apprehensive, but excited about what lay ahead.

At that moment, one of his camera team, Daniel Demoustier, walked in carrying bags of clothes he'd bought at the market. Among the purchases was a green fleece, far too big for him, but necessary for the cold desert nights that lay ahead.

Everybody was busy preparing – checking their kit, the 4 x 4 vehicles, the fuel and food and water. Fred Nérac, a French force of nature in his forties who loved good restaurants, fine wine and skiing, was also on Terry's team. He was out trying to source 'a few nice things for the camping trip'. He meant, I presume, food. He was always well supplied and well prepared.

I remember once working with Fred on a story about a serious avalanche in the French Alps, in which British tourists were killed or missing. I arrived hopelessly attired, in suit and overcoat. I'd been covering a diplomatic story in Paris. Within minutes, Fred had taken me to a ski shop, buying all the kit I needed. We had permissions, complimentary lift passes, and a guide to take us to the affected area. He had it all planned, right down to the piece to camera on the slopes, with him skiing backwards. We sent the pictures and a voice track back to London, and then headed out to the restaurant he'd already booked. Fred was a class act.

The final member of the team was a Lebanese driver, fixer and translator, Hussein Osman, who I had met a year earlier in Beirut and who had been driving me around Kuwait in the build-up to war. Quiet but loyal, brave and efficient, he was now running around making sure they had enough fuel for the days ahead.

Everyone was busy preparing for something I felt you could never really adequately prepare for. What lay ahead was utterly unpredictable, uncertain and in the lap of the gods. War, once it starts, is impossible to anticipate with any precision. Things go wrong, plans go awry and intentions go south. It is a truism of war that 'no plan survives contact with the enemy'. And another favourite with British troops is SNAFU ('situation normal, all fucked up').

So, in such circumstances, how can you prepare? It didn't stop us trying. My team, consisting of cameraman Mike Inglis, producer Derl McCrudden, soundman Ted Denton and two satellite engineers, Steve Gore-Smith and Alan Bugby, did all we could to make sure we had everything that we could possibly need in our four vehicles. The most important items for Inglis were a large box of teabags and a kettle. Mike didn't mind going to war so long as he had a brew every morning. For me, it was tinned tuna and crackers. I could survive for weeks on that and bananas. Odd, really. All Steve seemed to worry about was the new satellite dish ITN had bought for the job, the Swe-Dish. Light, mobile and mounted on a 4 x 4, it would, we hoped, enable me to anchor the evening news each night live from inside Iraq. Our plan was ambitious but perfectly doable. In fact, it was to be a huge success.

A day or two later, we moved out from the Sheraton and drove sixty-odd miles to the desert border area and set up camp.

Terry and his team had left earlier and were already filming in the heavily militarized no man's land between Kuwait and Iraq. The build-up to war was complete; the desert had become a giant, dusty military car park full of tanks, armoured vehicles and impatient troops. Hundreds of thousands of them.

On our first night in the desert, ITN wanted us to present the *Evening News* to test the satellite dish was working and all was well. Mike Inglis aimed his lighting rig at a couple of army Land Rovers near a makeshift press information centre (PIC) set up by Colonel Chris Vernon and his team. It worked as a backdrop, and the broadcast went smoothly. The communications were easy and the picture was clear. We were under way.

Afterwards, we decided to pitch our tents at the PIC and get some food – and, more importantly, some sleep. Unfortunately, it soon became clear that we were not welcome. The British reporters 'officially' based at the PIC, including a team from ITN, had apparently made it pretty obvious to the military media people that they didn't want us there. They were unhappy that we were trying to take the benefits afforded by the PIC – food, decent accommodation and protection – while not having to submit ourselves to the other side of the deal, i.e. control and censorship.

And they were right. That is exactly what we were trying to do. Their opposition to it was understandable. I would probably have done the same. It just didn't seem like that at the time.

And so it was, in the morning, we were kicked out and went off to fend for ourselves.

We moved south, back towards the Kuwaiti border, and found a flattened area surrounded by berms of sand on four sides, which provided near-perfect cover. We pitched tents and made it our home, or rather the others pitched their tents. I couldn't be bothered, and slept perfectly happily for two or three nights in the car.

This small area also became our studio in the desert as we counted down to war and broadcast nightly back to the UK. Weeks of diplomacy, against the backdrop of the huge military build-up and big anti-war protests at home, had failed to lead to a peaceful solution. President George W. Bush appeared on television, live from the Oval Office, to announce the start of hostilities, and soon bombs began falling on Baghdad. It was only a matter of time before hundreds of thousands of British and American troops would cross the Iraq–Kuwait border and head north towards the capital.

On the Friday night before the war began, I spoke with Terry on our Kuwaiti mobiles. He had already filed a number of reports from northern Kuwait and he was happy. He told me he was bedding down for the night alongside some American tanks and armoured vehicles. He said his plan was to cross with them and then make his way along the Basra road. Neither he, nor I, thought he would get very far before they would encounter road-blocks. But I wished him well and told him we would be heading for a port near Basra called Umm Qasr. We had been told the British would be airlifting troops into the area to secure the port as soon as possible. It would be an important staging post for supplies. Our decision to head there seemed like a sensible plan.

'Go well, mate,' Terry said. 'See you on the other side.'

On the Saturday morning, at first light, we moved off. By now Terry had already crossed into Iraq. He had awoken to find the Americans had already gone, and he wasted no time in giving chase.

As for ourselves, we had arranged a rendezvous with a friendly British military policeman who was looking after one of the main crossing points into Iraq. He had agreed to smooth our way across. We were on our way in our convoy of four vehicles when my producer Derl, who was in the lead car, signalled for us to stop. We pulled over and he jumped out brandishing his mobile phone. He had received a text message from London. 'Call Newsdesk Urgent', it read.

We didn't think much of it. That is pretty standard stuff from the ITN foreign desk, and more often than not there would be nothing particularly urgent about the message whatsoever. Still, Derl called, and it was answered, unusually, by the deputy editor Jonathan Munro. Munro asked where we were. There was an urgency in his voice. Derl told him we were at the border about to cross into Iraq and we were anxious to get going. 'Don't,' yelled Munro. 'Stop exactly where you are. I am ordering you not to cross that border.'

He told Derl something about an ITN team encountering trouble in Iraq and that they were halting our deployment. It soon became clear it was Terry's team. He, Daniel, Fred and Hussein were all 'missing'.

Later, I called Jonathan back. He confirmed they were unaccounted for and went further. ITN had received reports there had been a gun battle and it was likely they'd been caught up in it.

'Are they alive?' I asked.

'We don't know, we think so. Just don't cross, just wait,' he said, and ended the call.

I felt sick to the pit of my stomach. But, shamefully, not only because of Terry and his team. I felt sick also because I was being prevented from doing something I had thought about every minute of every day for the past few weeks.

Our initial reaction was anger that we were now unable to do our jobs. Mike Inglis was particularly annoyed that they were stopping us doing what we had long planned for. This was the moment. The war had begun. The invasion of Iraq was under way. British troops were about to be in action just a few miles from where we were standing, and we were being told not to go. We were all furious.

We stood at the roadside and watched as the British troops and heavy armour went over the border. It was immensely frustrating. Soldiers gestured to us to follow them in, and we couldn't. More than once, we thought 'to hell with London', but we didn't cross. We stayed where we were and missed the beginning of one of the biggest stories we'd ever cover.

But, slowly and painfully, it began to sink in that perhaps the foreign desk wasn't telling us everything they knew… or at least suspected. We calmed down, and it soon hit us that Terry and his team might well be in serious trouble. No contact with London or us meant bad news. Just how bad would become clear in the coming hours.

Gradually, more information came through. Only snippets, the barest details, but all of them bad. We heard something about them being caught in crossfire, something about vehicles burning, something about no word from Terry. Something about ambulances and Basra. Our anger turned to desperation for more news. By now, nothing else mattered. Not the story, not the programmes, not the war. We just wanted to know our mates were OK. But they weren't.

Another call from London. Munro again. This time it was to tell us a morsel of good news. Daniel Demoustier was alive, had made contact and was walking back towards an Iraqi border crossing. Munro gave me the name of the crossing and asked Mike Inglis and me to go meet him. We looked at the map; it was about ten miles away. We set off.

We got there before Daniel, so we had to wait for him to come across the border. And then I saw him. A dishevelled, dust-covered, hunched-up figure, walking, stumbling towards us. He was alone.

He was held briefly at the border point, frustratingly close to us, and then he came through. We embraced. He looked dazed and shocked. He had the vacant stare of a man who had seen bad things. He had cuts and grazes and his hair was matted with dust and mud and a little blood. In fact, his hair seemed brittle, standing up. Is that possible? I just remember it being like that. Was it shock? It must have been.

Then he started talking and didn't stop. It was muddled and incoherent and endless. We tried to slow him down; Mike Inglis led him to the car and we drove south towards Kuwait City. And all the while, Daniel talked.

He told us he had been driving north towards Basra, he and Terry in one vehicle, Hussein and Fred in the other. He told us how they drove past some American tanks in the fields either side of the road. 'But there was no roadblock, nothing to stop us. The traffic was moving. Everything was OK. We could see a bridge ahead and then Basra.

'And then the shooting started. Heavy shooting. I tried to get into the well of the driver's seat, I just got my head down. It was too much firing,' he said. 'Too much.'

He told us how he thought he saw Terry was hit, but he wasn't sure. He thought he saw him open the front passenger door and fall out of the vehicle. It was all a blur. A terrible blur.

'I just don't know what happened to him or Fred or Hussein. I just don't know. I'm sorry.'

He was crying now, but didn't pause even to catch his breath. It was a long stream of terrible, awful detail. The gunfire, the noise, the smell, the fear, the heart-stopping fear, the blur, the guilt... yes, guilt, that he was out and breathing and talking and safe, and the others – his colleagues, his friends, his buddies – were not. And, and, and...

He trailed off for the first time since he fell into our arms at the border.

Then he started again. Sitting upright on the back seat of the car. He told us how he managed to get out of the vehicle and crawled across the road into a ditch. How he just tried to make himself invisible as the firing continued. He mentioned something about the car exploding, how it was on fire, how he could do nothing to get nearer to the other guys. 'I couldn't see them. Where were they? I couldn't hear them. It was just firing all the time.' He told us how he was pinned down and terrified and frozen to the spot.

Mike and I looked at each other. We both feared the worst for the others. I felt sick. I asked Daniel what he thought happened to Fred and Hussein in the other car. 'I don't know,' he said. 'I just don't know.'

We drove to the military checkpoint where vehicles were being stopped from coming further north. We didn't want to cross in case we weren't allowed back in to the closed border area. We had arranged to meet a member of the ITN team who would drive Daniel back to Kuwait City and to hospital to be checked over.

Before he left us, Daniel showed me the sleeve of his over-sized fleece, the one from the market. There was a bullet hole through it. The fleece was baggy enough that it had missed his arm. One thing was obvious, Daniel was lucky to be alive. What had happened to Terry, Fred and Hussein remained unclear. There was still hope they were alive.

We returned to the desert and our tents. It was a terrible time. Someone produced a bottle of whiskey, illegal in Kuwait but we didn't give it any thought. We drank and we talked about Terry and Fred. There was tracer fire in the distance. The story we should have been covering didn't seem to matter now. Nothing much did.

We were asleep in our tents in northern Kuwait that Saturday night when David Mannion was called into an edit suite at ITN's HQ in London. Some footage had come in from Basra. It was filmed by an Iraqi camera team in a hospital morgue, and showed bodies piled up after an incident on the bridge earlier that day.

David took one look. He knew it was his mate. He knew it was Terry. 'I just recognized him straight away,' he told me much later. 'It's not something you should ever have to see, your best mate dead, but it was him. I knew it.'

David left the edit suite, got straight into his car and, for the second time that day, drove out to the Buckinghamshire home of Terry's wife Lynn to break the devastating news to her. It was an appalling night for Terry's family, for David and for everyone at ITN.

I woke early on the Sunday morning. By now Derl had spoken to the desk in London. It had been confirmed: Terry was dead; Fred and Hussein were missing. The words 'presumed dead' weren't used, but they were implied. We were all devastated. Mike Inglis, one of Terry's best friends, made tea and cried. We all cried. Day one of the war. Day bloody one. And Terry was gone. I could not believe it was happening. We drank our tea in silence. But we were all thinking the same thing. What on earth do we do now?

What we did was go out and film whatever we could; we had a programme to put out. The Sunday evening broadcast was dominated by the death of Terry. We went live from the desert and the presenter, John Suchet, asked me about him. It was the hardest report I have ever done. As I spoke on air I noticed Mike Inglis, behind the camera, welling up. I never thought for a moment that on day two of the war our programme would essentially be one story, and that story would be about the death of one of our own.

But that is war. People die, hundreds of people every day. And you never know any of them. But someone knows them, someone out there does. And they grieve and mourn and cry their hearts out. We just don't see it. Or we seldom do. War is most often about anonymous death.

But on that day, in that war, it wasn't. We did know them. We knew them well. I couldn't have presented the programme that night. I didn't have it in me. Suchet did a brilliant job, sounding composed and calm and in control. Not easy, not in those circumstances. Not easy at all.

Afterwards, Derl phoned the news desk. David Mannion answered. He told Derl that we had done a great job in appalling circumstances and he told him to hang on. He put the phone on the desk, leaving the line open. He then addressed the newsroom, allowing Derl to hear it. He paid tribute to his best mate and then to everyone involved in that day's coverage.

'It was touching and sincere,' Derl told me later. 'He then came back on and spoke to me. And for a man who was grieving, I always felt he was remarkable in being able to give more than he took in those moments.'

The phone call over, it was just the six of us in the desert, sitting on the berm staring at the sky. It was 2 a.m. Over towards the port city of Umm Qasr, just across the border, tracer bullets 'danced in the night sky' as Derl put it. We sat there saying nothing. In the distance, the sight and sounds of the war we should have been covering. I noticed Derl was welling up. Mick Inglis did, too. 'I know, mate. It's hard, isn't it,' said Mick.

It was the worst day of my professional life.

But Terry had said in Kuwait, 'We just have to do our job, it's important.' I'd thought he was right then, and I felt even more that he was right now. We had to do our job.

That was not the immediate view in London. There was paralysis, and understandably so. Nothing like this had happened at ITN. And no manager, however well trained, organized or prepared, can be expected to deal perfectly or even adequately with a situation like this.

David Mannion called to say he still didn't want us to cross the border. He suggested we return to Kuwait City. Or even return home. I understood why he was saying that. But I had no intention of doing it and I am not sure he meant it either. I think he just felt he should say it. What else was he supposed to say? He had just sent his best mate to war and he wasn't coming back.

My heart went out to Mannion. The best, boldest, most instinctive television newsman I had encountered was going through utter hell. It was so cruel.

I called a meeting of the guys on the team and I told them that Dave Mannion was talking about us pulling back. 'Does anyone want to do that?' I asked.

Silence. Mick Inglis looked at the ground and wiped his eyes. Still silence. Nothing from anyone. Derl then said that if anyone wanted to go back then we should all go back. If just one of us wanted out, we should all go out. Steve Gore-Smith murmured agreement. I felt he might possibly want to leave. It was his first taste of war, and it was a particularly bitter one. I thought he would want to go. If he did, it would have been a disaster. He was the technical genius who kept us on air. We needed him.

Ted Denton, the youngest member of the team, in his early twenties and a brave, funny London lad who had wanted to do sound and found himself at war, then piped up.

'Well, I ain't fucking going anywhere,' he said. 'I only just fucking got here.'

Laughter in the desert for the first time in forty-eight hours. 'Let's crack on,' said Inglis. 'If we go back to Kuwait City, what would Terry think? What would he say?'

'That's me and Ted then... What about you lot?'

Everyone said they were in – including, thank God, Steve Gore-Smith. Our war was about to begin. In the worst-possible circumstances, but we were under way.

I phoned Mannion and he asked me to talk to Stewart Purvis, the editor-in-chief, who had also wanted us to hold off. I couldn't get hold of him but I spoke to Jonathan Munro, whom I had come to trust and admire. He was dealing with the whole thing better than most of us. 'You should continue, but there are new rules,' he said. 'You check in every two hours and we discuss every move you make.' We agreed. On reflection, Munro would have made a good editor of ITN, but he was later lost to the BBC.

We eventually managed to attach ourselves to a small team of Royal Engineers heading for Umm Qasr. Finally crossing into Iraq proper was a huge relief, but everything we did, every move we made, was thought through and negotiated with London. In truth, it became a cumbersome way to operate. It wouldn't survive contact with real stories, and it didn't. Gradually things loosened up. But the backdrop to everything was Terry's death.

The Royal Engineers were just what we needed. A group of soldiers who were not attracting much press attention and who liked having us around. We followed them into the port, where we were met with a giant portrait of Saddam Hussein, defaced and damaged, and a checkpoint manned, mercifully, by British troops. In the port itself, very little shipping, but one important vessel had arrived, the Royal Navy supply ship *Sir Galahad*.

It had just docked, having been delayed by storms and the discovery of mines strewn across the port waters. On board were about 650 tonnes of food, medicine and fresh water. It was much-needed humanitarian aid for local Iraqis displaced by the fighting, and the Ministry of Defence believed it sent out an important message about British intentions in the war. It was also a perfect, and safe, location for that night's *Evening News*. I was able to say for the first time, 'Good evening from inside Iraq...' It was long overdue.

And then we had a stroke of luck that was to make our lives much easier than we could ever have imagined. We came across a base set up by Royal Marines who were staging patrols of the port area and seemed welcoming and chatty. I was able to meet the commanding officer of 42 Commando, Colonel Buster Howes, who was around my age, immensely likeable and a gem of a guy, clearly on the way up. He immediately invited us to stay the night at the base. In fact, he insisted. But there was a hitch. He had an embedded news team who he had to give priority to and who may not welcome our presence.

'Who is it?' I asked. 'It's Bill Neely and Dave Harman from ITN,' he said. 'Surely you know them?'

Obviously we did. Bill is a good mate and a class act, and he was generous in the extreme about letting us hang around. I immediately agreed that he would take absolute priority on all breaking stories; my only concern was to present the *Evening News* from our dish each evening. Bill quickly saw the advantage of having an ITN satellite dish at the same base as him. It broke all the rules of pool coverage, but he didn't care, I didn't care and Buster Howes couldn't give a damn. We opened up our direct phone line to the UK, invited the marines to make calls home and became the most popular news team in Iraq. I am sure it also broke every rule in the military book but it was great for morale, and our relationship with Buster was based on a trust that I hope we did not breach.

Buster was a guest on our programme, and the profile of 42 Commando was higher than it would otherwise have been. Everyone was happy. It was a deal, done on the ground, that benefited all sides and offended no one. It worked.

One night, we anchored the programme from a roundabout in front of the base gates. In the middle of the roundabout was another giant mosaic portrait of Saddam Hussein. Buster provided security for the show. His marines formed a protective shield around us, and the machine gunner in the nest above the base entrance overlooked the entire presentation area, which had been floodlit by Mike Inglis. We were pretty conspicuous, but well protected. Just before we went on air, there was a huge bang in the middle distance. Derl buckled as if to take cover, Ted flinched and Inglis said, 'Fuck, what was that?' The marines didn't so much as twitch. We were in safe hands. We never found out what caused the explosion.

These were difficult days, though. On one occasion, we went filming near a local market and saw a water tanker where residents were filling containers. The war was causing hardship and hatred. A couple of Iraqi men turned on Mike while he was filming and he had to fend them off. It was an ugly moment that threatened to get out of control and was an early sign of what was to become the story of Iraq. Local resentment was to turn into a low-level insurgency that would eventually make the occupation of Basra a nightmare for British forces, and would cost lives and reputations. We jumped in the car and made a rapid exit.

One evening, Buster called me into his office. He wanted to brief me about the imminent assault on Basra. We pored over his maps. He was generous with details and I was grateful that he trusted me. It was for my information so we could work out our movements, and was not for reporting. It was immensely considerate and showed a confidence and an awareness that struck me as exceptional. Buster would, in fact, go on to become Commandant General Royal Marines and later the defence attaché in Washington DC. I was not remotely surprised.

But for now he was a colonel in Iraq and he was doing me a huge favour. We were heading into Basra.

My thoughts that night turned to Terry. This was to have been his moment. Had things turned out differently he would now be at the gates of the city or even already inside it. I am sure he would have had one of the first reports from inside Basra. It was all so desperately unfair.

The night before the move into the city, Buster put us in touch with some military media guys who agreed to escort us in. There was little protection. They were in soft-skinned Land Rovers and were lightly armed. But they seemed to know what they were doing and where they were going, and that was good enough for us.

In the event, it was not the easiest of journeys. We found ourselves negotiating a heavily mined road, gingerly making our way around unexploded mines that had only been partially buried. The army officers thought it had been done in a hurry by withdrawing Iraqi forces.

Our guides decided to leave the tarmac road and drive across some muddy, boggy ground towards an industrial estate. I was not at all sure it was a good idea. It was getting dark, it was eerily quiet and I didn't like it at all. Even Mike Inglis was uneasy. We ended up spending the night with a unit of Special Boat Service guys who wouldn't tell us anything and didn't want us around. In the middle of the night they were packing up and leaving. They were to be some of the first British troops into Basra. We had no idea.

When we eventually reached the outskirts of the city there was gunfire echoing through the streets. We saw British snipers firing into a nearby building. It was apparently a mopping-up operation involving troops attached to the Desert Rats.

But we were being told Basra was largely under control. We were taken to Saddam's palace, which had become a British headquarters. That night it was: 'Good evening from newly liberated Basra ...' It felt good. Basra and Baghdad were effectively taken, the war was progressing well from the coalition point of view. And it was a successful programme, including reports from across Iraq, from Washington DC and, of course, from London.

During the broadcast I noticed Buster Howes walk behind the camera while we were on air. He smiled. 'Welcome to our new abode,' he said.

We were there for several days and it was a lively time. On several occasions, shells would land close to or inside the palace grounds. There was still resistance out there. One day, we ventured out into Basra itself; it was chaos. Shops and hotels were being looted. We saw televisions, lamps and furniture being carried out, or simply lobbed from upper-floor windows of the Sheraton. Part of the building was on fire. At one point, our vehicle was surrounded by an angry crowd of locals banging on the roof and windows. Things were becoming tense and threatening, but there was little hint of the violence that would engulf the city over the coming months and years. The war was a success; the post-invasion years were a disaster for which George W. Bush and Tony Blair would pay a heavy political price, and hundreds of their troops would sadly pay a much higher one.

While we were in Basra we were joined briefly by two former SAS security guys sent out to Iraq by ITN. They were not only out there to help protect us. They were there mainly to find out whatever they could about what had happened to Terry Lloyd and his team. They wanted to find Fred Nérac and Hussein Osman, hopefully alive, but if not then at least their bodies. Their families were suffering the most awful ordeal. An ITN producer, Nick Walsh, had also been assigned to try to find out more about exactly what had occurred on the road to Basra. There were too many questions and not enough answers.

After another few days we had to make the decision about whether to head to Baghdad, which had by now fallen to American forces. The foreign desk was keen for us to get there to present another couple of programmes from the capital. The security guys were initially optimistic about getting us up there by road. But one night a couple of Western journalists were ambushed and badly beaten while making the drive. Others were missing, feared kidnapped. The atmosphere was changing rapidly. The advice given to us was not to go unless we could persuade the military to fly us up. That proved impossible to organize. It would be drive or nothing. I called a meeting of the team at the palace. No one fancied it.

I was quite relieved. Our war was over. We were going home.

But if our assignment was over, the battle to find out the truth about Terry was only just beginning. Slowly, painstakingly, Nick Walsh was putting together a picture of the events that unfolded on the road to Basra.

He managed to obtain some photographs of the scene just after the shooting. They came from an American photographer who was embedded with the American troops nearby. It turned out he had been with the US battalion involved in the firefight. He said he'd been stopped by US Marines from going nearer to the scene of the attacks.

Nick also managed to talk to a spokesman for the battalion, who was by now in Baghdad. Through him, he reached the captain whose tank crews had, it turned out, opened fire on Terry and his team. This is what Nick wrote about the encounter:

He said that the tanks had seen a white pickup truck with a machine gun mounted on it coming from the direction of Basra. It was flanked by two cars marked as TV vehicles, speeding towards them. The white pickup was filled with Iraqis. Through telescopic sights, one of the soldiers had seen an Iraqi put on a gas mask and load the mounted AK-47 machine gun. He claimed the Iraqis fired first. His men thought the Iraqis were suicide bombers and had stolen the ITN vehicles. They thought they were being attacked.

It was the first real account of how it happened. Eventually more detail emerged, and the story gradually came together. It appears that the ITN team were driving towards Basra until they saw the Iraqis approach. They turned the vehicles around but were chased by the Iraqi truck. This was the scene witnessed by the Americans. Several vehicles coming at high speed towards them. And this was when the firing started.

But there was more. Nick also managed to meet the driver of a makeshift minibus ambulance who claims to have picked up two wounded Iraqis and Terry Lloyd. Crucially, he said Terry was wounded by Iraqi fire but was still alive when he placed him in his ambulance. 'But then as we drove away,' he told Nick, 'we came under fire again.' Ballistics experts have since confirmed Terry was shot in the head by an American bullet. All the evidence suggests it was fired while the vehicle Terry was in was driving away from the Americans.

In October 2006, a coroner ruled that Terry was unlawfully killed by American forces. Coroner Andrew Walker said he would be writing to the Director of Public Prosecutions 'to seek to bring the perpetrators to justice'.

'Terry Lloyd died following a gunshot wound to the head,' he said. 'The evidence this bullet was fired by the Americans is overwhelming... There is no doubt that the minibus presented no threat to the American forces. There is no doubt it was an unlawful act of fire upon the minibus.'

After the inquest, Chelsey Lloyd, Terry's daughter, said that the value of the inquest had been demonstrated and that the culprits should now face a court of law. She was determined to pursue the case, and so too was ITN. But there was no court hearing and there was no justice.

The final word, legally at least, came in July 2008. The head of the Crown Prosecution Service (CPS) counterterrorism division, Sue Hemming, said it was not possible to say who fired the shots that killed Terry. She agreed that forensic evidence indicated he had been injured by shots from Iraqi forces and then he was hit by US fire. But there would be no prosecution.

'Having considered all the evidence gathered by UK authorities and the evidence from the US, together with advice from counsel, we have decided there is insufficient evidence for a prosecution,' Hemming said. 'I understand that this will be very upsetting news for the family and friends of Mr Lloyd but I can reassure them that every care was taken in pursuing lines of inquiry and reviewing the evidence.'

I remember reading those words at the time. They seemed to me weasel words. It had all the hallmarks of a CPS inquiry that went through the motions and little more. I do not imagine for a moment there was any real pressure put on the Americans to identify the perpetrator.

I am convinced the US Department of Defense had little time for the whole issue. And I am equally convinced the Ministry of Defence in London had no wish to 'go to war' with their allies and pursue the case with determination and vigour.

But the fact remains, and I'll say this again, that all the evidence points to Terry having been shot in a makeshift minibus ambulance travelling away from the American troops who opened fire. I hear what people say about the 'fog of war', I understand the argument that Terry and his crew had put themselves in a very dangerous situation. They had chosen to be there. But it is, on the face of it, a war crime. And, at the very least, the coroner's ruling that he was killed unlawfully should have been put to the test in a court of law.

There was no justice for Terry or his family. Like many others who knew Terry well, it angered me at the time. Then it became an overwhelming sadness that, despite Andrew Walker's conclusion, there was to be no closure. No satisfactory ending. No justice.

David Mannion was worn down by it all, and it had a lasting and very noticeable impact on him. But he was philosophical, under the circumstances. 'The fact is, Mark, there isn't much more we can do,' he told me. 'The Americans know that one of their men fired the bullet that killed Terry. But they will never say who it was. They probably haven't even bothered to find out. And they will certainly never allow him to speak for himself in a court of law. That's it. That's where we're at after five years of fighting. I think we're done.'

He was exhausted and defeated. I am not sure that the exuberant, warm, emotional, inspirational, driven man I respected and admired has ever been quite the same since. Terry's death took a terrible toll on his family, but it also wounded his boss and his mate grievously. It is so terribly sad.

Ten years after Terry's death, I returned to Iraq with his daughter Chelsey and Daniel Demoustier, to make a documentary about the events of that terrible day. Chelsey was visiting Iraq and the scene of her father's death for the first time. It was harrowing and emotional but ultimately rewarding, she said. She said she felt 'strangely at peace'.

We also managed to track down the commander of the platoon involved in the firefight. Vince Hogan, who had since left the US Marines, agreed to meet Chelsey in a coffee shop in Virginia. They talked for half an hour about his memories of the day. Hogan said he wouldn't do anything differently had the same scenario unfolded today. 'We felt under threat,' he said. 'You have to make split-second decisions and you have ultimately to protect your men.'

In an interview with me, he said he was horrified when he heard that journalists had been killed.[*] He was sympathetic, kind and helpful to Chelsey.

As we left that coffee shop, she told me on camera that she no longer had feelings of vengeance or a desire to see men prosecuted for her father's death.

I am not sure I could be so generous.

---

[*] Fred's and Hussein's bodies have never been found. It is a truly hideous situation for their families. My heart goes out to them.

GETTING AWAY WITH IT... NO
INTERVENTION AND NO JUSTICE

RAQ BECAME THE costly mess that still haunts Tony Blair to this day. The result: countless deaths of Iraqis and Western troops, the rise of ISIS and the ongoing trauma in that country. His disastrous decision to join the US in going to war, in some ways, has its roots in the Rwandan genocide.

Rwanda is a scar on the conscience of the world. But could it have been prevented? Of course it could. All that was needed was a recognition of the moral imperative, a rapidly deployed force of a few thousand properly equipped fighting troops, and a willingness on the part of the UN to follow up with a meaningful plan for temporary occupation and stabilization. Scandalously, none of the above occurred. Nearly a quarter of a century on, it seems incredible that a genocide could have taken place without the international community doing something to stop it. But that is what happened.

As the violence began, there was a UN force in Rwanda with a mandate to assist in the implementation of the Arusha Peace Accords which were reached in the summer of 1993. But when ten Belgian troops were killed, that country's government pulled out the rest of its force and quickly the United Nations

Assistance Mission for Rwanda (UNAMIR) was further reduced from 2,100 to just 270. The slaughter progressed unimpeded by any outside forces.

Just as my attention, and that of almost every other Western journalist in Africa, was firmly on Johannesburg and the election of Nelson Mandela, the United Nations was preoccupied with the war in Bosnia and attempts to get peace talks going there. Rwanda paid the price.

It wouldn't have taken much to halt the genocide. With 2,100 UN troops already in Rwanda, it would only have required a few thousand more to have given Roméo Dallaire, the Canadian commander of UNAMIR, a real chance to prevent the bloodshed, or at least the scale of it.

General Dallaire insisted to his bosses at the UN in New York on many occasions that there was genuine evidence that 'genocide' was being planned by Hutu extremists. On 11 January 1994, three months before the violence began, Dallaire sent an urgent fax to New York, addressed to Major General Maurice Baril, the UN secretary-general's military adviser. It quoted a reliable informant – a former security aide to President Habyarimana who became known as 'Jean-Pierre' and who had been responsible at one time for training the Interahamwe militia. He was considered by Dallaire to be a thoroughly credible source. Dallaire said in the fax that there was a plan for the 'extermination' of the Tutsis and that huge supplies of weapons had been brought into Rwanda and stockpiled for the purpose.

Dallaire sought permission to do two things. He wanted to raid the arms caches around Kigali and elsewhere. 'It is our intention to take action within the next 36 hours,' wrote

Dallaire. 'Recce [reconnaissance] of armed caches and detailed planning of raid to go on late tomorrow.'

The other issue he brought up was a request from Jean-Pierre that he and his family be protected by the UN and evacuated out of Rwanda. The reply was astonishing. Dallaire was not only denied permission to mount the raid, but he was told to tip off the government of President Habayrimana – the very president whose inner circle was behind the genocide plot. The UN also refused permission to evacuate Jean-Pierre from Rwanda. Needless to say, the raids never happened and the informant broke off contact, fearing for his and his family's lives.

Years later, Dallaire was quoted as saying: 'If I had had one reinforced brigade – 5,000 men – well trained and well equipped, I could have saved thousands of lives.'

I have spoken to at least three senior military men in the UK who agree with him and who believe the job could have been done with an even smaller force. One told me: 'The problem is not manpower, or weaponry or money, the UN had all that was necessary at its disposal. The problem was political will. And when that is lacking, you're dead.'

It is a story of terrible blunders by an organization that failed the people of Rwanda.

I've heard some argue that the United Nations could not have sent in a fighting force with an aggressive mandate because it would have been accused of committing aggression rather than promoting stability. That is nonsense. The evidence of an imminent, well-planned genocide was mounting, and in those circumstances any criticism of an intervention would surely have been muted and minimal.

I have also heard the argument that it would have been illegal to send in troops because the government of Rwanda would certainly not have consented to such action.

Well, that too is irrelevant. The UN could have invoked Chapter VII, which permits it to use force against the will of a party, even a member state. This has been done several times since the end of the Cold War and is feasible, but only if international support exists. The only military move by Western states was to send aircraft – not to get troops in, but to get their civilian nationals out.

There is absolutely no doubt that, with the political will, there was a way. But there was precious little will. In fact, there was none.

The two main international actors in this real-life tragedy were France and the United States – both, of course, permanent members of the Security Council. The French were never interested. They had long-standing links to the genocidal Hutu regime and had ignored many government atrocities before.

And the United States was also hell-bent on staying well clear of Rwanda. Indeed, it went further, and blocked the authorization of reinforcements for UNAMIR. Why? Well it just so happened that Bill Clinton, president at the time, had learned a harsh lesson about intervening in African civil wars just a few months earlier.

In October 1993, six months before the genocide, eighteen US Special Forces men were killed on a single night after a disastrous raid on the Somali capital Mogadishu. Two US Black Hawk helicopters were shot down, the bodies of US soldiers were dragged through the streets and the images were broadcast around the world.

Among the consequences of the failed assault were a 2001 Hollywood film called *Black Hawk Down*, and more immediately and far more seriously, a complete re-evaluation of America's relationship with Africa – in particular, a new wariness when it came to interventions in humanitarian crises on that continent.

To make matters worse, the doctrine of only using 'overwhelming force' was the predominant thinking in Washington at the time. The task of moving a huge US contingent to a remote, land-locked African country that they didn't particularly care about and where their national interest was certainly not threatened, was something they simply were not up for taking on.

Of course, they could have mounted an airlift of UN or even US forces into Rwanda. They didn't want to do it. They even refused to allow American technology to be used to jam the Hutu extremists' radio broadcasts that were the key to spreading the messages of hatred and prolonging the killing.

Bill Clinton and the then US representative at the UN, Madeleine Albright, have since recognized their mistake and apologized for their part in withdrawing UN forces from Rwanda as the genocide started. Kofi Annan, then under-secretary-general for peacekeeping, who was responsible for the communication with the UN force commander in Kigali, has also expressed regret that he personally didn't do more.

It was an appalling, collective failure of international politics and diplomacy. But the media must share the blame, too. As I've already said, journalists, including myself, totally failed to appreciate what was happening in Rwanda until it was too late. We all thought, or most of us did, that it was a typical central African story of tribal bloodletting. It wasn't. It was genocide. The outside world got it wrong.

And a few years later, I personally witnessed a good example of just how simple an effective intervention in Rwanda could have been.

In May 2000, a fresh bout of savagery was threatening to engulf yet another African country. This time it was the former British colony of Sierra Leone, where a civil war had been raging for ten years or so, but this time the outcome was very different. And that was largely due to the foresight and actions of a young, little-known, British military commander, David (now Sir David) Richards.

It was, I'm afraid, a typically African scenario. A rebel militia, in this case the Revolutionary United Front (RUF), was terrorizing vast areas of Sierra Leone and were on the verge of taking the capital, Freetown. When we arrived in the country, an assault on Freetown was expected at any moment. Many people were fleeing, fearing the butchery of the drug- and drink-fuelled rebels, whose signature atrocity was to hack off the limbs of their enemies and any civilians who stood in their way, including women and children.

Just for good measure, the RUF fighters were also holding scores of Zambian UN peacekeepers prisoner. The Foreign Office in London and the US Department of State were advising their nationals to leave Sierra Leone as quickly as possible. The British government went further and ordered a task force of naval ships and helicopters to evacuate hundreds of stranded Britons and other nationalities before the capital fell.

So it was that, under cover of darkness, I watched RAF Chinook helicopters descend from the night sky to pick up several groups of very relieved expats from the grounds of the Mammy Yoko Hotel, where they had been advised to gather for their safety.

They were flown to Lungi Airport on the coast, which had been secured by a couple of hundred British paratroopers, and then transported by RAF Hercules aircraft to the safety of Dakar in Senegal. It was a smooth operation that lasted through the night and into the next day.

The evacuation complete, that was supposed to be it. The British forces were meant to withdraw from Sierra Leone and leave the people of Freetown to their fate at the hands of the much-feared Revolutionary United Front. That was the plan... until David Richards decided otherwise.

I was preparing to talk to Brigadier Richards about the evacuation when he postponed the interview and disappeared for several hours. I was mystified by his behaviour, but the BBC correspondent on the ground, Allan Little, had heard a suggestion that Richards was planning a more extensive operation than a simple evacuation.

'I think he's up to something,' said Little, without giving away what that 'something' was. Little was one of a handful of BBC correspondents I hugely admired. He was competitive, but not unpleasantly so, a thoughtful and quite brilliant writer, and unusually trustworthy and communicative for a rival reporter.

It turned out that Richards had nipped off to see the country's president, Ahmad Tejan Kabbah, who was in hiding somewhere and preparing to scarper in his helicopter, parked readily on the lawn of his safe house.

Richards had gone to inform him that the British force of eight hundred heavily armed paratroopers would not be leaving after all. Instead, they would be overseeing the battle against the approaching rebel army. The Brits would stay there, supply arms and ammunition to government forces, train them as best they could in the time available, and Brigadier Richards would take personal command of the war. In other words, this ambitious young British army officer had just decided to take sides in an African civil conflict, without any serious consultation with a senior politician in the UK.

It was a quite extraordinary intervention, and one that changed the course of the war and reshaped the future of the country.

When Richards returned to see us at the hotel in Freetown, he had made his mind up. He told Little and me what he was planning, we both looked at each other in some surprise and then realized the story was about to get an awful lot more interesting. Richards told me he had taken the decision because he was convinced he had everything he needed to win the war very quickly. The rebel army was basically a brutal but disorganized rabble who were only equipped with AK-47s and machetes. He believed, rightly, that the fear they instilled in the wider population was not born of any great military prowess, but rather of an inhuman savagery that Richards felt could not be left unchecked. However, he also recognized it was a risk. 'If this goes wrong I'm done for,' he said. 'But I promise you, it won't.'

I believe the mere fact the decision was made and publicized probably delayed the expected assault by the RUF. It bought much-needed time.

There remained the small problem of getting permission from London for the rapidly conceived escapade. But timing is everything, and in Tony Blair he had a prime minister emboldened by Britain's role in the NATO intervention in Kosovo a year or so earlier, and who was prepared to see Sierra Leone as another early test of a fresh approach to foreign adventures. It fitted Blair's new attitude of 'liberal interventionism'.

This was a bold doctrine outlined in a speech the previous year in Chicago. In it, Blair proposed a set of guidelines for military action that stressed Western morality and humanitarian values. He identified five major conditions that should be satisfied when considering intervention and confronting dictatorships:

- Be sure of the case; sure it will do more good than harm.
- Exhaust all diplomatic options.
- Be sure that the military options can be prudently, effectively and sensibly undertaken.
- Be sure it will endure for the long term.
- It should serve national interest.

He also said, 'Non-interference has long been considered an important principle of international order... But the principle of non-interference must be qualified in important respects... Now our actions are guided by a more subtle blend of mutual self-interest and moral purpose in defending the values we cherish.'

So, Sierra Leone seemed a pretty good fit; most, if not all the conditions were met, particularly if you agree that a peaceful former colony served the national interest better than a war-ravaged one.

Richards certainly persuaded Blair of the case for action. And most importantly of course, it worked. Within a few weeks the country was tugged away from the brink of mayhem. The rebels were forced back, the captured UN troops were rescued, some basic functions of government were restored and eventually the peace held. David Richards's force gave way to thousands of UN blue helmets; British advisers began training the police force and a new Sierra Leonean army; and eventually the enemy was largely subdued.

Within a couple of years, elections were taking place, the RUF leader, Foday Sankoh, was on trial for multiple murders and 65,000 rebels had surrendered their arms.

Every time I think about Sierra Leone, and every time I have talked to Sir David Richards since, I can't help thinking of Rwanda.

I'm convinced that a similar intervention there would have unquestionably saved hundreds of thousands of lives. Like Sierra Leone, the aggressors were largely ill-equipped, untrained peasants. A rapid intervention by a professional force would surely have contained the violence, or if the deployment was early enough, pre-empted it. And if a large UN force had followed, deployed right across Rwanda, stability would have returned. It would have been hugely difficult, but some sort of political agreement may have been possible. Genocide in Rwanda was not inevitable. Something could and should have been done.

But the truth is the world's approach to intervention shifts with circumstances and time. As I said earlier in this chapter, America's bad experience in Somalia governed its approach to Rwanda. The US basically decided it was pointless sending troops to what they considered third-world hellholes when there was no real national interest at stake. And in Rwanda, there was no national interest.

It was, in part, the shame of the West over Rwanda that led to Blair's more open-minded approach – discussed at some length, I should add, with Bill Clinton.

So, Blair was right before he was wrong; because just as his Chicago doctrine was used to justify the successful interventions in Kosovo and Sierra Leone, so it also underpinned Blair's rationalization of the Iraq War. Blair certainly thought there was a case for war and he certainly thought it would do more good than harm.

To understand his thinking, you have to remember the context. And for that you have to listen to what he said to the Chilcot Inquiry into the Iraq War in 2010. The crucial thing, he argued, was that the 9/11 attacks changed everything:

If September 11 hadn't happened, our assessment of the risk of allowing Saddam any possibility of him reconstituting his [weapons of mass destruction] programmes would not have been the same... The point about [9/11] was that over 3,000 people had been killed on the streets of New York, an absolutely horrific event, but this is what really changed my perception of risk, the calculus of risk for me: if those people, inspired by this religious fanaticism, could have killed 30,000, they would have done.

It led Tony Blair to make three assumptions: that Iraq was, at least, capable of making weapons of mass destruction; that it was deceiving the UN inspectors; and that any WMD produced by Saddam Hussein could be acquired by terrorist organizations who could use them to mount devastating attacks.

Hindsight, of course, is crucial in all this, and when I interviewed Mr Blair after the Chilcot Report was published, he repeatedly made two points: he did not have the benefit of hindsight, and if presented with the same set of circumstances again, he would make the same decision.

And to the Chilcot Inquiry, he said this:

It is a decision, and the decision I had to take was, given Saddam's history, given his use of chemical weapons, given the over one million people whose deaths he had caused, given the years of breaking UN resolutions, could we take the risk of this man reconstituting his weapons programmes, or is that a risk that it would be irresponsible to take? The reason why it is so important... is because, today, we are going to be faced with exactly the same types of decisions.

And he was right. We have been faced with those types of decisions since – most seriously and recently, the question of whether to intervene in Syria; and to a lesser degree, whether to pre-emptively assassinate terrorists and their leaders who are believed to be planning atrocities.

Following the disaster that Iraq became, 'intervention' was a dirty word once again. Politicians and strategists are thinking twice about committing troops and resources, and as a consequence, vulnerable and oppressed people living under ghastly regimes across the world are paying the price right now.

But look at Blair's own five conditions for intervention and ask yourself whether they applied to Iraq. Was he sure of the case? Well, he convinced himself of the case on the basis of what we now know to be false intelligence. Had all diplomatic options been exhausted? No, and the Chilcot Report is scathing about that. Could military options be sensibly undertaken? Yes, that was the easy bit in Iraq (or at least the initial invasion was). Were they able to endure for the long term? Absolutely not, it turned very quickly into the murderous quagmire many people had predicted. And did it serve the national interest? Arguable at the time, but with hindsight, clearly not.

If Iraq was a disaster, how do we describe the ongoing catastrophe that is Afghanistan? Here is an intervention that was mounted with worthy aims and widespread support, but again lost its way very quickly and has never recovered.

In the beginning, it all seemed clear enough. After 9/11, George W. Bush, with the support of Tony Blair, launched Operation Enduring Freedom on the grounds that the Taliban leaders, who were then in control in Kabul, were refusing to hand over Osama bin Laden and his al-Qaeda cohorts. Few could argue with the reasoning, and in the wake of the appalling attack on innocent civilians in New York, it won support around the world. The stated goal was to track down bin Laden, eliminate the terror group in Afghanistan and attack the military capability of the Taliban. This is part of Bush's address to the nation on the night the airstrikes began:

> More than two weeks ago, I gave Taliban leaders a series of clear and specific demands: Close terrorist training camps. Hand over leaders of the Al Qaeda network. And return all foreign nationals, including American citizens, unjustly detained in their country. None of these demands was met. And now, the Taliban will pay a price. By destroying camps and disrupting communications, we will make it more difficult for the terror network to train new recruits and coordinate their evil plans. Initially the terrorists may burrow deeper into caves and other entrenched hiding places. Our military action is also designed to clear the way for sustained, comprehensive and relentless operations to drive them out and bring them to justice.

'The United States of America is a friend to the Afghan people,' he also said.

Well, I am not at all sure what the Afghan people would think about that now, nearly two decades since the war began. Because this has turned into a brutal, costly, troublesome intervention that shows no sign of ending. It is consuming civilian lives, perpetuating a corrupt, incompetent central government in Kabul, and has done nothing to bolster security for either America or, crucially, the people of Afghanistan.

Certainly, on several trips to that country since 2001, I have yet to meet many Afghans who feel the United States is their friend. On the contrary, many tell me that life under the Taliban was infinitely preferable to the life they now lead in a war-wracked country. The truth is that the intervention in Afghanistan meant different things to different people and took on a life of its own. In London and Washington, the whole mission went through a number of rationalizations. It turned from a well-conceived military operation to disrupt al-Qaeda and its terror network, weaken the Taliban and alleviate suffering, into a much broader and less well-defined intervention designed to bring widespread security, build a new society and democratic infrastructure, aid reconstruction and facilitate the emergence of some sort of functioning state. In short, it was nation-building, and the truth is it hasn't worked.

I remember one trip with British forces in Helmand in 2007, where I was specifically told by the Ministry of Defence that I would need to cover not only the military progress being made, but also the 'extensive work being done on reconstruction and development in the area'

When we arrived at the British base at Lashkar Gah, it was soon pretty obvious that this would not be quite so simple. They wanted to take us to a water project in a local village, but unfortunately 'the security situation does not permit that at the moment'. So, in effect, the British troops were too busy fighting the war to help ferry the media and officials from the UK-led Helmand Provincial Reconstruction Team around various projects. It was one small example of a much wider problem. Nation-building under fire doesn't work, and that has been the main issue in Afghanistan. Never has there been a secure-enough environment for state-building to take place in any meaningful way. The war has never ended.

And it's not through lack of trying. The United States has spent almost one trillion dollars on the war itself; and another $117 billion on relief and reconstruction. It has been the most expensive attempt to rebuild a single country in the history of the United States. They've spent more, in the present-day dollar equivalent, on Afghanistan than the Marshall Plan delivered to the whole of Europe after the Second World War.

And what has America got for its money? Well, 2,400 US servicemen and women have been killed, thousands more wounded and hundreds of US military contractors have also died. And war-related violence has also claimed the lives of over 30,000 Afghan civilians. Has the sacrifice been worth it? Not if you look at the official reports compiled by a key American figure in all this, the Special Inspector General for Afghan Reconstruction, John F. Sopko. In his most recent reports sent back to Washington DC, Mr Sopko is brutally honest and unsparing in his criticism of the American involvement in Afghanistan. His words are worth repeating here.

On the question of helping prepare the Afghan forces for the fight against the Taliban, he said this: 'The United States failed to understand the complexities and scale of the mission required to stand up and mentor security forces in a country suffering from thirty years of war, misrule, corruption, and deep poverty. We still need to address the problems of defining mission requirements, and of executing these missions adequately.'

These are astonishing conclusions seventeen years into a mission.

And on development and reconstruction he had this to say:

> The United States currently lacks a comprehensive strategy to guide its reconstruction efforts in Afghanistan. It also lacks overarching plans with clearly defined metrics to guide its work in a number of key areas such as anti-corruption, counternarcotics, health, education, gender, rule of law and water. The lack of planning and related strategies means the US military and civilian agencies are at risk of working at cross purposes, spending money on nonessential endeavors, or failing to coordinate efforts in Afghanistan.

Again, this is a breathtaking critique. And there are two other points to make about the state of Afghanistan right now. According to the World Bank, despite the intervention and the expenditure, levels of poverty, unemployment, violence, crime and corruption are all on the increase.

And in the war itself, the Americans and the Afghan security forces they train and support are bogged down. The central government in Kabul controls only about 57 per cent of the country's districts, which is around 64 per cent of the population. The rest is under Taliban control.

It is why Donald Trump is ordering a new push to defeat the Taliban once and for all. But there's no new strategy. Trump spent the 2016 election campaign denouncing policy on Afghanistan as a 'total disaster', and railing that the costly conflict drained America of enormous resources at a time of more pressing needs at home for American taxpayers.

And yet, as I write, the Pentagon is outlining a Trump-endorsed plan to commit yet more troops and resources to the war. It reflects a growing concern among US military leaders that battlefield setbacks for Afghan forces against the Taliban are leading to a still-deteriorating security situation inside the country.

Interestingly, the president pledged to end the strategy of nation-building to concentrate on winning the war. 'I share the American people's frustration,' he said, 'over a foreign policy that has spent too much time, energy, money, and most importantly lives, trying to rebuild countries in our own image, instead of pursuing our security interests above all other considerations.'

So there you have it. The era of state-building in Afghanistan is suddenly over. They tried it and they failed. And what a mess it is.

The failures of intervention were worse than even the most cynical observer could believe. In his extraordinary book about American involvement in Afghanistan, *No Good Men Among the Living*, the journalist Anand Gopal investigates a counter-terrorist operation in January 2002.

Gopal recounts how American intelligence had identified two locations which were believed to be 'al-Qaeda compounds' housing senior operatives of the terrorist network. US Special Forces were sent in at night by helicopter. During the raid the commander, Master Sergeant Anthony Pryor, was set upon by an unknown assailant. He reacted by killing the attacker with his pistol; he and his Special Forces comrades then shot dead several others, seized prisoners and departed like swashbuckling Hollywood heroes.

But, as Gopal explains, there was a problem. The intelligence was wrong. Pryor's unit had not attacked al-Qaeda, or even the Taliban. They had in fact attacked the offices and accommodation of two senior district governors, both of whom were actually opponents of the Taliban and who were helping the Americans at the time.

The American team had shot dead guards, handcuffed one of the governors to his bed and executed him, sent in AC-130 gunship helicopters to blow up most of what remained, and left a calling card behind in the wreckage saying 'Have nice day. From Damage, Inc.'

And it gets worse. Many of the prisoners they took were tortured before the mistake was recognized and they were released with apologies. It turned out a so-called Afghan informer had falsely informed the US that his political rivals were from al-Qaeda in order to have them killed.

Gopal writes:

The toll... twenty-one pro-American leaders and their employees dead, twenty-six taken prisoner... Not one member of the Taliban or Al-Qaeda was among the victims. Instead, in a single thirty-minute stretch the United States had managed to eradicate... the core of any anti-Taliban leadership – stalwarts who had outlasted the Russian invasion, the civil war, and the Taliban years but would not survive their own allies.

The US, a friend of the Afghan people? Somehow, I don't think so.

I was supportive of the decision to go into Afghanistan in the wake of the attack on the Twin Towers. I can remember sitting on a hillside in northern Afghanistan watching American aircraft drop huge bombs on Taliban positions to the north of Kabul and thinking that this was a just war and a worthwhile war if it meant ridding that country of the terrorists who had planned 9/11.

But as the months and years passed, it was increasingly obvious that British and American troops were getting ever deeper into a war they simply could not win.

In many ways, the British had the worst of it. From 2006 they were given Helmand Province, the centre of the Taliban insurgency and consequently the area of some of the worst attacks and most intense fighting anywhere in Afghanistan. Furthermore, the British were supposed to control Helmand and defeat the Taliban with only a few thousand troops and inadequate resources.

In the summer of 2009, I headed to Helmand Province to cover the beginning of a long-planned operation to secure canal and river crossings and establish a British presence in one of the main Taliban strongholds. It was called Operation Panther's Claw, and involved the Welsh Guards and the Black Watch and was overseen by Brigadier Tim Radford. We flew into Camp Bastion, the main base in Helmand, and a day later we were in a Chinook helicopter for the short hop to the smaller British camp at Lashkar Gah.

I felt guilty as I settled in the canvas seat and buckled up. Scores of British troops were being killed and injured because of the lack of helicopters in Helmand. Most had to travel by road, and that involved a huge risk of improvised explosive devices (IEDs). They were the Taliban's most effective weapon and were taking a disproportionate toll on British lives. The trip by road was deemed too dangerous for us, but OK for the troops. I found that hard to accept. We didn't have to be there, we were choosing to be there. *They* had no choice.

So, I sat there in helmet and flak jacket peering out at the lawless, Taliban-infested terrain below and hoped for the best. They were known to take potshots or launch missiles at military choppers, although it was rare for them to score a hit. It was, though, with some relief that we descended into the dust and stifling heat of Lashkar Gah. The base is well defended, and has to be. The enemy is not exactly at the gates but they're not far away.

We found our accommodation tent, I threw my kit onto a camp bed and went off for a meeting with Brigadier Radford. He seemed pleased to see us and asked to see me alone for half an hour. He wanted to outline the plan for the operation but he first wanted to make sure that he could trust me. It was fair enough. I told him that whatever he told me would remain confidential until the operation started. We got along. I liked him, and he tolerated me.

But it was a harrowing start to the visit. Within a couple of hours, as the sun was going down, we were standing on the parade ground with hundreds of troops and other personnel, listening to the camp clergyman pay tribute to four soldiers who had lost their lives in the previous days. Three of them had been killed by IEDs. It was an emotional ceremony, and that night in the mess tent, several of the troops mentioned how unhappy they were about the lack of proper protection in their military vehicles, and the lack of helicopters to move them around the battlefield. 'It's not the Taliban killing us,' said one, 'it's the Ministry of Defence.'

I was taken aback by the anger. They all seemed convinced of the justness of the war, but much less impressed by the resources they were being given to fight it. The American philosophy is 'overwhelming power'; the British one seemed to be 'whatever we can muster'.

Operation Panther's Claw began on our second night in Helmand. We had a reporter on the front line and I was presenting *News at Ten* from the base.

The information we were getting suggested it had begun well, and within a couple of days I was flying with Brigadier Radford to Babaji Fasal, an area that had been cleared of Taliban by a few hundred troops of the Black Watch, 3rd Battalion, Royal Regiment of Scotland.

The operation followed what the Ministry of Defence described as 'one of the largest air operations in modern times' and involved Apache and Black Hawk helicopters and Harrier jets. We found the Black Watch troops exhausted, covered in dust and hunkered down in a compound that gave them protection. Their commander, Lieutenant Colonel Stephen Cartwright, told us it had been an extremely tough fight and they had only managed to push the Taliban a mile or so out of the village.

He took us into the village itself and it was deserted. Just a few of his men patrolling. For some reason, I interviewed

Brigadier Radford on the forecourt of what seemed to pass as the local garage, with two old fuel pumps out front. He chose the location because it afforded some protection from Taliban snipers out in the countryside. Interview over, we filmed a little more before heading back to the helicopter and returning to Lashkar Gah to edit a piece reporting the first success of the operation.

The following day, Brigadier Radford called me into his office and he showed me a photograph of a mangled British military vehicle. It was a write-off, and I feared more troops had been killed in an IED.

'No,' he said. 'Fortunately the driver of this vehicle survived. It was in that village we filmed in yesterday. He was checking out the fuel from one of those pumps we were standing next to.'

He laughed. It was the exact spot on which we had conducted the interview. We had been standing on the IED. 'We just weren't heavy enough to detonate it,' he said. 'Thank God you're a lightweight.'

I didn't think it was funny.

In many ways, Panther's Claw epitomized both the success and the futility of the British involvement in Afghanistan. In military terms it was a victory, in the sense that the aims of the mission were satisfied. They had secured the areas they wanted to and forced out the Taliban.

But it was achieved at a terrible cost. Ten British soldiers died in a five-week campaign to take an area the size of the Isle of Wight. And here's the thing that will be hard to accept for the relatives of those who died: the area of Babaji Faisal is now back in the hands of the Taliban. As are huge areas of Helmand which were taken at one time or another by British forces over the past few years. It is the story of the war. Incredible bravery on meagre resources, short-term success, but ultimately pointless. Much of what was 'achieved' in Helmand looks now to have been basically lost.

Gradually, it began to dawn on politicians and the public that this was not a war that was going to be won in any final sense. There would be battles won, there would be setbacks, but there would be no victory in the true sense of the word.

In 2012, six British soldiers were blown up in one IED attack while they were on patrol. It was a defining moment in many ways. I wrote a column for the *Sunday Mirror* asking why on earth the war was still going:

Is it no more for this Afghan war?

The war has invaded all our lives – but still it goes on. Why?

Most wars are doomed when they invade the lives of the public and the public starts saying 'No more'. Well, next week, just like last week, Afghanistan will invade our lives again. Not just the lives of a bereaved wife, mother or father. But the lives of all of us.

The moment will come on Tuesday when six coffins containing the bodies of the soldiers killed in the worst single attack on British troops in this conflict will return home.

Such repatriations have happened before, of course. They've happened time after time. So many times, in fact, that the emotion-drenched ceremonies were in danger of becoming what they most certainly were not... routine.

But this time it will be different. It will be different because I sense the public mood is changing in a quite dramatic way. Over the last few years, when the fallen were returned, there was sadness and tears and grief, but also a feeling that it is the inevitable consequence of war. And this was coupled with the belief that this was the right war, the war to rid Afghanistan of al-Qaeda, to track down the mastermind of 9/11, Osama bin Laden, and to put a new government in place.

Well, that's all happened. But still the war goes on. And now fewer and fewer people understand why.

We can't win it in any recognised military sense. At least, not without putting troops into Pakistan. And even then it's unlikely. In fact, it would only make things worse.

So people ask, 'Why?' And when the bodies still come home, the sadness becomes tinged now with anger.

The war invaded our lives in another way last week too. It was when an American soldier went berserk, slaughtering 16 men, women and children as they lay sleeping in their beds. We know these things happen in war and perhaps we shut our minds to it when the war is perceived to be 'worth it'.

But when the cry is already 'What on Earth are we doing there?' such atrocities stamp on our sensitivities, they tear at our tolerance and make the call for an exit from Afghanistan ever louder.

Politically, too, things are starting to go awry. President Karzai, corrupt and weak, is making great play of telling NATO to keep its troops out of Afghan villages and in their bases. It is very difficult to fight a war on that basis. And this war can only be fought with the consent of the Afghan government and people.

And then there's the Taliban deciding to withdraw from any talks about peace with the Americans.

PM David Cameron and US President Barack Obama are both speaking bravely about 'real progress' and finishing the joint mission in Afghanistan.

And in a way they are right to do so. But the war has invaded all our lives. The cost in cash and in fatalities is being questioned. And there's no greater challenge to politicians overseeing a conflict than a growing cry of 'Why?'

Just after the deaths of the six soldiers, I interviewed the then defence secretary, Philip Hammond. The exchange went like this:

MA: What would you say to the families of young soldiers about to deploy to Afghanistan, and who are maybe thinking, 'Why on earth are we there?'

PH: We are there because our national security interest demands it.

MA: But it doesn't, does it; our national security interest doesn't demand it. There's a bigger security threat from Pakistan or Somalia than from Afghanistan right now.

PH: If we cut and run, you can be sure you will see a resurgence of international terrorist training in Afghanistan.

So this was the problem. After eleven years in Afghanistan, the international community was in a situation where they couldn't leave, because the security situation would deteriorate. The Afghan national forces simply were not – and still are not – up to the job. It is the war with no end. It is an expensive mess.

Now, clearly, American and British troops fought, and some still fight, with remarkable courage and tenacity in Afghanistan. There are numerous stories of incredible bravery and sacrifice that have been told and recognized many times.

I can speak best of the British forces that I worked with in Afghanistan. And having spent time with them; having slept, eaten and drank alongside them in various godforsaken hellholes, and been protected by them as well, I can testify to not only the courage, but also to the decency, warmth and friendliness they showed to the Afghan people in the most hideously difficult circumstances.

But could I say now, as things stand in Afghanistan, that it has been a sacrifice worth making? I honestly don't think I could. And it breaks my heart to say that.

So, intervention is littered with failures and difficulties. The best of intentions often end up buried in an unforeseen quagmire. But that doesn't mean intervention is wrong. It can work and has worked, in Kosovo, Sierra Leone and East Timor. But these missions all had something in common. They were limited in scope and time and commitment, and most important of all, they were doable.

Interventions that become wholesale exercises in nation rebuilding, that try to impose Western ideals on a culture not fully understood or appreciated, are likely to end in chaos and failure. Or in the case of Afghanistan, just never end.

But if there's now often little political will for international military interventions around the world, you would assume there would be unanimous support for international justice for those guilty of atrocities, war crimes and genocide.

Well, your assumption would be wrong. The International Criminal Court (ICC) has the idealistic goal of putting on trial the perpetrators of the world's worst atrocities – genocide, major war crimes and crimes against humanity. Over 120 countries support it, but the United States is not one of them. Nor is China, nor Israel.

And that's not the only problem. There are several flaws. Without an international police force, it relies on the cooperation of member states, some of whose leaders may one day be wanted for prosecution by the court. Also, the wheels of international justice turn frustratingly slowly. The ICC was founded in 2002, and it was ten years before it secured its first conviction.

Furthermore, nine out of its eleven investigations to date have focused on Africa, leading to claims of neo-colonial bias. It's also massively expensive; over one billion dollars has been spent, but it has thus far only convicted four people.

The ICC has two main purposes: to provide justice and peace of mind for victims and their relatives; and to act as a deterrent to others. On both counts, it has not been very successful. Victims are frustrated by the long delays and the frequent failure to convict, and atrocities continue unabated. The international community has failed to prevent terrible crimes in Syria, and attempts to refer the conflict to the ICC were blocked by Russia and China.

In 2005, the ICC issued an arrest warrant for the warlord Joseph Kony, whose guerrilla group, the Lord's Resistance Army, was responsible for the deaths of more than 100,000 people in the Central African Republic. From 1987 to 2006, the armed group also abducted more than 20,000 children to use as soldiers, servants or sex slaves, according to Unicef.

But despite a search involving Ugandan and US forces, Mr Kony continues to avoid capture. Though Ugandan soldiers did manage to recover Mr Kony's bathtub, which his slaves carried around for him in the bush for years. So no bath, but also no justice. His victims deserve better.

The genocide in Rwanda and war in Yugoslavia had their own international criminal tribunals and both have been severely criticized. The Rwanda court sat for about fifteen years, cost around £1.5 billion, and after a genocide in which up to a million people were killed, indicted only ninety-three people.

It took the Yugoslavia court twenty-two years to arrest and convict Ratko Mladić, the Bosnian Serb commander dubbed the 'Butcher of Bosnia'. He was responsible for the massacre of nearly 8,000 Muslim men and boys at Srebrenica, as well as the four-year siege of Sarajevo during which nearly 10,000 civilians died.

He was sentenced to life imprisonment, but at the age of seventy-four. The relatives of his victims will be asking, 'Why so little, so late?' Many of them are still looking for the remains, the bones, of their loved ones. It will not seem like proper justice to them.

And what message does it send to victims in Syria or in Yemen? What hope does it give them? And what message does it send to the tyrants of today?

A better way forward than cumbersome and slow international judicial processes may be independent national inquiries, backed by prosecutions within national court systems supported by outside legal help. Such prosecutions would ideally begin while the crimes and the evidence are recent and the witnesses still alive. They could, if necessary, be staged in neutral countries. It already happens to some extent: Sweden and Germany have both investigated and prosecuted war crimes in Syria using evidence partly gathered by human rights organizations in the country, under a mechanism created by the UN in late 2016.

There has to be a system with more teeth and more urgency than that which currently exists. At the very least, there has to be an international consensus that war criminals must be tracked down and not allowed to disappear because it's too difficult to find them or because some political deal is done to give them immunity. As the journalist Janine di Giovanni, who's covered Bosnia, central Africa, Rwanda and Syria, has said: 'Then perhaps the Robert Mugabes, the Bashar al-Assads, the Joseph Konys will know that they will never get away with what they did. That we will hunt them down, that we will find them, we will get them. That they will never hide or walk away.'

Unfortunately, as it stands, they will instead be bolstered by the likelihood that no international force will come to stop or arrest them, and that international justice will probably never catch up with them. And this, in the twenty-first century, is an abandonment of every conceivable moral obligation.

ANCHORMAN

THERE ARE TWO truisms about working in television news: you have the most fun as a reporter, but you make the most money as a newsreader. Trust me, I've done both.

It's also true that this state of affairs is not fair; reporting is much harder work. It involves long, often unsociable hours; repeated, unpredictable interruptions to family life; tedious drives, endless flights, and accompanying it all, the nagging, ever-present fear of missing a big story.

An anchorman or newsreader has none of those worries. All he or she is required to do, for the most part, is look presentable and read clearly, with correct pronunciation and without too many slip-ups. You earn your money when big stories break while you are on air – or, heaven forbid, things go wrong in the studio – but otherwise it is pretty straightforward.

My daughter Beatrice summed it up nicely when aged about five. Her class was asked by the teacher to tell everyone what their parents did for a job. 'My mum's a doctor and my dad reads out loud at night,' announced Beatrice.

The former *Newsnight* presenter Jeremy Paxman is openly contemptuous of the job of news presenting. 'You need a skill or two to be a successful newsreader,' he writes, 'mainly the ability to knot your tie, put your trousers on the right way round, and to sound as if you vaguely know what you're talking about.'

Very amusing, and not far wrong – apart, obviously, from the fact that he seems to assume it is a job for men...

But given how simple it's supposed to be, I was, in the beginning at least, a pretty terrible newscaster. I was nervous, hesitant, and rattled through the script just to get it over and done with. I would also sometimes develop a bead of sweat on my upper lip that made me look shifty and unconvincing – all qualities, if that's the word, not regularly associated with delivering the nation's news of an evening.

I was inexplicably promoted before I was remotely ready and was asked to present an evening news programme with Kirsty Young. After a few links she turned to me and, in that soft but firm Scottish voice of hers, said, 'Just slow down, Mark. We really do have to make this last half an hour!'

It was often rabbit-in-the-headlights stuff. A joke started going round.

Q: In a room full of secret service agents how can you tell which is Mark Austin?

A: He's the stiff one.

I also had the unerring knack of, every now and then, looking at the wrong camera. The red light on top of the 'live' camera should have been the clue, but even that proved too difficult.

In the early days I was named 'Wally of the Week' by the *Daily Star* newspaper. Twice. The first occasion was when

I warned viewers who didn't want to know the score of an England football match, the highlights of which followed the news, to 'look away now'. We then put up a caption with the score and I remained silent... until the director cut back to me and I said, 'Great win there for England.' It was an ad-lib from nowhere. Utterly inexplicable!

The second occasion was for another programme, on which I was supposed to announce that the African nation of Eritrea had won its first ever World Athletics Championship gold medal in a particular event. But I actually said the medal was won by Ethiopia, a country that just happened to be at war with Eritrea at the time.

Punctuation – or the lack of it – is another pitfall awaiting the inattentive anchorman. One night on *News at Ten*, I was supposed to open the programme with the following sentence: 'Good evening, paedophiles in Britain who fail to notify authorities when moving home will in future face the wrath of the law.'

Unfortunately, the pause after 'Good evening' was rather shorter than it should have been, and it sounded very much like I was saying 'Good evening paedophiles...'

Cue much Twitter faux-outrage and hilarity along the lines of 'You speak for yourself, mate...' Within minutes, Jonathan Ross, who happened to be watching at home, was posting a video of the mistake to his five million followers. It wasn't helpful. Before the end of the programme, and completely unbeknown to me, it had gone viral and the ITN press officer was getting calls from newspapers anxious for a comment.

When I came off air I returned to the newsroom completely oblivious to my gaffe, until I picked up my mobile phone and noticed a text message from my daughter: 'You're all over social media. Congratulations.' I logged on to Twitter and all became embarrassingly clear. Thanks, Wossy.

It got worse. On the following Friday, the clip got another public airing, this time on the BBC's *Have I Got News for You*. Paul Merton's quip was right on the money: 'And people say commas aren't important!'

He's right, but the BBC isn't immune either. One of their news presenters opened a programme like this: 'This is BBC World News. I'm Jonathan Charles kept hidden for over two decades and forced to bear children...' A little comma there may have helped.

On another occasion, I fell victim to a lack of concentration and too much punctuation. I was reading out an introduction to a very serious story about an earthquake in Pakistan. Thousands of people had been killed and we had sent our top reporters to the scene to cover the aftermath.

What I was supposed to say was that our international affairs editor Bill Neely 'saw first-hand relief efforts getting under way'. Instead, because of a rogue comma, I actually said he 'saw, first, hand relief efforts getting under way'.

There were gasps and not a few chuckles in my earpiece, and my co-presenter, Mary Nightingale, turned to me with a look of horror on her face as the videotaped report from Neely mercifully began to play. 'Did you really say what I think you said?' said Mary.

'Yes, I think I did.' I replied.

It is slightly depressing when you have covered some of the biggest stories of our times that the most common question you get asked is: 'What's the worst mistake you've made on television?'

As you see, I have plenty of contenders.

But because of technological advances, the job of newscasting has dramatically changed over the last fifteen years or so, and it no longer just involves reading a script from an autocue. Mobile and lightweight broadcasting technology now enable news anchors to get out to the scene of big stories and present entire programmes from location.

This is something I have done a lot of over the last couple of decades. It enables the newscaster to have a role in actually reporting on the story and to have ownership of it in a way that I think really resonates with the viewer. It makes the job more difficult, but also more rewarding.

I agree it is pointless sending news anchors out of the studio to simply read a few scripts. That's a complete waste of time and money. The key for anchors on location is to add real value to the programme by being there. It is something I felt very strongly about at ITN and was keen to do at every worthwhile opportunity.

It was a huge privilege to work for ITN, a pioneering news organization whose great tradition, it always seemed to me, was built on the very best eyewitness reporting by gifted correspondents, who transported the viewer to the heart of the story. And I was also convinced it was at its best when taking the programme on location to front original journalism, highlighted by compelling camerawork and sharp writing. I believe combining experience as a reporter or foreign correspondent with the job of anchor can make a real difference to the coverage.

Presenting from location, when the story warranted it, added to the sense of an ambitious, risk-taking, news organization that offered an exciting and different product to the BBC. They had decided, two or three years ago, to cut back on location anchoring, in the face of growing criticism about the way licence fee money was being spent.

Rather than embracing and exploiting that difference, ITV News, under new leadership, chose to become more like the BBC. It was a strange way, in my view, to take the fight to the opposition and to try to attract some of their viewers. It was all rather odd and sad. Long, studio-based interviews or conversations with correspondents now eat up precious minutes that could be given to first-hand reporting.

One of the reasons I was given was that they no longer had the money to do it. I am sure that is partly true, but news coverage is about choices. I am not convinced this was the right one. At Sky News there is no such reluctance to present coverage from the scene, in fact it is part of their raison d'être and one of their strengths.

ITN's former editor, Deborah Turness, was a great proponent of taking the show on the road. She was hugely imaginative and bold and came up with some cracking ideas – among, it has to be said, numerous less good ones. But that was her way, and by and large it worked! She was fearless, risk-taking and unswervingly loyal, and it was her who sent me on one of the most amazing trips of my lifetime: to the Antarctic.

Climate change was one of Deborah's obsessions, and she came up with a series called 'Three Degrees from Disaster'. The investigation highlighted that if temperatures were to rise by just 3 degrees Celsius more, we could reach the point of no return. Melting ice caps would lead to a dramatic rise in sea levels, threatening the lives of millions of people around the world.

The then ITV News science editor Lawrence McGinty travelled around the world to see the environmental hotspots where climate change is already most obvious. His amazing journey covered the massive destruction of the Brazilian rainforest, the deserts forming in China due to drought, the risk of flooding in the Seychelles and the melting ice sheet in Greenland.

The series was a success and the decision was made to take the reports further. Deborah called me into her office and said, 'I want to send you to the Antarctic. I want us to be the first TV news programme to anchor live from there.'

It was typical Turness. The result was a week-long special in January 2007 called 'The Big Melt'. During the week, Lawrence McGinty and I would travel around the continent to measure the retreat of the ice in one of the coldest, most remote places on earth. It wasn't easy, and just getting the satellite dish to Antarctica was an adventure.

The main dish – weighing 650 kilograms and measuring 2.4 metres in diameter – was flown on a Hercules by the RAF into Port Stanley in the Falkland Islands. The plan was for HMS *Endurance* – the Navy's icebreaker – to collect it and transport it to Antarctica.

But another important piece of kit for the dish was travelling to the Falklands by air, via Chile. Unbeknown to us as we left the UK, it was offloaded at Punta Arenas and never made the flight to Stanley.

It was a disaster. The only way the equipment could get to Antarctica was on HMS *Endurance*. We decided we needed to charter a plane to get the thing to the Falklands in order to meet the ship. But then the weather closed in and the charter couldn't take off. Our week of special reports was days away, and everything now hinged on this piece of satellite dish kit, a charter company that was losing interest, the weather in Chile, and a ship in the Falklands that was about to leave. It didn't look good.

Somehow we managed to get the equipment to a Chilean Antarctic base, and we persuaded the *Endurance* to make a detour to pick it up. We then jumped on a British Antarctic Survey Dash-7 plane for the five-hour flight into their base at Rothera, which was to be our home for ten days.

As we descended through the light cloud, it was utterly enchanting to see the Antarctic for the first time. Just endless sunlit whiteness below us: pristine, beautiful and largely untouched by man. It was breathtaking natural beauty. We were at the bottom of the world, where humanity – despite its best efforts – had been unable thus far to do its worst, and it lifted the spirits. It was a wonderful moment. There were just four of us in the team: McGinty, myself, cameraman Eugene Campbell, and the crucial man, satellite engineer Steve Gore-Smith.

I say crucial... and he was. Our problems were not over. After mandatory safety training – which involved roping ourselves into and safely out of a crevasse – Steve had to start building the dish, and then he had to somehow find the satellite. 'Not easy,' as he indelicately put it, 'from the arse end of the world.'

Antarctica, January 2007. Presenting the ITV *Evening News* from one of the most remote locations on earth!

Antarctica, January 2007. Crevasse training before we could go anywhere.

And with cameraman Eugene Campbell... checking his focus!

With ITN Editor Deborah Turness in the ITN studio in London, 2007.

The ITV *Evening News* studio with Mary Nightingale, 2009. A virtual studio without the computer graphics.

Hurricane Sandy in America, 2012. Preparing to do an interview with US correspondent Robert Moore.

In the *News at Ten* studio with Julie Etchingham, 2016.

In the crowds on The Mall for the Diamond Jubilee, 2012. A year earlier, similar reporting duties for the royal wedding ended in farce. Mobbed by scouts!

Meeting the Queen at a journalists' charity reception in 2014. Mary Nightingale and Sophie Raworth also in the greeting party.

In Rwanda, twenty years after the genocide, with Immaculate Mukanyaraya, who hid from the slaughter in the trees below.

In a so-called Reconciliation Village in Rwanda, twenty years on. The Hutu militiaman on the left lives next door to the woman (*centre*) whose family he butchered. An extraordinary experiment in reconciliation.

My two loves: cricket…

…and drumming. Here playing the O2 Arena in London during the 'Newsroom's Got Talent' charity competition in September 2010. Who'd have thought it?

Royal Television Society Presenter of the Year, 2015.

Great fun... A cameo appearance – one of many – on 'Ant and Dec's Saturday Night Takeaway', 2015.

With my daughter, Maddy. A photo for the promotion of our documentary on anorexia.

Love this picture. Reporting live for Sky News from the roof of the Washington bureau in 2018.

And it wasn't. Steve was struggling. For fourteen hours he battled, through howling winds and temperatures that plummeted to minus 20 degrees, to find a wretched signal. I'm tempted to say 'day turned into night', but of course it doesn't in January in the Antarctic. It is always day; there is no night.

Fuelled by regular cups of tea from Eugene, Steve eventually made a successful transmission at 5 a.m. on our first day of broadcasting. The opening programme went without a hitch, and I managed to conduct a live interview with Tony Blair in Downing Street. Even he was impressed.

McGinty was in his element, and did a fascinating report about how scientists measure temperatures in the Antarctic going back thousands of years. He filmed a research team drilling down into ice sheets in some of the remotest parts of the southern wilderness. They would extract cores made of ice that had fallen as snow hundreds of thousands of years before.

One of the scientists, Rob Mulvaney, explained the next step: 'Trapped in the ice are tiny bubbles of the atmosphere. Now this is the real actual atmosphere of the past. We can take out the air from those bubbles, measure the air for greenhouse gases, like carbon dioxide, and measure how it has varied through time.'

It was utterly fascinating. The analysis showed there have been eight ice ages in Antarctic history, and each was followed by a big melt. 'The levels of carbon dioxide today suggest we are in for another,' claimed Mulvaney. 'In the last hundred years, we've put the same amount of carbon dioxide into the atmosphere as we'd expect in the difference between an ice age and a warm period. That's a lot of carbon dioxide.'

The week went well. Bizarrely, Princess Anne turned up at the base on one day and gave us an interview. She was out there with her husband on a trip related to a charity linked to the explorer Ernest Shackleton. We'd had no idea she was coming.

I loved every bit of the trip. Although I did nearly die.

I was filming on a small rigid inflatable boat (RIB) among the giant, stunning icebergs floating close to the base, and I was doing a piece to camera very close to one that towered over us. Halfway through my piece about melting ice shelves, we heard a frightening, very loud creaking sound. The boatman swung the RIB around. He knew what was coming. Suddenly, and before we could escape, massive chunks, the size of cars, began falling off the iceberg. They crashed into the sea, a hundred metres or so from where we were. The boatman did well, and so did Eugene, who kept filming as it happened. It was dramatic TV, though it could very easily have been my last-ever piece to camera. But I suppose if you're going to die, die in Antarctica. It really is – crashing ice boulders aside – the most tranquil, idyllic and wonderful place.

I am conscious that I began this chapter by saying how simple newsreading is. Well, it is, until things go wrong. Then you earn your crust. And when you're on location, there's a lot that can go wrong.

It did in Beijing, when I was presenting *News at Ten* live from a position overlooking Tiananmen Square. It had taken weeks of hard work to get permissions and everything set up. The communist regime doesn't like Western news organizations broadcasting live from the square. The memory of the

1989 massacre coverage still haunts them. It is still incredibly sensitive. I have been arrested on that square more times than I can remember.

Anyway, all was set. Until, that is, I got the 'three minutes to air' count in my ear. We were still printing out the scripts from our laptop, but I had a small teleprompter that was working so I was relaxed. Suddenly, there was a spark from the power supply, a small bang and everything went off. Autocue, lights, printer... nothing was working.

'Two minutes to air,' I heard in my ear. *Two minutes to disaster*, I thought to myself. The top of the programme was complicated and pre-planned with a specific grab that I had to describe precisely. I had to get the script right, but I didn't have one. Nothing. The producer, Alex Chandler, was on the phone to London; the engineer, Kelvin, was trying to at least get the light back; and I was consumed with a gathering panic that was not conducive to addressing the nation sensibly.

Alex was furiously handwriting the opening script. *Good lad*, I thought, *we'll be fine*. We should have been, but I can safely say he has the worst handwriting on the planet. I could barely read it.

The *News at Ten* music sounded. Deep breath. Alex talked me through the script; I was still jotting stuff down as we went on air. Mercifully, the headlines were recorded. When they cut to us, I smiled and said, 'Good evening from Tiananmen Square in Beijing'... then tried desperately to come up with a reasonably coherent introduction.

It is odd. So often in the field, you do not have scripts and certainly not a teleprompter. And you talk with ease and from memory and it all works smoothly. But when you think you have scripts and an autocue and then suddenly you don't, it befuddles your brain. Anyway, we got through it... just.

There was also the night I drenched Sir Trevor McDonald live on air. It was in Hong Kong when I was Asia correspondent for ITV News, and the handover of the British colony to China was the climax of a thoroughly enjoyable assignment. Our coverage on the night of 30 June 1997 had been long planned, and I will never forget it. Not only because of the historical nature of the event itself, but also because it very nearly ended in catastrophe for ITN.

As resident correspondent and bureau chief, it was really down to me to ensure it all ran smoothly. Trevor, then presenting *News at Ten*, was to anchor proceedings live from Hong Kong, and I had found the best-possible vantage point for him. The roof of Hong Kong's best hotel, the Mandarin Oriental – with its magnificent views across the busy harbour – was to become our open-air 'studio' for the big night, giving the programme a spectacular backdrop.

However, the one thing I hadn't planned for was the tropical monsoon. There was no cover up on the roof, and the storm was fast approaching. Cristina Nicolotti, the producer, started barking orders about someone getting hold of some sort of shelter. Eventually, a flimsy canopy was erected and I breathed a sigh of relief. But as we went on air, it soon became clear it was about to give way under the sheer weight of rainwater that was pooling on top. Trevor did his best to ignore the chaos around him, and during a break in the programme I tried to push the water off the canopy. Unfortunately, I only succeeded in soaking Trevor and his scripts. As we went back on air, the wind picked up and the rain was now driving into us. As a result, Trevor was unable to read the autocue through his splattered glasses. Somehow, he battled through, I managed to deliver my live summing-up at the end of the programme, and a possibly career-ending disaster was averted.

It was an unforgettable night in many ways, and particularly memorable for me, because my youngest daughter Beatrice was one of the last British babies born in colonial Hong Kong. Happy days.

On another occasion, I almost missed a news programme altogether. I was in Beirut covering the war between Israel and Hezbollah in 2006. Cameraman Eugene Campbell and I had gone to film a bomb-damaged hospital in a Hezbollah-controlled suburb of the city. It was a quick trip before I had to present the lunchtime news from our hotel terrace. Unfortunately, it didn't turn out as we planned. While we filmed the hospital we were detained at gunpoint by Hezbollah fighters. They were upset because the hospital was still being used to treat a number of their wounded fighters and they didn't want them filmed. We had no idea that was happening.

We were taken into the building and led down some dark stairs into the gloomy basement. It was all very unsettling. They were hostile and aggressive and they wanted Eugene's camera and tapes. I was beginning to think we could be in serious trouble. Would we get kidnapped, or worse? All sorts of ghastly scenarios rush through your mind.

It was pretty tense for a couple of hours. But Eugene, a tall, likeable and very genial Irishman, gradually took the heat out of the situation and persuaded them we were there to film what the Israelis were doing to Beirut. I suddenly realized I had about forty-five minutes until the programme. Eugene explained my predicament and told them they could keep him, if they let me go to present the news. It was a courageous and generous offer, which they accepted. I didn't like leaving him there, but he insisted I took the driver back to the hotel. 'Just make sure you send him back... and if I'm not back by tonight, fly in another cameraman.' That's why I love the Irish. He was released an hour after me.

Newsreading also catapults you into the strange world of a kind of B/C list celebrity. You become famous simply by dint of appearing on people's televisions every night. Most of us have precious little talent that is deserving of anything approaching celebrity status. We can't act, we can't sing, we don't do stand-up and we don't, as far as I know, tackle the great scientific challenges of our age or discover life-changing medicines. None of that stuff. We just read the autocue. It's an underserved, unwarranted and slightly embarrassing fame. And if you're not careful, it can also lead to trouble. That happened to me when the *Radio Times* asked for an interview in 2008.

One consequence of becoming a face on the telly, particularly a newsreader, is that for some reason your opinions and views hold more weight or are deemed more interesting than people in other jobs. I've never quite worked out why. There are plenty of folk in many walks of life who have far more interesting views than me.

This is complicated, and made even more inexplicable, by the fact that you're not really allowed to have views due to your position. You have to be impartial and uncontroversial and essentially dull. But, despite all that, your views are sought, as indeed mine were by the *Radio Times*. It did not turn out well.

Near the end of the interview the journalist suddenly asked me about recent controversial comments made by the news presenter Peter Sissons, who'd said that many newsreaders had not 'earned the right' to do the job.

All my alarm bells sounded and all my instincts said, 'deflect this one', and yet in I waded. I told her that I knew what he meant and that I thought a number of newsreaders were chosen mainly for their looks and lacked a proper reporting background.

Here is what I said: 'I do think there are a number of pretty young women and handsome young men without a solid journalistic background reading the news nowadays, and I think it's a shame for them.'

The interviewer then asked whether I thought you have to have covered wars to be able to read the news. I answered: 'No, of course you don't have to have been to a war zone to read the news, but it probably does help.'

The interview was seized on by the newspapers. The *Daily Mail* headline screamed 'Top ITN newsman Mark Austin blasts TV autocuties'. It then listed and showed the pictures of five women presenters who they said were 'possible targets for his criticism'. The list included two friends, my *News at Ten* co-host Julie Etchingham and the *Newsnight* presenter Emily Maitlis, both of whom are, it goes without saying, television journalists of the highest quality. I was mortified.

The whole tone of the piece was that I was being sexist and I should be taken to the stocks and pelted with rotten tomatoes. The *Mail*, the *Guardian* and *The Sun* all pointed out, too, that I had recently been voted the 'Sexiest Newsreader Ever' in a *Sun* online poll; an award I obviously put above most others but which, incidentally, was greeted with hysterical laughter by my wife and two daughters. But the point was made. I was not only sexist, but a hypocrite as well...

The papers had their fun, but predictably they completely missed the point I was making. What I was trying to say was that young presenters, both women *and* men, were too often going straight into presenting and not bothering to go on the road as reporters, which is good experience and immensely enjoyable.

It wasn't a sexist point but a general, non-gender-specific one about becoming a news presenter without reporting experience. I even had to go on *Woman's Hour* to explain myself to a mercifully understanding Jane Garvey.

It was much ado about nothing, but it was a salutary lesson about newspaper interviews and about engaging at all in the TV sexism debate.

And, of course, it is a debate that still rages, and quite rightly. There is no question in my mind that women in TV news – particularly, but not uniquely, presenters – have to put up with much more nonsense than men. I have seen it over many years. They are viewed in a different way, judged in a different way and treated in a different way, and it is frankly lamentable.

In my early days at BBC News and at ITN, it was obvious pretty quickly that both were essentially run by men for men. There was an almost laddish culture in the newsrooms, built around war stories, sport and the pub. It must have been excluding and intimidating for women trying to make their way in the profession. One of the few women in any position of power when I joined ITN in 1986 was known to her face as 'Stiletto'. She was a very tough, very impressive foreign editor, but she must have found it undermining. In fact, I know she did; a female colleague of hers has since told me so.

The culture was deeply ingrained when I started, so it was easier, I suppose, to just accept it than to challenge it. It is no excuse, but that was what I, and many other young male journalists, did. It was a culture that not only tolerated unacceptable behaviour but almost made it an 'accepted' part of the job that young women had to put up with. I didn't give it as much thought as I should have done, and I don't think many men did. And therein, to be honest, lies much of the problem. In retrospect, I think my generation should have spoken up about what was clearly not right. We didn't.

My former ITN colleague Mary Nightingale told me stories of 'sexist nonsense' that became routine. She's written about the news editor who superimposed her face on a Page 3 pin-up and plastered it all over the newsroom. 'Where's your sense of humour? I'm only having a laugh,' she was told when she complained. 'It's just the way things were,' she said.

Some years ago a senior TV news executive told me – only half joking – that the key for male presenters was that women viewers wanted to sleep with you and male viewers wanted to have a pint with you. And if you presented alongside a woman the ideal was that viewers suspected you may be sleeping with each other! I kid you not.

It was the sort of thinking that almost encourages predatory behaviour in the workplace.

For women, appearance is made part of the job in a way that it is not for most men. I've heard women presenters being asked to change clothes, or to wear a certain hairstyle or different make-up. I've heard (male) managers discuss how to approach a female presenter about wearing sexier, less boring tops: 'She needs to liven things up a bit.' I was even asked whether I would raise the issue with a colleague myself. I said I wouldn't, and left it there. I should have made more fuss. I regret not doing so.

Superficiality is the stock in trade of television news, and not least when it comes to presenters. For a female TV presenter the right look is a job prerequisite that is deemed every bit as important as her ability to write scripts or conduct interviews, perhaps more so. It is a beauty standard not required of most male presenters. And if women fall short, their usually male bosses – and, sometimes, newspaper columnists – will let them know about it. Their appearance is public fodder.

The most I've ever been asked to do is straighten my tie or get my hair cut. Having said that, I did get a trashing for my appearance in *The Sun* once. In his column 'Telly Talk', Charlie Catchpole wrote: 'Moira Stuart and Mark Austin looked like beauty and the beast on the BBC news at the weekend. Beside immaculate Moira, Mark seemed to have been dragged through several hedges backwards. His hair must have been blow dried in a wind tunnel at British Aerospace and, if he'd shaved, I can only presume he's used a potato-peeler by mistake. Well below the mark, Mark!'

Well below the belt, Charlie! I knew Catchpole and I took it on the chin. It was amusing and I did look a bit scruffy on the telly in those days. But the criticism of a woman's appearance is altogether more pernicious. The criticism of me was comical, but because women on TV are often defined by their appearance and it is seen as an essential part of their job, the criticism they face is insidious.

And it has only become worse with the introduction of social media. Fiona Bruce, the BBC newsreader, has spoken about the 'hideously misogynistic' online abuse that high-profile women on TV receive: 'I'm astonished at the freedom with which a depressingly large number of men feel they can say what they want... about women. I look at my daughter and think, "God I didn't think this was coming your way". I really didn't.'

Fiona concedes that things are changing slowly and suggests its thanks to 'talented reporters', including BBC chief international correspondent, Lyse Doucet: 'Because when you listen to Lyse, you don't think, "What is she wearing?" Most of the time it's a flak jacket! What you think is, "God, she's in the middle of Aleppo risking her life."'

And she's right. There are a number of women reporters who are able to go quietly about their business and who are being judged on little else than their work. When you watch Lyse, or Channel 4's Lindsey Hilsum, or CNN's Christiane Amanpour, or Orla Guerin of the BBC, or ITN's Penny Marshall, or Alex Crawford of Sky News, you are seeing a woman at the very top of the game. They are role models who inspire young women and young journalists generally, and who are helping to change things.

But CNN's Amanpour says it was never easy to establish herself in a man's world: 'I did think I had to behave like a guy, there's no doubt about it. I did think that I couldn't be touchy-feely in a macho world. And it stays with you. It's not good.'

Amanpour and I both found ourselves in our first war zone at the same time. We were in Bahrain and Saudi Arabia for the Gulf War in 1990. She believes being a woman was actually an advantage in that situation: 'It was not only me; I had a camerawoman and a female sound recordist. We were given the job because we were women... CNN said, "We are sending these women to the most patriarchal society in the world, Saudi Arabia." What it did was give me a profile,' she told me, 'and because I was a woman I got a lot of preferential treatment from a lot of the men there, particularly some of the Saudi princes.

'I remember when we got to Saudi Arabia. The brother of the current crown prince was a bigshot then, and he drove me and my crew all the way to the Saudi–Kuwaiti border and we got the first shots of Iraqi tanks in the "no man's land" and we scooped everybody... and all the men from the American networks had smoke coming out of their ears.

'I would say, throughout my career, being a woman was a massive help because I was at the cutting edge of women being put in these jobs.'

But she says, being a correspondent, she was treated differently to female presenters: 'There is no doubt. I have also experienced male bosses dictating to female anchors what style their hair should be, what streaks and strands and colours should be in their hair, how high the hemline should be... the glass desk so you see the legs. Women did it. They hated it, but did it reluctantly.

'It still exists. It's a beauty contest. I never dyed my hair, I never did my teeth, I never did anything like that, but I was not in the studio under the lights day in, day out.'

Yes, things are definitely improving. Women presenters are being given more opportunity and greater roles in television news, and not before time. But the problem is that it is still mainly men appointing them or promoting them.

So it is changing slowly, but the real progress will come when it is women making more of the decisions in television newsrooms and above. Deborah Turness was a brilliant and inspirational editor of ITV News who went on to become president of NBC News, and Fran Unsworth has recently been made the head of news and current affairs at the BBC. There should be more and will be, in time.

Amanpour agrees: 'It's changing slowly, but until there are more female presidents of companies, until there are females who actually do the hiring and firing and create the ethos of the company, it is going to be a very hard slog.'

The recent revelations about Harvey Weinstein and the sackings of powerful male TV presenters such as Matt Lauer and Charlie Rose in the United States will undoubtedly hasten the pace of change in Hollywood and on television.

Cristiane Amanpour sees a direct connection between everyday sexism in the workplace and the allegations of sexual misconduct that led to the #MeToo movement: 'One thing leads to another in such a permissive environment. If women are considered second-class citizens, or third-class citizens, men can with impunity disrespect us and consider us less than equals and that is a civil rights issue. It is a civil rights issue, a human rights issue.'

The 2018 Golden Globes in Hollywood was seen as a watershed moment for women. They wore black on the red carpet, with pins on their lapels saying 'Time's Up', and many female stars made speeches or references to women's equality.

And the night will be remembered for a powerful speech by Oprah Winfrey, which some saw as a dry run for a possible presidential campaign: 'For too long women have not been heard or believed if they dared speak their truth to the power of men. But their time is up. Their time is up. Their time is up.'

It was a night of inspiring speeches, of protests well made, and of optimism that things are changing. But the awards were still dominated by men. 'And here are the all-male nominees,' said Natalie Portman, the presenter for the Best Director award, pointedly.

There is, of course, a direct line connecting Trump's election, the women's marches and the #metoo movement that emerged in late 2017. It was, in part, a backlash against the conditions that allowed Trump to win the presidency despite the credible allegations of sexual harassment and assault made against him. The momentum has also propelled record numbers of women running for political office. You can make out the contours of a movement that could shape American politics sooner than we think.

I am worried, though, by some of the coverage of the issue. When Matt Lauer was fired from NBC's *Today* show in America, he was replaced by a woman, long-time reporter Hoda Kotb. It was widely welcomed and it broke the long-established tradition of a male–female presenting format on morning shows. It was the right move at the right time, in many ways. But in making that point, Brian Stelter, the CNN media correspondent, said this: 'It's a logical move for NBC, especially in the wake of Lauer's abrupt exit amid complaints about inappropriate sexual behaviour at work...'

Now, I see what he's getting at. But his sentiment seems to be that it's a logical move because clearly no male presenter can be trusted not to behave in an inappropriate way. And that is, frankly, outrageous. The guilty party here was Matt Lauer; not men in general. But it's hard to make that point when the bigger issue – the often appalling and unfair treatment of women in the workplace – is the one that rightly has all the momentum. And, of course, women shouldn't have to work in an all-female work place to feel safe.

And money is part of that unfair treatment, too – pay, of course, is at the heart of the gender equality debate. And a group of female presenters and reporters at the BBC took umbrage at the pay inequality exposed at the corporation after it was forced to list those earning more than £150,000.

The women wrote public letters of complaint and threatened action unless the gender pay gap was closed. The BBC's China editor, Carrie Gracie, actually resigned over the issue, a move that caused considerable embarrassment to the BBC. Hers seemed an open-and-shut case, as it was revealed she was earning 50 per cent less than her male colleagues doing an equivalent job.

But, when it comes to presenters, the pay issue is fraught with difficulty. I have always negotiated with my agent the best contracts I can. It depends when you negotiate, with whom you negotiate, and your importance to your employer at any one time.

I have no idea what my female presenter colleagues were earning at ITN. But sometimes you negotiate different hours or a different number of days. Sometimes one presenter has much more experience than another; sometimes the roles differ in a way that is not obvious to the viewer. It's complicated.

But when there is a clear pattern of women being treated unequally, then sexism obviously exists. And at the BBC and some other broadcasters that was certainly found to be the case. However, the BBC dealt with the issue in a blundering fashion. First, they agreed to publicize the pay of their staff; then they made great play of highly paid male presenters agreeing to pay cuts. This is nonsense. It is not about some men earning too much, it is about women earning too little.

It is a highly paid world at the top of the TV presenting ladder, but it is also competitive. I do not begrudge anyone earning as much as they can achieve. I do believe that the pay gap must be closed... but upwards for women, not downwards for men.

Cristiane Amanpour backs Carrie Gracie: 'Women should be paid the same for doing the same job. It's not rocket science, and until that happens we won't be taken seriously.'

The correspondents' office I walked into at BBC Television Centre in the early eighties was an almost exclusively male habitat. Kate Adie was the only woman in there, apart from the office PA. She was one of the very few women correspondents around at that time; she was certainly the most famous.

Kate was very helpful to me when I joined, and made a point of telling me to put real thought into the writing. 'The pictures are the important thing in television,' she told me, 'but good pictures can be made really special by the right words... and sometimes the right words are no words.'

I have never forgotten that. What she means is that sometimes the pictures tell the story and words get in the way, detract from what the viewer is seeing. Sometimes no words are needed. It was a great piece of advice.

She was renowned for her courage under fire, but she was pretty gutsy in the office, too. I really admired the way she held her own in the alpha-male-dominated environment of the BBC correspondents' office. She was a fearsome customer, even when you were on her side.

When I left to join ITN, I felt like I was off to sup with the devil. They were the enemy in her eyes, and she could barely conceal her contempt when I quit.

A few years later, we came up against each other when we were both reporting in Bosnia. We were using the same satellite dish, operated by a news agency, for our live reports back to London. I had a ten-minute window just before the BBC's slot.

Sometimes in live telly, things change, and on this occasion my report was delayed a few minutes because of another breaking story. I was just about to go on air when Kate came up to me shouting something about how it was her turn and she needed to get in place. I managed to mumble that I was about to go live when she shoved me out of the way, took her place in front of the camera and demanded to be switched through to the BBC.

She actually pushed me aside without any concern for my programme whatsoever. Technically, we had encroached into the BBC's satellite time, but many reporters would have let me do my live piece and then taken their place. Not Kate Adie. No way. I was the competition and she was giving no quarter. It was extraordinary.

Kate was a very impressive journalist who blazed the trail for women reporters and proved that war reporting and dangerous assignments were not a male preserve. There was a fearlessness about her, and an ability to cut through the nonsense that was remarkable.

Amanpour – who followed where Adie led – believes we are on the verge of real change not just in TV but in wider society, too: 'A hash tag doesn't make a movement and doesn't change laws, but I think we are at a watershed moment. Things are moving. They really are moving. Women have been playing nice, but sometimes you have to kick a door open and that is what this is about. That is what Trump and the women's marches and Harvey Weinstein is all about. It's given a quantum leap to the movement.'

She's right, and the industry will be a better place for it.

MADDY

WHEN YOUR LIFE is largely about witnessing the suffering, misfortunes and difficulties of other people, it is uncomfortable, disconcerting and not a little painful to find yourself at the centre of the story. I say this with sincerity, even though I was responsible for the decision that made it so; that put myself, or should I say ourselves, in the full glare of the public spotlight.

I am talking about the illness that almost took my daughter's life. I am talking about the time in my working life when day after day for many, many months, I would turn up to read the news but only go through the motions. I am talking about the time I thought I would leave in the morning only to find later that my daughter had not survived the day.

I was presenting *News at Ten* and I was determined that the two or three million people watching every night wouldn't realize that anything was wrong. I don't know why; I suppose I wanted to shut it out. My daughter Maddy had fallen ill with the eating disorder anorexia, and it was threatening to tear our lives apart. In the beginning, going public about what happened to her was the furthest thought from my mind. It was private and there is still a stigma attached to eating disorders specifically and mental health in general. It was too raw an issue, too intrusive and unfair on Maddy. In fact, we went to great lengths to hide her condition even from good friends. We simply did not want it out there. We just wanted her to recover.

Mercifully, in time, she did. I will explain later why we decided to tell our story, and I hope you won't judge us for that. I still do not know whether it was the right thing to do or not. You will have your opinion, but we did what we did and I will try to give the reasoning as best I can. But, first, this is what happened.

It was November 2012, and I was having breakfast in the George Hotel close to the United States Congress in Washington DC. It is a friendly, well-run boutique hotel just a few hundred yards from the ITN offices in the capital. I liked it, felt at home there and particularly appreciated its very impressive wine cellar. I was happy, and our coverage of the final days of the Obama election campaign was going well. I had just spent a couple of sunshine-filled days filming around the Rappahannock River on the Virginia coast. We were interviewing Ryan and Travis Croxton, two brothers who jointly owned a thriving oyster company, but who were hopelessly divided when it came to re-electing Obama. One was Democrat, one Republican. I can't for the life of me remember which was which but they were good talkers, interesting interviewees and we filmed them out on one of their many boats on an unseasonably warm day. It made for good pictures, a nice story that was in a sense a microcosm of America, and we were about to edit the piece for that night's *News at Ten*. Things were good.

And then the call came. It was my wife and she was clearly upset. She told me she was anxious about Maddy, our eldest daughter, who had slowly been losing weight over a number of weeks. I hadn't been remotely concerned. She was an athlete who had been training and racing hard that summer and was desperate to get her 800 metres time down. She had competed a few months earlier in the Olympic trials and wanted to improve. If she was losing a little bit of weight, that didn't seem to me to be a major issue. Little did I know what a problem it would turn out to be. I basically persuaded Catherine that everything would be OK, ended the call and walked across to the office to edit our piece.

The following day, Catherine called again to say she had spoken to Maddy, who had assured her that everything was fine. She insisted she could easily put the weight back on and she would do so once her eighteenth birthday later in November was out of the way. I felt reassured by the conversation and supposed that the weight loss was more to do with the party we'd planned for her than anything else. It seemed to me pretty normal behaviour for a girl about to celebrate her eighteenth with a big bash. I was even less worried than I was the previous day.

I thought nothing more about it until I flew home a few days later, with Barack Obama now re-elected to the White House. Maddy's party was a lot of fun and involved 120 of her friends in an apparent hurry to get as drunk as possible in a marquee in the garden of our house in Surrey. I had done my best to prevent total chaos. The vodka being served at the bar was watered down, I had bought low-alcohol rosé wine and I had employed security guys from ITN, former marines who accompanied us to war zones around the world, to search guests on arrival for supplies of alcohol. It was necessary. They confiscated enough bottles and half-bottles of spirits to virtually fill a wheelie bin. We managed to get through the night without serious incident, apart from a fight involving a guy who had already injured his neck in a rugby game that day and was wearing a neck brace. We threw him out.

But as the party wore on, some parents who also came to the party commented about how thin Maddy looked and asked if it had occurred to me that she had lost too much weight. I decided to talk to her about it the following week.

The conversation did not go well. Maddy was defensive and hostile and didn't want to engage. She became angry and non-communicative and wanted to close the subject down. She told me it was her life and her body, and pointed out that, since she was eighteen now, I couldn't do anything about it anyway and she could do whatever she wanted. I reacted badly and it ended in a shouting match. It would not be the last time I would badly misjudge things during her illness. And it very soon became clear that that is exactly what it was. An illness. One I didn't understand. One I didn't know anything about. And one I did not deal with at all well. It was the beginning of the most traumatic time in our family life. It was the beginning of a descent into hell.

It was Maddy's school housemistress, Andrea Saxel, who decided enough was enough. I took a call from her at home one day, and she told me very directly that she was extremely worried about Maddy. She knew the signs and believed that my daughter was in the grip of anorexia. Maddy needed help and quickly.

I immediately made an appointment with our local GP and drove over to the school to pick her up. When I arrived, she was in Mrs Saxel's office, tearful and frightened. But, as I was to find out, not frightened enough to pull herself out of it. That, by the way, was mistake number one: 'pull yourself out of it' is not a demand that sits well with an anorexic.

We drove in silence to the GP, who was understanding and sympathetic. She weighed Maddy and then asked me if she could speak to her alone. I have no idea what was said between them. What I do know is that within a couple of weeks we were sitting in front of an eating disorder specialist at a local hospital in Farnham, and the news wasn't good.

She had spent about an hour with Maddy before we were called in, and it was all very matter of fact: 'Maddy is very unwell and my diagnosis is anorexia nervosa. It is not dangerous at the moment, though it could become so. But I am hopeful that with the right treatment she can make quite a quick recovery. It won't be easy though. I have to warn you.'

My wife Catherine – an A & E doctor – knew how serious this was, but kept calm and asked quite detailed medical questions. I was determined that I could shake my daughter out of it and make her see sense. That was mistake number two. There was no question of 'making her see sense'. By now, sense to her was not eating; sense to her was to take as much exercise as possible. And sense to her was that we, her parents, were now the enemy.

We wanted to make her do what she implacably did not want to do. She did not want us or the specialist, or anyone in that unit, to be in her life. She was, in short, on a very rapid path to self-destruction.

The specialist had talked about the 'right treatment'. It was to prove the beginning of a very steep learning curve. Talking about the right treatment was one thing. Being able to access it, or even identify what it should be, was something else altogether. Maddy was given an appointment once a fortnight where she would go in and get weighed and talk to a nutrition-ist if one was available. They would give her a meal plan and advise her on how to cope and start eating again. That was it.

It was to make very little difference. Maddy – or rather this demon called anorexia that now possessed her – was absolutely determined to limit her intake of food to just a few calories a day. Calorie counting and food avoidance became the domi-nant theme of her life. Very quickly she became horribly thin, adamantly uncommunicative and intransigent.

Mealtimes became a battleground, arguments became ever more bitter and our relationship became toxic, if you could even call it a relationship. I was shut out of her life. It was poisonous and terrifying. I was convinced I was watching her slow, inexorable death.

She was there, but she was gone. It is the only way I can describe it, really. She was alive but she was dead. Dead inside. Wasting away. The daughter we loved so much had left us to be replaced by an emaciated, ghost-like figure we could never rec-ognize as Maddy. And it all happened so quickly. One moment she was a vibrant, strong, energetic and beautiful young girl. The next, she had begun the rapid, dangerous descent towards self-destruction. That's what anorexia does.

I didn't understand it at first. Cancer I understand. Diseased cells multiplying, spreading, invading and destroying. But this was my daughter wilfully destroying herself by not eating, or at least by not eating enough. At first, I thought it was crass, insensitive, selfish and pathetic. Until I began to understand. And I deliberately say 'began' to understand, because even now, several years on, I don't really understand. Not fully. Not really.

I remember once that Maddy seemed to relent. We were having breakfast one day and she asked if I wanted porridge. I jumped at the chance and said I'd love some. She wanted to make it and I watched her pour the porridge oats into a saucepan of water rather than milk. I urged her to put some milk in and she relented, but she only put in the bare minimum. I noticed a jar of clotted cream in the fridge and thought that if I got the chance I would pour it all in without her knowing. I didn't get the chance, of course. She was protective and watchful. This was porridge on her terms, and nothing would change that. In the event it was a small victory, but it didn't last.

Maddy seemed hellbent on self-destruction and it broke my heart. The daughter I thought I knew became remote, conniving and filled with cunning. She would do anything to avoid eating. She would lie and lie again, and then explode with rage if we challenged her. She was abusive and vile, and seemed possessed by something she could not control – or worse, did not want to control.

She showered me with contempt. I couldn't say anything to her about it because she was in total denial. As a parent, you have to make a decision, and I made the wrong one. I decided to go on the attack. I told her she was being ridiculous. I told her to get a grip and grow up. And I told her to 'just bloody well eat, for Christ's sake'.

I drew a parallel to the appalling plight of family friends who had a young daughter who had passed away from leukaemia. 'She didn't make a choice, did she?' I said. 'She was desperate to live but despite all the medical help available, she couldn't. That is a tragedy. But you, you are doing it to yourself.'

On one terrible night, as she lay on the kitchen floor in front of the Aga, I said something I bitterly regret. She was refusing to get up for dinner and was curled up there for warmth. Anorexics get so cold. Maddie was only interested in a cup of hot tea. I told her she was going to kill herself and then I said it: 'And if you really want to starve yourself to death, just get on with it.'

'If you really want to starve yourself, just get on with it.' Was I really saying that to the daughter I loved?

And here's the worst thing about it. For a moment, for one ghastly split second I think I actually meant it. I was exasperated and at my wits' end. I wanted the whole dreadful situation just to go away.

She didn't respond at all, which only made things worse. Within moments I wished I hadn't said it. But it was too late. I still don't know what she thought about hearing her father say that. I am not even sure she remembers. I hope she appreciates now it was me talking to anorexia and not Maddy.

But I began to think this was going to destroy me as well as her. The fact remained I was her battering ram. Everything I did and said was wrong. I couldn't bear it.

What I failed utterly to grasp was that she was seriously mentally ill and could not see a future for herself. Not grasping that was a big mistake. Once you accept it is a mental illness and should be treated as such, it is somehow easier to accept. Without understanding that, you forever think it is simply a case of getting food down her neck. It is so much more complicated than that, and I did not appreciate that.

Things worsened, and we tried to get her into the local eating disorder unit as a day patient. They didn't have any places. We were desperate. We were totally failing to treat her or help her at home. My wife was becoming ill herself from the stress of it all. Imagine being a doctor, a job you've chosen because you want to help and care for people and make them better. And yet you can't even help your own daughter. You can't treat her. Imagine that. That is what my wife went through. She struggled to cope. In fact, she couldn't cope. Neither of us could.

Maddy urgently needed help and treatment. But what treatment and where? We hit problems right from the start. The main problem, it seemed to me, was that she needed rapid, early and significant medical intervention. But she couldn't get it because she wasn't acutely ill enough to warrant a hospital bed. She wasn't thin enough to trigger admission to a full-time eating disorder unit. And, at eighteen, she wasn't young enough to qualify for children's mental health treatment.

Just think about that. *Not ill enough.* One would have thought that enough was now known about the predictable path of anorexia that the most sensible and economically sound response would be quick and intensive intervention by trained doctors and psychiatrists. But the fact is there are not the resources for that. Her GP was a lifeline, but the best we could get early on were fairly regular outpatient specialist appointments that came and went with no real apparent improvement.

Maddy would say exactly what the specialist wanted to hear, would somehow find ways to boost her weight just before appointments and then starve herself again afterwards. And because she was eighteen, we had no legal power to make her go anywhere for treatment or do anything. We had no access to her medical records unless she gave express permission. At one stage I was told she would have to be an inpatient in a local adult facility, being treated alongside very ill, long-term mental health patients with severe problems. That would have been disastrous.

It was hopeless. And here's the thing. If our family, with an A & E doctor and a pushy journalist who can quite often get things done, starts to crack and fall apart, what hope is there for other families battling the system? What hope for single parents? What hope for those unable to afford private medical help? 'No hope' is the answer as it currently stands.

It quickly became clear that the only option was private inpatient treatment. It costs thousands of pounds a week. So the fact is it is out of reach for the vast majority of people in this country. We had health insurance, but the money quickly runs out under most schemes; it would only cover a quarter of the four to six months that we were told was the least Maddy needed. But, fortunately, we had the money. We would make it work.

The unit did its best, but this was a very expensive regime of forced feeding, no exercise (you could only climb the stairs to go to bed at night), accompanied toilet visits to prevent patients throwing up the food consumed, and monitored sleep to make sure they didn't exercise while in bed.

It was probably what Maddy needed, but it was a disaster. She was put in a cramped dormitory with eight other girls, all of whom seemed intent on bucking the system somehow and taking in as little food as possible. They would also exercise in the beds, keep the windows open so they would shiver, and constantly go to the toilet, where some of them locked the door and, out of sight of the nurse supposed to keep an eye on them, would jog on the spot in the loo for several minutes. It was crazy. Maddy actually deteriorated there, or at least her mental state certainly did.

We could see Maddy becoming more and more depressed and we decided it was the wrong place at the wrong time. She resisted it and hated it and threatened to kill herself. There had already been one recent suicide there and we didn't want another. I told the people who ran the unit that I would be taking her out. It caused huge problems. A senior doctor was summoned and he told me it would be highly irresponsible to do so. She was too thin and too weak to leave their care. I phoned my wife to tell her that they were insisting Maddy stayed. She wanted her home. The doctor then threatened to section Maddy. That would have involved calling the police and going through a legal process to detain her; and that would be on her record forever and have implications for the rest of her life. It was not going to happen. I gathered up Maddy's things, put them and her in the car and we fled.

On the journey home, Maddy was weak and looked very unwell. I worried it was a huge mistake. I even thought about taking her straight to A & E. In the end, I decided to take her home. Catherine had set up a monitoring system in Maddy's bedroom and had moved a mattress alongside her bed. It resembled a hospital emergency room. Catherine would sleep there until it was safe to leave her. She would check her heart rate regularly. The real danger at that time was heart failure. Her organs were slowly giving up on her. We felt alone and vulnerable and abandoned – and this is with a doctor in the family. How on earth other parents cope, I simply do not know.

The impact of all this on families is devastating. As a father I remember feeling lost, excluded and reviled. I didn't grasp the issues of body image and weight control and I found them difficult to talk about. I floundered, and in the process, I think, ended up poisoning her against me still further.

And all the while, Maddy was shrinking away. She was painfully thin, constantly pale and cold, so cold all the time. Her arms and legs became stick-like, her face gaunt, her eyes hollow. Her skin was blistering, her bones were increasingly brittle. Her body was closing down. We were watching her slowly die and we could do nothing about it.

We soon had a breakthrough of sorts. The day patient unit at the local hospital in Farnham finally had a place for her. She would be picked up by ambulance in the morning, have breakfast and lunch under supervision at the unit and various sessions of counselling. She would be home for dinner and at weekends. It didn't make much difference at first. Maddy would eat very little at home because she was forced to eat substantial meals at the unit during the week.

She also began getting up early and disappearing for walks. Initially it would be twenty minutes or so, but eventually she would be gone for a couple of hours. Morning after morning she would do this. I would get up at 5.00 a.m. and go into her room to persuade her not to go. I locked doors and hid keys, but she always found a way out. She started going out earlier and earlier – 4.30 a.m., 4.00 a.m., then 3.30 a.m. She would go whatever the weather. She would walk in rain and bitter cold. I remember waking one morning with thick snow covering the garden. Her footprints marked the route she had taken. I will never forget seeing that. It was 5.30 a.m. and my sick, frail, desperately thin daughter was crossing some field or walking along some wooded path, all alone, vulnerable and consumed by this terrible thing called anorexia.

I never imagined for a moment I would write about this. I have covered war, atrocity, famine and natural disasters the world over, and I am paid to find the words to describe what I witness. But when a crisis comes crashing headlong into your own family, when the life-and-death struggle is your own flesh and blood? No thanks. Too close. Too raw. Too uncomfortable. Too exposing. Too self-important, even. This we kept quiet about.

But the truth is I can't keep quiet about it, and I won't keep quiet about it because something needs to be done to help the victims of anorexia. As a country, our response is bordering on the pathetic. It is a mental illness like all the others. And, almost uniquely, it is a mental illness that can directly kill.

And Maddy was continuing to weaken. She had developed bone marrow failure and was covered in sores as her skin was breaking down. She hadn't had a period for months. Her body was ceasing to function.

I was presenting *News at Ten* each night, trying to concentrate on what I was supposed to be reading but in truth thinking only of Maddy and whether she would survive the night. She was five and half stone, down from nine and a half. Things were bleak.

Then, mercifully, and almost from nowhere, things began to improve. The work being done by the nurses and key workers at the day unit was beginning to pay off and have an impact. It was tough when it had to be, gentle and cajoling at other times. It was run by good people who cared and it probably saved her life.

Maddy had also made a decision. She wanted to get better. It was the first time she had said that and meant it.

Maddy spent a year there, slowly regaining weight, but that wasn't the end of it. Afterwards she was left with debilitating depression. Even though she put weight back on, she didn't think she would get better. It frightened her. But, gradually, she did.

Looking back, Maddy traces the beginning of her recovery to a key worker and counsellor called Debbie. Debbie had told her at the end of one session that Maddy had three choices. She could either just carry on as she was and never get better. She could give up altogether and just die. Or she could make the choice to get better and recover. Maddy says it was a pivotal conversation and she vowed to try to get better.

We'd found a place run by the NHS that happened to be local to us and where she finally began to improve. We were lucky, so lucky to find it, and she was lucky to get a place there. It has limited resources but at least it exists. But my point is this: what happens to those who don't find a place like that? And why are there not more places like it? Most sufferers, it seems to me, are left to fall through the cracks in an inadequately resourced and financed system.

This was tragically illustrated in a Channel 4 documentary Maddy and I made after her recovery. We told the awful story of Lydia, a girl the same age as Maddy, at the same stage of the illness but who failed to find any significant treatment at all. While Maddy was being treated at Farnham in the day unit, Lydia was effectively abandoned. She had the misfortune to live in Norfolk, where the provision for eating disorders was poor. She was being seen, when possible, by a psychotherapist who was overworked and sometimes couldn't fulfil appointments. Following two cancelled appointments and one brief phone call, she disappeared one afternoon after saying she was going for a walk. Her body was found at the foot of Hunstanton Cliffs. It is a desperately sad story. It made Maddy very angry.

In an interview for the documentary, she confronted the health secretary, Jeremy Hunt, put the Lydia case to him and said, 'It's supposed to be a National Health Service not a National Lottery.' It was a fair point. The provision of care for eating disorders in the UK is a lottery. And very few win it. We found case after case of young women, and men, who were failed by the system. In fact, you can't really call it a system. There is no system. It is patchwork, ad hoc and inadequate.

Mental health problems in teenagers is the epidemic of our age. And despite promises, successive governments are not treating it like an epidemic. More than 850,000 children and young people have been diagnosed with mental health problems in the UK, and how many more have had no formal diagnosis but still suffer, often in silence, unwilling to share their despair?

So often girls with eating disorders – for it is overwhelmingly, though not exclusively, girls – are forced to wait months, even years, to get real help. And so often, where help can be found it is literally hundreds of miles from home, meaning parents have to make lengthy treks across the country just to see their child. It is expensive, inconvenient and just plain wrong in Britain in the twenty-first century. Affected families have enough stress to deal with without having to travel vast distances just to be with their sick daughter.

In the documentary we also focused on the case of Rachel from Nottingham, whose eighteen-year-old daughter had been allocated an eating disorder unit in Edinburgh, three hundred miles from her home. Rachel told us how the NHS would only pay for two flights a month but she made six trips in eight days, as any mother would want to do. She said the separation and the incessant travelling was 'inhumane'. This is what she told me: 'It's not only the illness that has been so tough, it's the separation, that's what's been traumatic. It's traumatic each end because I leave my other two daughters here with my husband and quite often they are upset, and then I get there and there's the feeling of euphoria because we are there together and she's looking a bit better and we spend the day together and then there's that separation again.

'It's a horrible feeling. I hate leaving her. Quite often I cry all the way to the airport, sometimes all the way through security. You see all the people giving me a wide berth, thinking who is this crazy, unhinged woman.

'One time, on the way to the airport, I just thought I couldn't carry on anymore, I just wanted the taxi to crash. But I've got to keep going, haven't I? Because I have two other daughters...'

It was harrowing stuff.

And she's right. That is exactly what it is... inhumane. And it sums up the way these patients are treated. Rachel has fought for several years to find the right treatment for her daughter. She's still fighting. She is a brave woman who decided to speak out.

I also met two young women suffering from anorexia, Vicky and Becky from Newcastle. There, the inpatient service had been cut back and there was virtually no outpatient treatment available. Vicky told me she had no support whatsoever. She had often thought about killing herself.

Becky also lacked outpatient support and had been told she wasn't ill enough to qualify for an inpatient bed in an eating disorder unit. She was in the process of trying to lose more weight so they would have to admit her. She was worried she would take her own life without proper help.

What sort of health service allows that to happen? Someone making themselves more ill to get treatment. It is madness.

And Newcastle is typical of many towns and cities across the UK. Even where help is available, it is often temporary, piecemeal and uncoordinated. Things simply have to change, and change soon. Norman Lamb, the Liberal Democrat MP doing so much to push the whole issue of mental health, says the government must take seriously calls to give mental illness the same level of commitment as physical health. But it is not happening. Get hit by a bus in this country and you will probably receive some of the best emergency treatment available. Get mentally ill, and there is a very grave risk that you will be abandoned.

What are needed are more specialist inpatient centres for sufferers up to the age of twenty-one. Girls with anorexia need immediate urgent inpatient care available to them. And they don't want to be in adult mental health units.

And in a world where getting an appointment with a psychiatrist or eating disorder specialist can take months, we need walk-in centres on the high street of every town and city in this country, manned by trained counsellors who know about anorexia and mental health. If it works, it would mean, at the very least, that sufferers could be identified earlier, help could come sooner and records kept of the visit. We must not let these girls and boys fall through the net. They will die. They do die. The story is in the statistics. It is reckoned that one in five chronic anorexics die as a result of the condition and malnutrition, or because they will take their own life.

I have asked Maddy several times what it was that triggered her illness, and she has yet to come up with a satisfactory answer. As I said, she was a promising athlete who ran 800 metres to a fairly high standard, winning national school events and taking part in Olympic trials. Was she running because she wanted to control her weight? Or did the pursuit of ever-faster times tip her over the edge? She denies that was the case. And after all, lots of young athletes push themselves to the limit in training without falling prey to anorexia.

I think the truth is there is no one reason. The nearest she has come to a plausible explanation was when she told me she felt her life was out of control and the one thing she could control was the amount of food that entered her body. Why she felt her life was out of control is the interesting issue. And there I think we enter the whole area of the growing pressure on modern teenagers through the ever-increasing use of social media. I am convinced there must be a link between mental wellbeing and an online world where girls are so often presented with supposed ideals when it comes to the way they look and the way they live their lives. It is a daily battering of fragile senses and sensitivities.

Again, Maddy has never identified that as a reason. But my fear is that an entire generation of youngsters are effectively taking part in a vast social experiment, the consequences of which may not be known until it is too late.

I wonder if the day of reckoning will come or whether it is already upon us. I am not arguing that social media is bad; it clearly has enormous benefits. But I am saying that I would not be enormously surprised if one day it was possible to prove a link between its use and teenage mental health issues.

What haunted me, and I imagine haunts most parents of anorexics, is the lurking question that perhaps we were somehow to blame. My daughter and the specialists rushed to tell us we were not, but it doesn't quell the nagging doubts that something we said or did may have pushed her into this dreadful condition.

I am pleased to say Maddy is much improved. We have our daughter back, where so often other parents do not. I am not sure that eating issues will ever completely leave her, but she is healthy, leading a normal life and is now at university. Others are not so fortunate. For many it is a very long and painful road to recovery, if recovery is possible at all.

About a year after Maddy recovered, she sent me a blog she had written about her illness and specifically about the effect she thought it had on her mum and on me. It was blisteringly honest and painfully observed. She writes about how she had felt, at the depth of her depression, that we, her parents and her siblings, had not wanted her around. Here is a small part of it:

I knew I was tearing my family apart, I'd watched myself shrink and the strongest people in my life began to show their cracks. My mother and father stood there feeling helpless and alone.

In my head, all I wanted was to lie in this grave I was digging for myself, but create a way in which my family could continue their lives without me, I wanted them to forget that I had ever existed so I could continue down my path of self-mutilation and slow suicide.

It was ghastly to read. I had no idea that she had been through such darkness. I wanted to push it out of mind. The illness itself had been hard enough to deal with. Now it seemed it was over, I wanted to brush it aside, even pretend that it hadn't happened, and get on with our lives. I certainly thought it was not something we should be writing about; that would surely only extend the pain we had felt.

But when Maddy asked what I thought of the blog, I said it was very good but hard for me to read. She told me she had found the process of putting her deepest thoughts onto paper cathartic. She felt better for doing it. And on reflection I had found what she said useful when it came to dealing with what we had been through. She then asked me if I would write something about what I was feeling during the worst of the anorexia.

I thought about it and then put a few thoughts down and kept them on my laptop. Every so often I would go back to it and rewrite parts or write some more, until I had what I thought was as honest an account as I could manage.

For months I did nothing with it. What I did do was write a piece about mental health and eating disorders for the Huffington Post website. I didn't mention Maddy at all, but rather just said it had affected my family.

A few days later I took a call from Martha Kearney, then the presenter of the BBC's *World at One* on Radio 4. She is a friend and a journalist I hugely respect. She asked if I would go on the programme to talk about the problems we had finding treatment for Maddy. I was torn; I wanted to make a noise about the lack of resources available for sufferers of eating disorders, but I was very reluctant to put her name and story in the public domain. In the end, Maddy and I decided we needed to talk about it, and in a way that would capture the attention of the public. So that is what I did. I spoke as honestly as I could about what she went through, how it affected us and the desperate need for more resources.

Predictably, the newspapers seized on the disclosure that I had at one point said 'if you want to kill yourself just get on with it'. It was a difficult few days but it certainly had an impact, and Jeremy Hunt faced some pretty tough questions from Martha as a result of it. I was glad I did it.

That led to an article for the *Sunday Times* magazine and subsequently to the documentary for Channel 4. I had huge reservations about my daughter taking part and being so open about her condition. But she was keen to drive the project forward. She wanted to do it. My concern was that the illness would in some way come to define her. I worried that she would become a poster girl for anorexia. We didn't want that. We simply wanted to get a message across in the most powerful way we could. I think we did that.

Maddy tells me she found the whole process cathartic and useful, and that it helped her deal with what she'd been through. I certainly hope that is true. I am very proud of what she did.

I just hope other parents and families in a similar situation find some encouragement in knowing people can get better and things can improve. I know we were very fortunate. We have our daughter back.

JOURNALISM

Two or three years ago, when I was presenting ITV's *News at Ten*, I was asked to speak about journalism to some fifth and sixth formers at Lancing College in Sussex. Sad to say that, despite their public school education, they were a bunch of liars.

They lied in a nice way, though. I asked them how many watched *News at Ten* regularly. Dozens of hands shot up. I said that I didn't believe them. 'How many of you really watch *News at Ten* regularly?' I asked. There was a lot of looking around and nervous twitches and then just a handful of pupils stuck their arms in the air.

I knew they'd been originally being polite, but the second show of hands was a far more plausible, though still not completely honest representation, I thought. When I asked them how they did actually receive their news, the answer came as no surprise. It was either on mobile news apps, or on Facebook or some other social media platform. And, clearly, this is what's happening across the country.

Among young people in the UK, social media has overtaken television as their main source of news. In a recent study by the Reuters Institute for the Study of Journalism, around 28 per cent of 18–24 year olds cited social media as their principal news source, compared with 24 per cent for TV. The trend in news consumption is clear, and in a decade or so it will become even more pronounced.

The Reuters study found that Facebook was the most common source – used by 44 per cent of young people to watch, share and comment on the news. Next came YouTube at 19 per cent, and Twitter with 10 per cent.

And it all raises a fundamental question – and one that was put to me after my speech at Lancing College: Has the digital era usurped the traditional "appointment to view" news programme on television? Is new media swallowing up the old?

One thing is certain. Ratings for programmes such as *News at Ten* on the terrestrial channels are on the slide, and have been for many years now. When I started working as a correspondent for *News at Ten* in the eighties, when it was presented by the legendary Sir Alastair Burnet and Sandy Gall, it was regularly pulling in 10 million viewers a night. But since the early nineties there has been a pretty steady decline. When I was presenting *News at Ten* with Julie Etchingham we would get audiences averaging around 3 million, while more recently it had fallen to about 1.9 million. Nothing to do with the presenters (I hope!), but rather the massively changing viewing habits of the nation. In some ways, mainstream journalism and the traditional methods of delivering it are under siege.

The telly is still holding out. Recent figures compiled by Ofcom on which news medium is most regularly used by adults are interesting. Newspapers are the main source of news for 31 per cent of adults, but declining rapidly. Radio is hanging on at around 32 per cent. The Internet, including usage on laptops and mobile devices, is at around 41 per cent and increasing. But TV still wins hands down, with 67 per cent of adults saying they regularly use it as a source of news. It also, by the way, remains the most trusted source.

But this won't last. The trajectory is pretty clear, and the box in the corner of the living room is on borrowed time. The rising use of other means of delivery, whether news apps or social media, is clearly undermining traditional business models and disrupting news organizations around the world.

Twenty-four-hour TV news channels, including Sky, for whom I now work, are constantly having to evolve to exploit new ways of delivering the news. In 2017, the total global digital audience for Sky News was 153 million unique browsers – up 15 per cent from the previous year. The social media audience for Sky News content topped 27 million.

Interestingly, the television audience remained stable over the year, with weekly total viewers up marginally to 5.2 million. John Ryley, head of Sky News, believes that's some achievement given 'the assault on "old" media from the mobile interloper'.

'Remember Riepl's Law: innovations in media add to what went before rather than replacing it – they coexist in antagonistic harmony,' he says. 'The non-stop television news channel is the production spine of our digital services. If we didn't have a TV channel, we would have to invent one. Remember, too, we are living in uncertain times – it's a golden age for journalism.'

But the growing challenge to TV news is clear. I can see that if pictures of a breaking news story or event are up on Facebook or Twitter in an instant, it can make our job seem less valuable.

I can also see how if opinion, reaction and comment on a story is running on social media, you might feel it neutralizes what we do on 24-hour news channels or traditional news bulletins. Your mobile phone means you have it all there in the palm of your hand, wherever you are. It satisfies the trend for news on the go, as it happens; information arrives in an instant – quick-fire, bite-sized, fast and dramatic.

And everyone, of course, can now be a journalist. The era of the 'citizen journalist' is upon us, and in many ways it is no bad thing. It is, I suppose, the democratization of news. Homemade content is everywhere now, and its growth has hugely influenced the style and direction of journalism. But is it a threat to traditional journalism?

Not necessarily. Citizen journalism is not going to replace or displace the mainstream but will rather be complementary to it; it really is not a case of one or the other. It is a case of the established media welcoming and embracing the new and seeing it as an advantage, a huge boost to the job of gathering news. It's the 'antagonistic harmony' that John Ryley talks about.

I mean, what are the chances of a TV news camera happening to be at the scene of a terrorist attack in London, for instance? Relatively low. But what is the likelihood of someone witnessing an attack having a camera on their smartphone? Extremely high. So, increasingly, the first images we see of any such event are invariably from a member of the public who has been caught up in the incident and who managed to record a few seconds of footage. That footage is often first uploaded to a social media site, but it still only gets real traction when it is picked up by the mainstream media and used as part of news coverage.

The advantages are enormous, and for news organizations it represents a real leap forward, but it also poses a serious challenge. The main news broadcasters like the BBC, Sky News and ITN have reputations built on authority, veracity and reliability. By and large they get things broadly right... and if they don't, they go to great lengths to put them right. There will be corrections and apologies if they make a mistake. It is all about reputation and credibility. News organizations rely on it.

But it goes without saying that it is much easier to get things right if you are generating the content yourself. You know where the pictures are from, who took them and what they represent. In other words, you can verify whatever it is you are publishing.

It is absolutely not the case with 'second-hand' material. So, the footage posted on social media may appear to be genuine, and may seem to be images of the event or incident you are interested in. But how do you know for certain? It is sometimes extremely difficult to tell, and there are many examples of footage posted online purporting to be something that it is not. It is a particular problem when it comes to coverage of wars – for instance in Syria, where it is very difficult for Western news teams to get access. It is quite normal in instances like this for producers in newsrooms to scour the Internet for footage of any particular attack. Finding it can be the easy part. Verifying it beyond all reasonable doubt is often virtually impossible.

Once when I was anchoring *News at Ten*, we had video footage of children covered in blood in the rubble of a house, which we were told was the aftermath of an air attack by the Syrian government regime. It looked genuine enough. It was heart-wrenching. We were about to include the images in a report on the programme when a producer realized she had seen very similar images a few months earlier. She checked and discovered the similarities were so great that it would be unwise to run them. She pointed out, for example, that one of the children was dressed in exactly the same way. We didn't include the pictures, and indeed it turned out they were several weeks old and were actually from a previous attack, or alleged attack, in another part of Syria. I noticed other broadcasters did include the images.

This is just one example of the difficulties posed by citizen journalism. How is it possible to discern the truth amid so much propaganda, misinformation, opinion and general noise? In the new digital ecosystem, how is it possible to know what is real news and what – yes, let's say it – is fake news?

Bending the truth is nothing new. The equivalent of today's deliberately erroneous tweets and posts can be found through-out history. Way back in the sixth century AD, the Byzantine historian Procopius revered the Emperor Justinian in official scripts but then secretly released all sorts of dodgy information in his history known as the *Anecdota*, to smear him. In Roman times, Octavian famously deployed disinformation as a weapon to gain victory over Marc Antony. And with modern develop-ments in mass communication, propaganda and fake news grew hugely in scale, particularly during the two World Wars. In the Great War, the British government used propaganda very effectively to rally and motivate the public against the threat of Germany. And, later, the Nazi party used the mass media expertly to build its image and then consolidate its grip on power in Germany during the 1930s. This was largely state-sponsored propaganda.

But in the twenty-first century, the term 'fake news' entered common speech to describe a very real cultural phenomenon: manufactured disinformation spread on the Internet to fool susceptible users. It usually involves small groups of people using social media to gain traction with untrue stories for various reasons. Some creators of fake news have financial motives. They look to use dramatic but totally spurious stories to win an audience for advertisers. But more often it is tied up with politics. The charges against Russian individuals and organizations for meddling in the 2016 US election point at all sorts of fakery going on. They posed as Americans and set up fake political groups, to disseminate often inaccurate information that disparaged the Democratic candidate Hillary Clinton and promoted the Republican, Donald Trump. They created fake Facebook accounts to pump out sometimes false information about contentious issues such as immigration and gay rights. Facebook has confirmed that Russians purchased $100,000 worth of advertising on its site – adverts that reached 126 million users.

Donald Trump used his Twitter feed to spread his own fake news during the US presidential campaign in 2016. He put out his – sometimes ludicrous – conspiracy theories suggesting, among other things, that Ted Cruz's father was involved in the assassination of JFK, that President Obama was not born in the USA and that climate change was a hoax.

His aides were at it, too. His adviser, Kellyanne Conway, went so far as to invent a massacre in Kentucky in order to justify and defend a ban on travellers from a number of Muslim countries. It was simply fake news. It was not true. She also came up with the phrase 'alternative facts' when trying to explain why the White House Press Secretary had claimed bigger crowds were at the Trump inauguration than at the Obama event.

And it all inspired a wildfire of fake news, fuelled and spread by his supporters online. How the Pope was backing Trump, how Hillary was selling weapons to ISIS... on and on it went until fake news was everywhere and false stories became *the* story.

And then, most insidious of all, Trump turned 'fake news' on its head and used it almost as a tool of power. He managed somehow to redefine the term so it became used to dismiss and delegitimize honest reporting by the mainstream media. At his first press conference as president-elect, he refused even to listen to a question from the CNN reporter Jim Acosta. 'You're fake news,' he yelled at him. In the following weeks and months, Trump accused several major media outlets of broadcasting or publishing fake news. It was repugnant. But it stuck, and it gained traction with his supporters. It was also done with some chutzpah, given that the Trump administration itself was pushing out all sorts of 'news' that was demonstrably fake.

The term 'fake news' is nothing but a euphemism for 'lies'. And lying is not good for journalism, which is fundamentally all about the truth. The moment journalism ceases to be about revealing the truth is the moment journalism stops mattering, and that is not worth thinking about. And it seems to me that fake news is the culmination of twenty years of dwindling trust in the establishment, in politics, in the political class and, yes, the media. That is not just bad for politics and journalism; it is bad for democracy.

How did it happen? It began, I think, with the build up to the Iraq War. A routine interview between John Humphrys and the BBC's Andrew Gilligan contained a passing reference to a 'sexed up' dossier. The very suggestion incurred the wrath of Tony Blair's communications director, Alastair Campbell, who launched an all-out assault on the BBC. This led to open warfare between the Beeb and Number 10, out of which all sorts of consequences tumbled, not least the tragic death of Dr David Kelly, a government scientist accused of leaking information to the BBC. It also led to the chairman and director general of the BBC losing their jobs, Tony Blair losing his reputation, and a lack of trust in the government on a matter as fundamentally important as taking the country to war.

The feeling, of course, that so much life and money was wasted on a conflict based on a false premise is hard to shed. But, more broadly, I think it led to a suspicion of government and politicians that has had lasting implications.

Of course, the Iraq War was just one element of the crisis of confidence in the establishment. In the years that followed, we had the scandal over MPs' expenses at a time when the country was facing growing cuts and austerity. We had the financial crash and the banking scandals and the seeming lack of anyone being held to account. And we had the phone hacking revelations, the closure of a major newspaper and the Leveson inquiry, which shone a spotlight into the dark corners of press malpractice and dishonesty.

It has been a corrosive, insidious process, which perhaps almost inevitably led to serious public disillusionment.

So what are we now facing? What we have is a perfect storm battering traditional journalism. We have the rise of sometimes unreliable citizen journalism, we have the emergence of the fake news phenomenon, and to top it all off we have a President of the United States doing his best to undermine mainstream journalism by constantly attacking it. Taken together, they are a real threat.

Now, on the face of it, the proliferation of fake news – the real phenomenon, not the Trump version – is bad for journalism because it undermines people's faith in what they see or read. In the end, consumers just won't know what or who to believe.

But far from making traditional journalism less relevant, fake news actually makes it more important than ever. It has never been more crucial to have trained journalists sifting through and checking and double-checking what is right and what is not.

Social media, at its best, is a convenient, informative and entertaining tool. You can get reliable newsfeeds, see what opinion-formers have to say and be directed to useful blogs and columns. But at its worst, it is a horrible mix of rumour, innuendo, speculation, misleading drivel and downright lies.

So surely it is the job of trained journalists, reporters and foreign correspondents to wade through that mush, that noise, that impenetrable fog of so-called news, to work out what is right, what is fact and what is fit to broadcast.

The role of journalists has always been to bear witness, to be there and to see with our own eyes. Our job is to tell it how it is, as best we can. Eyewitness reporting and analysis is what we are about, not half-baked truths.

The foreign correspondent, who crosses dangerous borders, enters inhospitable countries and reports in good faith what is happening in often perilous circumstances, is as important now as he or she has always been. The reporter who is trusted by the audience and who delivers an unbiased and impartial account of events is still an absolute must in journalism. It has remained a noble concept.

Just think of mainstream journalism as exactly that… a stream. That stream is now developing lots of little tributaries. Some of them feed useful, clean, pure water into the stream. Others, however, deliver toxic, polluted ghastliness that seeks to contaminate and poison. It is the job of traditional journalists to keep the mainstream as pure as possible.

It might all sound rather pompous but it is hugely important. It is startling how some established media have allowed themselves to become polluted. And I don't mean tabloid newspapers whose staple diet is entertainment rather than news. One of the most respected news and current affairs programmes, *Newsnight*, essentially repeated an Internet rumour about Lord McAlpine being a paedophile that was completely untrue. They paid a heavy price. It was a horrible mistake that cost the BBC's director general his job, and cost his organization £185,000 in damages and a lot more besides in terms of its reputation. For a moment, the much-admired *Newsnight* effectively became little more than an extension of Twitter.

When Internet rumour becomes good enough for established broadcasters, we know we are in trouble. Facts are our stock-in-trade, they are all we have to go on and we peddle half-truths and rumour at our peril. If the rigorous checking of information is not carried out, it gives succour to people like President Trump who try to claim that all is not what it seems.

So if there is an opportunity to reassert the importance of traditional journalism, there is also, it seems to me, a business opportunity. Just think about it. In an environment where news is increasingly unreliable and increasingly fake, where all sorts of garbage dressed up as news is washing around, how much more likely is it that people who care, consumers who want news they can rely on, will be prepared to pay for the real thing? I firmly believe that fake news may be the best thing to happen to the purveyors of real news. People may finally cough up for news they can rely on.

There are those who believe the mainstream media's sudden concern about fake news represents a desperate attempt to close down free speech, sanitize the web or in some way police what is published on sites such as Facebook.

Mick Hume, editor-at-large at the online magazine *Spiked*, says the 'top-level panic' about fake news in what he calls the 'post-truth' age is effectively about restricting freedom of speech 'in the name of "defending democracy". It doesn't get much more fake than that.'

And he goes on: 'The big threat facing Western democracy today does not come from a few fake news reports posted by foreign agents or teenagers in their parents' back bedroom. Far more dangerous to democracy are those at the heart of the Western establishment who want to re-educate voters about what they should know and believe, and establish fact-checking "gatekeepers" to limit democratic debate.'

It's an interesting take, but I don't believe the media elite is trying to shut down free speech; I think there is simply a genuine fear of the consequences of people being bombarded with – and, perhaps, believing – stuff that just isn't true.

Of course, there are many countries across the world where leaders despise and fear the very notion of a free, properly functioning media. They try to intimidate, or better still control, the news outlets. In those countries, journalists literally risk their lives trying to cover news and uncover the bad things going on. It seems to me that journalists operating in countries that have a relatively free press owe it to those who don't – to get into those countries, to shine a spotlight into murky corners, and expose and reveal what is really going on.

It is one of the dirty little secrets of the news game that many of the articles, photographs and videos we read or watch are produced by freelance journalists. News organizations are increasingly relying on freelancers – one of the consequences of budget cuts.

The advantages are obvious. The employer often doesn't have to pay salaries, insurance, travel and accommodation costs. Nor is it responsible for providing safety equipment like armoured cars, flak jackets and helmets. So, in other words, news organizations get the reporter on the cheap and bear none of the risks. But it is wrong.

In America, I interviewed Diane Foley, the mother of James Foley, one of the journalists kidnapped in Syria whose beheading was filmed by Islamic State terrorists and released to the world. James was a freelancer who went to dangerous places without the protection, security and insurance a staff photojournalist would expect and receive from their employer. Diane now works tirelessly for improved safety and treatment for freelance conflict journalists.

A few years ago, while working for ITN, I travelled with a cameraman to Mogadishu in Somalia – possibly one of the most dangerous capital cities in the world. We knew that as Westerners we ran a considerable risk of kidnap or worse. We also knew that as Western journalists we were particularly juicy targets for the Islamist militants or the gangs linked to them. We were determined to see for ourselves what was going on there and to report on the dreadful suffering, made so much worse by the conflict that still rages on the edge of the capital. But the innate cowardice that has been my protection in many a war zone through the years meant I would only make the trip if some sort of satisfactory security could be provided.

So we put ourselves in the custody of a local warlord called Bashir, who for a heavy price – $2,000 a day – provided thirty-six tough, battle-hardened and, crucially, heavily armed young men to watch our backs every step of the way. That they did so was, of course, a huge reassurance. That it was necessary is an indication of just how dangerous covering the news has become for journalists. And that we had to resort to such measures is, for me, a cause of considerable sadness, and in a sense guilt.

Sadness, because of what it says about what has happened to our trade. Where once the neutrality and independence of the media was widely recognized and respected, now it's clear journalists are being specifically targeted or sought out by those who fear the truth emerging. It's no longer enough to blame the messenger, it seems. Silencing the messenger is all too often the name of the game.

And guilt because of the glaring inequality that now exists in journalism. I could insist on that security in Somalia, I was insured and had the backup of a large organization with considerable resources which made safety a priority. But freelancers and local reporters working in dangerous countries have no such protection.

Local reporters such as Nur Mohamed Abkey, a veteran journalist in Mogadishu, whose body was found in an alleyway with gunshot wounds and evidence of torture. He was killed, say colleagues, because of his affiliation to a government-run station. He didn't have protection.

And Nasteh Dahir Farah, a freelancer and vice-president of the National Union of Somali Journalists. Recently married, he was shot dead as he was walking home from an Internet café. He didn't have protection, either. A colleague said simply: 'Someone didn't like his reporting.'

Someone didn't like his reporting. Just think about that. Someone didn't like what a journalist had written. So what did they do? They didn't try to put across their side of the story. They didn't attempt to persuade him of the validity of their arguments or their political creed. No, they just shot him dead.

There are many journalists like Nur Mohamed Abkey and Nasteh Dahir Farah in countries all over the world. In places like Mexico, Colombia, Zimbabwe, the Philippines, Iraq, Afghanistan and Pakistan, journalists are regularly murdered because of what they've written or said. Or because of a story they were investigating.

These are reporters who are not dropping in for a few days to cover a story and leave, but rather working and living with the constant threat of intimidation, violence and murder. And these are journalists who are paying the price for getting too close to the truth for some despot's liking. Despite the dangers, they've made a simple and very brave decision. They have decided it is their job to try to tell the truth about what is happening in their country.

These journalists know full well the risks of challenging the government or the militias. But they believe they must challenge, they must hold them to account, because they believe it is the right thing to do. They also know that if they don't, the chances are no one else will.

Meanwhile, the story of twenty-nine-year-old Ali Mustafa, a Canadian photographer, is illustrative of a freelancer's life – and death. I read his story on the website Medium; it was written by Jaron Gilinsky:

In early February... with a sparkling new Nikon, [he was] on his way to Syria. Ali crossed the border from Turkey and had the good (journalistic) fortune of being the only Western journalist in Hadariya, a rebel-controlled neighborhood of Aleppo. Thanks to his exclusive access, he sold photos by the dozen to [the photo agencies] EPA and SIPA, which were splashed on the front pages of the *Guardian* and *The Times* of London. On March 9th a government helicopter dropped a barrel bomb on a residential building. According to witnesses Ali went into the destroyed building with some young activists to try and rescue survivors. Suddenly, the chopper swooped back around and dropped another bomb. Ali's luck had run out. At the age of 29, on his second professional reporting trip, he was killed alongside seven Syrians.

So young… It was a story that filled me with sadness when I read it. But more than anything, it filled me with anger. As Gillinsky writes:

Nobody called Ali's family to notify them of his death. His sister found out through a photo uploaded by an activist on Facebook. His face was charred, but unmistakably his. Ali had no liability or life insurance policy when he was killed. The Turkish and Qatari Red Crescents recovered the corpse and transported it back to Turkey. His mother, who runs a small cleaning service, paid the Canadian government 6500 Canadian dollars to coordinate the repatriation, plus another 8000 for a flight and 7000 for the funeral. When all was said and done, Ali's family was more than 20,000 dollars in debt.

Now, there was no legal obligation for any of the news organizations he supplied to help his family financially or in any other way. But what sort of trade is it that treats its own like that? Things have to change.

Most obviously, there should be a recognized insurance policy for freelancers, and news organizations and agencies should contribute to the cost while the freelancer is providing for them. It really is a small price to pay.

We tend to think that most journalists who are killed are caught in the crossfire, or just happen to be in the wrong place at the wrong time. Some are, it is true, and their deaths are no less regrettable for that. But the horrific truth is that more than 70 per cent of the journalists killed in the last two decades were murdered in cold blood. And here is the scandalous statistic: in 80 per cent of those cases – yes, 80 per cent – the killers were not brought to justice.

So what we have are police and security forces who do not take the murders of journalists seriously – or worse, who are complicit in those murders themselves. It is nothing less than state-sanctioned killing and it is an outrage.

We journalists – all of us – share a belief that news and the spread of information is the foundation of democracy. We share a belief that good journalism should call bad governments to account. We share a belief that good journalism is about exposing abuse of power, corruption and malpractice, and not letting it go unmonitored and unchecked, unknown, unpublicized and untold. We share all these beliefs about our trade. But increasingly, such journalism and such beliefs come at a very high price; and, let's be honest, very few of us are prepared to pay it... and why should we have to?

When journalists are deliberately targeted and killed, it is a crime. When it happens during a conflict, it is a war crime. It is as simple as that, and governments and regimes around the world need to recognize it. Because at the moment it is difficult to be optimistic. If bad people in bad regimes see journalists can be killed with impunity, what hope is there?

It happened to my great friend and colleague Mick Deane,

a lovable bear of a man and a top-quality cameraman who guided me around the world's trouble spots in my early years as a foreign correspondent. He was shot and killed by what was assumed to be an Egyptian military sniper in 2013. He was filming with his team from Sky News outside the Rabaa mosque in eastern Cairo, where Egyptian security forces had just massacred hundreds of protestors. He was almost certainly deliberately killed.

As his wife, Daniela, wrote afterwards: 'Mick was an easy target... He was big and blond in a sea of protesters, hauling a bulky television camera. I think the security forces just got tired of seeing him there. So they decided to kill him. Not that I'll ever know for sure. They've never admitted it, of course.'

Three Egyptian journalists, including a twenty-six-year-old woman, were also killed that day. The security forces probably didn't want the story of the massacre to be told. So they shot and killed journalists. They murdered Mick. Yes, it was murder, of course it was, even though the coroner did not have the evidence to call it that. It was a murder carried out with total impunity. And that is a disgrace. But that is what happens when bad regimes do bad things they do not want publicized.

Before working with me, Mick had partnered another friend of mine, the foreign correspondent turned Sky News anchor Jeremy Thompson, and they became very close. After Mick's death, Thompson wrote: 'Mick Deane died as he lived, doing his best. Doing his best to open the eyes of the world to injustice.'

Mick was all of those things and more. He had great wisdom too, and experience. When I was a young Asia correspondent, he really was my guiding hand. He knew when to go on a story and when not to go. He would know which airline to fly, where to stay, who to talk to, who to trust and who to ignore. He would know drivers, local fixers and who you could rely on. He also knew how to enjoy himself. Boy, did he know how to do that.

I spoke at his memorial service and said: 'He was an "everything will be fine" man, and when you're an insecure, uncertain novice trying to make your way in this game, he was utterly indispensable.'

But Mick also knew the dangers of places like Egypt. He knew journalists are targets in many places around this world. He knew the risks. So much so that, at sixty-one, he was about to retire to the lakeside home in Italy he had built with Daniela. My heart aches for her. I really miss him.

Reporting has never been a safe profession, but what's changed is that nowadays journalists are regarded as targets, as fair game, as an extension of Western governments. Correspondents and aid workers are slaughtered on camera by barbaric Islamic State fighters who see the reporters as no different from enemy soldiers. It is a perilous job; more perilous than ever before.

And one reason is that modern technology in TV news allows us to broadcast, live if we choose to, closer to conflict zones than ever before. In the world of 24/7 breaking news, it is all about being live as it happens, at the scene, up to the minute. Exciting, breathless and edgy reporting from the front line as the bullets and the rocket-propelled grenades fly. Get that sound. Get that picture. Get it all. Because if we don't, the opposition will.

But wait, stop a moment, let's pause and think. Just because you can, doesn't always mean you should. Covering any conflict is dangerous, but as we've witnessed recently, covering conflicts and uprisings can be particularly difficult when there are no clear front lines and certainly no rules. The bravery of many journalists goes without saying, but it is perhaps important that the expectations placed upon them, or which they place upon themselves, do not expose them to an unnecessary level of danger.

And I see other reasons to worry. Rigorous cost-cutting within the media means there are fewer overseas-based correspondents who build up real experience on their patch. Instead, there is an increasing tendency to use so-called parachute correspondents, who are less able to assess dangerous situations in conflict-affected areas. I know, because I was one for several years. They do not have the same connections or contacts or knowledge, and will be more inclined to make errors of judgement. These are serious issues.

For me, the great sadness of television news at the moment is that just as we reach a golden age in terms of technology, allowing news to be delivered much more quickly and in so many different ways, the budgets for covering news are contracting.

I can see a future with less and less foreign reporting, proper journalism, eyewitness reporting across the world. Getting into where the story is, establishing for yourself what is going on and producing original pictures and script to inform the viewer.

Blank-canvas journalism is being there, finding out and discovering, and reporting what you find. No bias, no slant, no preconceptions, no agenda, no prejudice. It is pure journalism

– the hardest sort of journalism, because often it is in parts of the world that are difficult, expensive and dangerous to reach.

It is the kind of journalism practised by the John Simpsons, John Irvines, Bill Neelys, Lyse Doucets, Lindsay Hilsums, Jeremy Bowens and Alex Crawfords of this world. They are among the great exponents of blank-canvas journalism still on our screens. But for how long?

The balance of power is already shifting towards the news presenter as a personality. It is sometimes almost as if the person delivering the news is more important than the news itself. Some clearly think they are. The best news anchors are journalists first and celebrities second, if at all.

It really is ironic that it is so much easier to get your journalism out there, and yet smaller budgets mean there is less journalism being done. And if broadcast news is facing unprecedented challenges, then technological changes and cost-cutting are leaving many newspapers staring at extinction.

More than 170 local titles have closed in the UK in the last ten years, as readership is eroded by other sources of news and local media groups face declining advertising revenue and sales. It is immensely sad. The local newspaper where I began my career, the *Bournemouth Echo* (as it is now known), still survives, but in a radically altered environment – and for how long?

Local newspapers are an essential part of the journalistic food chain, with reporters in local communities playing a crucial role. They not only allow communities to know what is going on locally, but they also offer real democratic value. The presence of a journalist at a local council meeting, for example, makes local politicians more accountable and keeps tab on their behaviour.

And the same is happening to local newspapers in the United States. David Simon, the creator of the crime series *The Wire* and a former reporter on the *Baltimore Sun*, put his fears very clearly: 'The next ten or fifteen years in this country are going to be a halcyon era for state and local political corruption,' he said. 'It's going to be one of the great times to be a corrupt politician. I really envy them.'

His point, of course, being that as the number of journalists scrutinizing a politician's every move declines, so the opportunity to misbehave increases.

The British satirist on US TV, John Oliver, was even more colourful: 'Not having reporters at government meetings is like a teacher leaving her room of seventh graders to supervise themselves. Best-case scenario, Britney gets gum in her hair. Worst-case scenario, you no longer have a school.'

Many newspapers are slowly moving to an online presence to try to make money. But as Oliver points out, there's the danger of 'the temptation to graduate to what gets the most clicks. News organizations badly need to have leaders who appreciate that what's popular is not always what's most important.' Precisely.

The fact is, as I argued earlier, people are going to have to get used to paying for reliable news. Or, as John Oliver says, 'we are all going to pay for it.'

In his book, *We Chose to Speak of War and Strife*, the BBC's estimable John Simpson mourns the passing of the era of the great foreign correspondent. He writes about the *Daily Express* newspaper, which for around fifty years boasted one of the world's great stables of foreign correspondents: 'As late as 1968 thirty-five correspondents were still based around the world for the *Express*... By the early nineties the *Express* had one.'

His name was John Ellison; and eventually, says Simpson, 'he had to go too'. Just before Ellison left the *Express*, they met by chance at Heathrow Terminal 4, both on their way to different stories somewhere in the world. They spoke briefly and then went their separate ways. Simpson writes: 'I remember thinking I was saying goodbye to the last old-style foreign correspondent... shrewd, literate, good at languages, stylish, distinctly steely beneath the civilised exterior.'

So, given all of the above, do I feel pessimistic about the future of journalism? In some ways I do; it is pretty clear that the era of the foreign correspondent, blessed with the resources, support and, above all, time to do the job, is coming to an end. They are increasingly seen as an expensive luxury, and the contracting budgets of the major networks in America and the UK, and of the world's leading newspapers, mean they are being faded out fast.

Now, that is bad for journalists, for consumers, for accountability and for democracy. But on the other hand, there is no better time to be a journalist. This is in so many ways a golden age: there is more news, it travels more quickly and in so many different forms. It is analysed more quickly and delivered more quickly. While consumption of TV news is in slow decline, people are consuming news online in increasing numbers. It is not unusual for original, dramatic and interesting content to get millions of hits.

So journalism has to adapt to the new world, and part of that involves finding a way to get people to pay for it. This is the big challenge of our time for journalism. The BBC licence-fee model and the advertising model on commercial TV still sustain. But not for long. If a way can be found to more lucratively monetize online news, then I think the future is bright.

But, most important of all, the news needs to be right or it's dead. The truth matters. Now, perhaps, more than ever. Because, as I've observed across the pond over the past twelve months, the truth is under siege.

AND FINALLY... FROM TRUMPTOWN

A T 7.19 A.M. on Saturday, 6 January 2018, the phone by
my bedside sounded an alert. Donald Trump had sent out
the first of three tweets that, even by his standards, beggared
belief.

He had decided to address a question that was fast surfacing
in Washington: his mental fitness for office. Just a year into his
presidency, and this is what it had come to. This is what he said:
'Actually, throughout my life, my two greatest assets have been
mental stability and being, like, really smart... I went from
VERY successful businessman, to top T.V. Star, to President of
the United States (on my first try). I think that would qualify as
not smart, but genius... and a very stable genius at that!'

I honestly thought his Twitter account had been hacked. But
no, it really was Trump. He was reacting to the publication
of a book by Michael Wolff, *Fire and Fury: Inside the Trump
White House*. In it, Wolff claims that many of those close to the
president, including his former chief strategist Steve Bannon,
were openly questioning his fitness for office.

It is a wholly unflattering tome that depicts the president
as a childlike, ignorant, unread, impulsive, self-obsessed, fast-
food-devouring egomaniac. It was described as 'sensational',

'shocking' and even as 'the book that will bring down the president'. It was actually no such thing. Trump would have done better to ignore it.

But, most significantly, it did bring talk about the president's mental stability and fitness for office out into the open. Suddenly, it became part of the accepted discourse of the mainstream media.

Previously, it was only his Twitter enemies and his more extreme political opponents who were talking about the possibility of invoking the 25th Amendment, the constitutional provision by which the Cabinet and then Congress can vote to remove the president if he's deemed to be incapable of doing his job.

Up until this point, a group of Democrats in Congress had introduced legislation to force the president to submit to psychological evaluation, and a number of mental health professionals signed a petition calling for his removal from office after one of them wrote a book called *The Dangerous Case of Donald Trump: 27 Psychiatrists Assess a President*. But that was about it. It could all have been easily dismissed as armchair diagnosis and politically motivated character assassination.

With the publication of Wolff's book, that seemed to change. And it changed in large part because of Donald Trump himself. By engaging with the issue in his tweets on that Saturday morning, he risked, in a way, giving substance – even credibility – to the charge. Or, at the very least, he was giving the story 'legs', as we say in journalism.

He was guaranteeing that his fitness for office was *the* story of the next few days, and I remember thinking to myself that a 'very stable genius' would probably not have done that. There can be no upside for a president when the story is his own mental capacity to serve.

Questions about presidential mental health are nothing new. Abraham Lincoln was diagnosed with depression; John F. Kennedy took prescription drugs for anxiety; Lyndon B. Johnson was investigated for paranoid disintegration. But in all these cases, the details remained shrouded in secrecy for many years.

With Trump, it is not only in the public domain, but he encouraged it to be so with his bizarre tweets. Where was the benefit for him in doing this? What was the strategy? I simply couldn't understand it.

The criticism in the book, whether accurate, semi-accurate or plain untrue, obviously hit a nerve – and, Trump being Trump, he couldn't help himself. He had to lash out. It's who he is and what he instinctively does. Indeed, he went further and asked the White House doctor to undertake cognitive testing during what was supposed to be a purely physical health check.

The doctor, Dr Ronny Jackson, subsequently held a very odd press conference in which the very first questions from the media were about Donald Trump's mental fitness for office. He reassured everybody that there was no cause for concern. But, once again, Trump had ensured that the question of his mental acuity was right up there at the top of the media agenda. It was utterly bizarre.

In any case, the talk about invoking the 25th Amendment is way off the mark. It would require something far more serious than currently exists to provoke such a move. It is really designed to deal with cases where the president is so out of it that he is in no shape whatsoever to even agree to hand over authority. Whatever Trump's detractors may wish for, we are, as I write at least, a million miles from that. It is highly unlikely to happen.

The amendment was introduced in the wake of John F. Kennedy's assassination and the debilitating illnesses suffered by Dwight Eisenhower. It would need a crisis on that level to be enacted. And, politically, it is very difficult to see it happening. Before Congress even gets to vote on it, the vice president (personally selected by Trump) would have to call a vote of the Cabinet (personally selected by Trump), and a majority would have to agree he was no longer fit or able to be president. Only then would Congress assemble, and two-thirds of both the House and Senate would have to vote to remove the president.

It is such a high bar that it can virtually be ruled out. Trump should have ignored the whole issue about his fitness to serve, just as he should have ignored the Wolff book. But his tactic in response to the book was to write it off as 'fake news' and as part of the broader media conspiracy to undermine the presidency: 'Michael Wolff is a total loser who made up stories in order to sell this really boring and untruthful book...' he tweeted. He also threatened the publishers with legal action and injunctions.

By now, Trump's war with the media was reaching an alarming intensity. His 'fake news' taunts became unrelenting and unedifying. To be fair to Trump, his hostility to the media does have its roots in a genuine grievance. By and large, they cut him no slack whatsoever. The television mainstream media, in particular, has become tribal in its criticism. He can do no right.

Trump made a calculation. He would try not only to sidetrack the mainstream media, but he would, at every opportunity, seek to discredit it. It is the reason why 'fake news' has become his most oft-repeated mantra. And not only in the campaign, but since he entered the White House, too.

Major Garrett, the chief White House correspondent for CBS News, believes Trump is simply exploiting a disillusionment with the traditional media that had set in long before he became president: 'The mainstream media has had a credibility problem for some time now. Politicians and ordinary people have ceased to believe it in the same way that they used to… Donald Trump is driving that through more powerfully than any other president in recent American history.'

Trump's weapon of choice is Twitter. He's good at it, and it has become my morning wake-up call in Washington. You can rely on it. Pretty much every day, at around 7 a.m., the Trump stream of consciousness starts flowing.

He uses Twitter to rage, to vent his obsessions, to proclaim the success of existing policies and to hint at new ones, foreign and domestic, that he may or may not follow through on.

Make no mistake, there is method in the madness. He and his team are clever in the way they use social media. Trump uses it to test an idea, to distract from an issue that is not playing well for him, and to set his own narrative for the news day ahead. And, broadly speaking, it works.

But it only works because the media allows it to. A relatively small number of Americans use Twitter on a regular basis.

Therefore, what Trump is actually doing is using his Twitter feed to reach journalists who he knows will relay the Trumpian thought for the day to their readers, viewers or listeners.

And the more inflammatory the thought, the greater the certainty it will dominate the day's news agenda. Trump is using the news media he so despises, and the media is indulging a president they have contempt for.

The press must take some of the blame here. By allowing themselves to be complicit in this media madness, they are letting Trump off the hook. By lapping up his Twitter pronouncements, they do not expose the President of the United States to any meaningful cross-examination. It is an exchange consisting of bad-tempered contempt and criticism. The Twitter feed is replacing the press conference, and this is bad for journalism and certainly bad for democracy.

The problem is that studiously repeating and amplifying every Trump tweet simply confers more power on him and it allows him to control the news cycle so effortlessly. It is the stuff of the expert PR manipulator, the marketing guru or the persistent sales person and the media is often complicit in his clever use of it.

Donald Trump is by no means the first president to have an adversarial relationship with the media. The difference with Trump is that he seems not to believe in the fundamental role that a free press plays in democracy, and he actually threatens that role by spending a fair proportion of his time working to delegitimize the media.

It is one thing to despise the press. There are many reasons why Trump would want to do that. It has, for one, become unmerciful in its criticism of him. But it is quite another thing to work actively to undermine it to the extent that it is no longer believed.

President Obama often had a tricky relationship with the media, but in his final news conference he said this:

> I have enjoyed working with all of you. That does not, of course, mean that I've enjoyed every story that you have filed, but that's the point of this relationship. You're not supposed to be sycophants, you're supposed to be sceptics, you're supposed to ask me tough questions. You're not supposed to be complimentary, but you're supposed to cast a critical eye on folks who hold enormous power and make sure that we are accountable to the people who sent us here And you have done that.

And George W. Bush was equally understanding, saying: 'I consider the media to be indispensable to democracy. We need an independent media to hold people like me to account. Power can be very addictive and it can be corrosive, and it's important for the media to call to account people who abuse their power.'

Now, compare those quotes to any number of Trump's tweets on this issue. For instance, this one:

'The FAKE NEWS media (failing @nytimes, @NBCNews, @ABC, @CBS, @CNN) is not my enemy, it is the enemy of the American People!'

These are inflammatory words, and I am not sure that Donald Trump realizes the impact of what he tweets. In fact, shortly afterwards, staff at CNN received death threats from a man who said he would come to the CNN HQ and 'gun' them all down. The implications of a president demonizing journalists are frightening.

Jeff Flake, a Republican senator, pointed out in a speech from the Senate floor that it was Stalin who first used the phrase 'enemy of the people'. And there is a serious point to be made here. The president's 'fake news' onslaught is for domestic consumption. But it is also heard around the world, and it will comfort autocrats and dictators who do not tolerate any free speech, criticism or independent media. They will point to the United States, the supposed bulwark of democracy, and say 'journalists are bad people, untruthful and unreliable. It's fake news. The president says so.' How convenient for despots that is.

This is not theoretical, either. Flake made the point that the Syrian president Bashar al-Assad brushed off an Amnesty International report as a forgery. 'We are living in a fake news era,' Assad said. The president of the Philippines has also complained of being 'demonized' by 'fake news'; and, said Flake, a state official in Myanmar recently said, 'There is no such thing as Rohingya. It is fake news,' referring to the persecuted minority in that country.

And a president – especially one who, on a daily basis, accuses others of dissembling – probably shouldn't be a habitual purveyor of untruths himself. But that is Trump. All presidents speak untruths at some time or another, I am sure of it. But Trump is of a different order of mendacity. And it eats away at democracy.

As Jeff Flake said: 'The impulses underlying the dissemination of such untruths are not benign. They have the effect of eroding trust in our vital institutions and conditioning the public to no longer trust them. The destructive effect of this kind of behaviour on our democracy cannot be overstated.'

There are clear signs that Trump's attacks on the media are playing well with his support base, who have taken to holding aloft 'Fake News' placards in front of the cameras at Trump rallies. I saw them myself at an event for the Trump-backed candidate for the Senate, Roy Moore, in Alabama. The rally was addressed by Trump's former chief strategist Steve Bannon, who also picked out certain journalists in the room and ridiculed them in front of his baying followers. It was unsettling and dangerous. Many is the time I have been interviewing Trump supporters around the country, and they precede any comments they make with the accusation that we will misrepresent what they say because we are all 'fake news' anyway.

That a hypersensitive American president should seek to diminish and discredit one of the fundamental freedoms enshrined by the nation's founders is pretty remarkable; but it is utterly astonishing that millions of his conservative supporters across the county are so blithely complicit in and tolerant of such behaviour.

It is possible to see a scenario where if Trump's presidency starts to look like it is doomed, if his poll numbers plummet further and he finds it even more difficult to get legislation through, he will have a readymade scapegoat... the media.

But the irony in all this is that Trump is, broadly speaking, good for business. Ratings are up across the news networks and 24-hour channels. CNN trumpeted a 'ratings milestone' in 2017, earning its highest viewing figures on record; it was also the most-watched year for Fox News, the Trump-supporting network owned by Rupert Murdoch. And MSNBC saw the biggest gains in viewership of all the cable news networks. The *New York Times* also benefited from its best revenue growth in many years.

The prize in Washington was to get the first interview with President Trump for a British broadcaster. We tried on several occasions, as I am sure did the BBC and ITN. But the White House never really seemed interested in challenging interviews, and certainly not with non-American networks. In the end – despite months of effort – I was scooped by Piers Morgan. Now that is not a sentence I ever imagined writing and it actually brings me considerable pain to do so. But that is what happened.

A few weeks before heading to the States I was playing golf with Morgan and he said the interview was already in the bag. 'Not in doubt,' he said, as I stood hunched over a crucial putt. 'Only a matter of when.' It was annoying but Morgan and the president are old friends from when Piers took part in and, inexplicably, won a celebrity version of Trump's reality TV show, *The Apprentice*. Piers basically curried favour on Twitter as only he can, and his fawning posts came up trumps, so to speak. I found the grace within me to congratulate him by text. 'Thanks, mate,' he replied. 'I told you I'd get it hahaha. I'll get the next one too. Just to annoy you.' Nice. And he quite probably will. There was certainly nothing in the first one to unduly trouble Mr Trump!

The truth is, the Trump train is still intact, still on the tracks and may remain so for some time. A senior British diplomat in Washington is certainly of the opinion that there is an increasingly clear route to two terms of Trump: 'If the economy keeps roaring along and the Democrats don't get their act together, it is more likely than not that this Trump presidency could last eight years,' he told me. 'I think we need to be planning for that.'

The point is this... Over the first year, there has been media focus on the president's temperament, judgement and character, all of which do not make him an ideal president. But that is an incomplete picture of the Trump presidency, and it is in some ways a distraction from what he is getting done. It is unfair to Trump not to consider his achievements, and they are considerable.

They relate mainly to the economy, which since he has been in office has been firing on all cylinders. Growth is well up on the average for the eight years that Obama was in office. The stock market is coming off record highs, but the economic fundamentals remain very strong and unemployment is down to a sixteen-year low. Manufacturers are more optimistic than they have been for many years. Many big companies, such as Walmart and Apple, are promising more spending and more jobs. Trump is claiming he is already turning America around, and with some justification.

Most economists say that the economic performance during the first year of any presidency is largely down to his predecessor, but Trump should get the credit for good economic news going forward.

And Trump is also desperately trying to keep his promises to his supporters. He had six clear priorities when he was on the campaign trail: he said he would cut taxes, pull out of the Paris climate change accord, try to renegotiate the North American

Free Trade Agreement (NAFTA), deregulate the government and industry, move the US embassy in Israel to Jerusalem and build the wall on the border with Mexico.

He has done, is doing, or is trying to do all of them. He has also kept his promise about the Supreme Court, putting conservative judges in place, which will have a lasting impact.

Strangely, a booming economy normally translates into good poll numbers. But Trump has a problem here... people don't seem to credit him. A former Clinton adviser, James Carville, famously coined the phrase, 'It's the economy, stupid.' What he meant was that it has always been the state of the economy that ultimately determines the way people vote. In other words, other issues are on the sidelines. When it comes to putting a tick in that box, the overwhelming consideration is the economy.

Trump will worry that the connect between the economy and the presidency seems to have been broken – although his approval ratings are ticking upwards.

And polling numbers are one thing; an actual election is quite another. It may well be that if the economy continues to thrive, that when it actually comes down to it people would be prepared to vote for Trump again in 2020. But Trump being Trump, he even drives his own staff to distraction sometimes.

In a stage-managed opportunity to talk up the impact of his tax reform measures, they sent him to a cylinder factory outside Cincinnati in Ohio. They wrote a speech explaining how many of the workers there had received big bonuses as a result of the corporate tax cuts.

Mid-speech, he broke away from the autocue and started berating Democratic lawmakers who didn't applaud him during his State of the Union address. He called them 'treasonous' and 'un-American'. It was guaranteed to grab all the headlines, and it did. The exasperation and frustration of his speechwriters can only be imagined.

Trump had figured that calling the Democrats un-American would play well with his support. But Republicans as a whole see the economy as the clincher in the mid-term elections, not Trump's 'treason' comments, which would probably have alienated more people than they won over.

The Trump presidency is proving the most extraordinary of modern times. It is astonishing to watch it unfold first-hand, and I honestly have no idea how or when it will end. There are some here who believe he is doing lasting damage to some areas of government, the environment and the judicial system. Elizabeth Drew, the veteran observer of the Washington scene, says: 'Nixon was bad, but this guy is so corrupt and greedy and oblivious to the norms of democratic governing that the Trump/Russia scandal could be more threatening than Watergate.'

Having lived in America for a year now, it seems to me this country is not a happy place. Hopelessly divided, angry, insular, polarized, unequal and, above all, fearful. There are many representations of the angst and the unhappiness in American society. The horrific and almost weekly mass shootings in schools and churches, the opioid crisis, the racial tensions in part caused by the police shootings of unarmed black men, the continuing allegations of sexual harassment and the unfolding narrative of powerful men and predatory behaviour, the growing income inequality, and the sense of pessimism that pervades many working-class areas where jobs have been lost and hope has evaporated.

President Obama must take at least some of the blame. Ten years ago he came into office offering such hope and optimism despite the global economic crisis. I was in the United States at the time and there was joy among the centre and left, who genuinely felt that America was on the verge of something special. He was a popular president who managed the recession with skill, but his rhetoric scaled much greater heights than his actual achievements, and he battled with Congress and struggled to get things done.

And then came Mr Trump. Maybe we should think of him as a symptom rather than a cause. Maybe we should view Trump as the political manifestation of the angst that prevailed and still prevails here. For it is difficult to believe that, in any other election in modern times, Trump could have won the nomination of the Republican Party, let alone the presidency. A non-politician who has never served in the military, he would have had little chance. He also benefited from a particularly poor performance from his Democrat opponent, Hillary Clinton.

So, unlikely as it may have been, this is his time. He has real populist appeal just when America's broader mindset is disillusionment with mainstream and establishment politicians. And he has a chance to put in place policies that could lift many of his blue-collar supporters out of their workless despair. He could find ways to do it.

He's trying to get a massive infrastructure spend through Congress, though his heart doesn't seem to be in it. He's also kept a campaign promise to impose tariffs on steel and aluminium imports. Cheap steel dumped by China has cost thousands of jobs in America.

It may be that his tax cuts will help the process, improve the mood and lift the spirits here. There are signs that they seem to be having the intended effect – they're boosting corporate earnings, stoking investment, and in some companies, they are trickling down to workers in the form of higher wages. But it does look as if, over the long term, higher earners will proportionally get a bigger tax cut than lower earners, and that will only worsen income equality here.

And this goes to the heart of the problem in America, and of the big challenge that faces President Trump. For a vast number of Americans, the whole idea of rising living standards, which has defined this country for so long, is no longer a real prospect. While 90 per cent of children born in 1940 ended up earning more than their parents, only 40 per cent of those born in 1980 have done so. And expectations are worsening. In a 2016 poll, only 38 per cent of Americans thought their children would be better off than they themselves are.

Now, income inequality has long been tolerated in the US because of the high levels of social mobility. It is the combination that gave rise to the American dream. Yet today the opportunity to live the American dream is much less widespread.

Interestingly, a John Hopkins University study found that poor black and Hispanic people are much more likely than poor white people to report that they live better than their parents did. Low-income whites are seeing the erosion of the American dream.

There are many reasons for that. Technology and automation threw millions out of manufacturing jobs, and many have not retrained or found new work in the service industries. They now exist in decaying towns where depression, drug-taking and suicide are on the increase. The combination of shrinking blue-collar jobs and a readily available supply of drugs such as heroin and fentanyl is a lethal one. In some areas, there has been a significant increase in premature mortality.

Carol Graham, author of *Happiness for All?: Unequal Hopes and Lives in Pursuit of the American Dream*, says, 'Desperate people are more likely to die prematurely, but living with a lot of premature death can also erode hope.' She paints a bleak picture.

And those people who are suffering eroded hope are the very people who Donald Trump has identified and is promising to help. The danger for the president is that by playing to the fears – and, it has to be said, the prejudices of his base – he may simply be contributing to the sense of decay in some parts of America.

His cynicism and rage may fuel the anger of his supporters and satisfy his core support, but it leaves much of the country depressed and anxious about the political direction their country is taking. The language of politics has become coarsened and hate-filled and intolerant, and any sense of common purpose and bipartisanship appears to have been sidelined.

But Trump's 'Make America Great Again' mantra also hints at optimism. The official theme of his first State of the Union address, in January 2018, was our 'new American moment', as he called it. And what made the speech work was the way he brought into it the heart-lifting stories of the carefully chosen American heroes who attended the set-piece event and who seemed genuinely moved by the applause and the standing ovations they received.

These were the 'forgotten men and women' who Trump promised to help during the election campaign – the army sergeant who rescued a wounded comrade in Syria; the North Korean defector who limped to freedom on his crutches; and the parents of two teenage girls murdered by the notorious MS-13 street gang.

It proved to be one of Trump's triumphs. He delivered it well and it struck a chord. In the days after the State of the Union, his approval ratings shot up and the Republicans reduced the Democrats' lead in generic polling for the midterm elections.

The speech also reinforced Trump's strategy of an economic nationalism that promises higher minimum wages, increased government spending and restrictions on trade and immigration. If it works, and President Trump can improve the lives of the people putting their faith in him to do so, it will be the making of his presidency. It will certainly be among the most important measures of it.

One of the world's leading economists, Kenneth Rogoff, certainly thinks Trump's economic policies have some merit. 'The policies are not as crazy as the person,' he said.

When I travelled across Alabama, in December 2017, I found young people in desperate need of work and who trusted Trump to deliver. Most said they were prepared to give him a chance, but if he didn't produce jobs, higher wages and cuts in immigration they would look elsewhere.

And that is quite possibly what is happening across America. The country has entered a new political era of voter discontent and unlikely election victories. Nothing is normal anymore. The American dream is over for many of this country's citizens, and more and more of them are angry about it. It is partly what won the election for Trump.

But the big question is whether the president can deliver on his promises to the disaffected who voted for him. The tax cuts may not do it. He needs to deliver jobs and hope, too. Re-establishing the coal and steel industries to their former glory is unrealistic; and there is a question whether his tariffs and protectionism will help, and whether that infrastructure plan will materialize.

It is too early to say and as with all presidents, delivery will be the key. But here's the point: if Donald Trump fails to make life better for those who voted for him it will be a similarly discontented electorate in future elections. They will be seeking an alternative, maybe even the polar opposite. It seems un-American and unlikely, but it could be a left-of-centre Democrat as the next president. Stranger things have happened.

I am writing this at the end of a few weeks that have been truly breathtaking, even by the standards of the Trump administration. And it sums up the helter-skelter world of this White House.

In just over a month, Trump has yanked the United States out of the Iran nuclear deal that almost everyone, including the International Atomic Energy Agency, said was working; he's slapped swingeing tariffs on steel imports from key allies; he's held a historic summit in Singapore with North Korea's Kim Jong Un, a brutal dictator whom he described as 'funny, smart, and talented'; and he's ordered children to be separated from illegal immigrant parents and then rescinded the order after pictures appeared of children sleeping in cages in makeshift detention centres.

There you have it. A few weeks in Trumptown, in all its mercurial, aggressive, audacious, bold, shameless, heartless and offensive glory.

There is pervading Washington a constant sense that something is coming, relating to the investigations and court cases. Ask Washington insiders what it is and they can't answer, other than to say that it could be Russia or just as likely a very persistent porn star.

Whatever you say, Donald J. Trump has shaken things up in a country with a complacent and virtually moribund system of politics, where money, lobbyists and establishment long-servers dominate, and presidents of both political persuasions find it increasingly difficult to get anything done. He's seized on issues ignored by politicians for years: poverty, the costs of industrial decline and immigration, drug addiction and the struggles of working-class whites.

He has also played to the dark side of populism – indulging racists and bigots, insulting opponents, summarily discarding senior advisers who don't agree with him – and he has done so in a bullying and mean-spirited style. He has vulgarized the public dialogue.

But in so doing he's also woken up America. His actions have re-energized the Democrats, galvanized the #metoo movement, more women than ever are standing for political office, and

America's students are organizing and agitating over guns like never before. The conservative author David Frum traces a 'new spirit of citizen responsibility' to Trump's election in 2016. Trump, in fact, may well have been exactly what America needed.

The other day, I found myself at a big Washington social event attended by some notable Democrats. The conversation was all about how terrible 'it' is. How unprecedented. How disastrous. How shameful. How difficult it would be for America to recover. How 'it' was doing lasting damage to American institutions, the courts, the criminal justice system and the environment. It was almost as if they couldn't bring themselves to say the words President and Trump consecutively.

I understood what they were saying. But, heading home, I began to wonder whether their sense of crisis was a little exaggerated, whether, rather than representing an existential threat to America, Trump is, at worse, just another of the periodically recurring maladies of American public life. After all, this country, with all its optimism and hope, always manages to move forwards and not back.

America has survived mad presidents and bad presidents. It has survived slavery, civil war, segregation, the Great Depression, the Second World War, McCarthyism and Nixon's Watergate. It has survived much worse than Donald J. Trump, for goodness' sake.

It's possible, I suppose, that, ultimately, the current sense of foreboding will pass and America will reset its politics to normal. Or even, having had this shock to the system, normal-plus. Whether it's four years or eight years of Trump, the country may one day look back and think the magnitude 8 political earthquake, the upending of everything, the challenge to orthodoxy, the chaos and enduring sense for many of national embarrassment, may actually have been worth it.

Or maybe not…

ACKNOWLEDGEMENTS

T HANKS FOR THIS book go to many people but not least Derek Wyatt, who, in a chance conversation near Sloane Square, suggested Will Atkinson as a publisher. Thanks, of course, to Will and to everyone at Atlantic Books, in particular, their thoughtful and persistent editor James Nightingale. The book was vastly improved by him and by Gemma Wain, who cast her eye for style and accuracy over a manuscript badly in need of both. Thanks to my endlessly patient and talented camera-men, Andy Rex, Mick Deane (God rest his soul), Jon Steele, Eugene Campbell, Mike Inglis, Mark Nelson, Tony Hemmings, Mickey Lawrence, Ben England and Dave Harman, among many others, who have searched memories and memory sticks for badly needed detail. Their power of recall was on the whole far more valuable than mine. I am grateful, too, to my agent, Anita Land, for gently encouraging me to do it and to my father, Mike, for bullying me into doing it.

Thanks to John Ryley at Sky News for paying me to go to Washington DC to watch Trump close-up for a year, and for providing the Georgetown apartment in which most of this book was written. In DC, Elizabeth Drew was generous with her time and her opinions, which have been formed over a long and distinguished journalistic career. Our fizz-fuelled chats were indispensable. Others in DC were gracious with their off-the-record briefings. They know who they are.

I also must thank the team at Sky News in Washington, Emily Purser and Cordelia Lynch for their thoughts and patience and Duncan Sharp and Dickon Mager for retrieving my manuscript when lost or misplaced on my laptop. Thanks, too, to Laura Brander, Steve Gore-Smith, David Stanley and Ken Cedeno for providing or taking photographs. Laura Holgate and Roohi Hassan were crucial when it came to raiding the ITN archive for me when they should have been producing programmes.

I owe a debt of gratitude to Jeremy Thompson whose jobs I seem to have filled all around the globe; where he went I followed... Asia, Africa, DC.

And thanks finally to my Editors at ITN over the years, the legendary Sir David Nicholas, Stewart Purvis, Nigel Dacre, David Mannion and Deborah Turness, for allowing me to cover the stories and events that helped shape this book. I am eternally grateful to all of them for their confidence in me, and for their guidance and support.

PICTURE CREDITS

Section one

Publicity photo, c.1988 (*ITN/REX/Shutterstock*); Covering the Open Golf for ITN, 1990 (*John Curtis/REX/Shutterstock*); Reporting the Mandela inauguration, May 1994 (*ITV News*); Rwanda, 1994 (*ITV News*); Post-interview team picture with President Nelson Mandela, 1994 (*ITV News*); Mark Austin and Nelson Mandela (*ITV News*); Mozambique floods, March 2000 (*ITV News*); Winning an Emmy (*Matt Campbell/AFP/Getty Images*); Freetown, Sierra Leone, May 2000 (*Trinity Mirror/Mirrorpix/Alamy Stock Photo*); Presenting the ITV *Evening News* from Kuwait, 17 March 2003 (*Courtesy of Steve Gore-Smith*); Writing scripts in the Iraqi desert, 25 March 2003 (*Courtesy of Steve Gore-Smith*); Studio in the desert, 26 March 2003 (*Courtesy of Steve Gore-Smith*); Convoy en route to Basra, 6 April 2003 (*Courtesy of Steve Gore-Smith*); Inside Iraq, 8 April 2003 (*Courtesy of Steve Gore-Smith*); Terry Lloyd (*ITN/Getty Images*); Team photo, Basra, Iraq, 10 April 2003 (*Courtesy of Steve Gore-Smith*)

Section two

Presenting the *Evening News* from Antarctica, January 2007 (*Courtesy of Steve Gore-Smith*); Crevasse training (*Courtesy of Steve Gore-Smith*); With cameraman Eugene Campbell (*Courtesy of Steve Gore-Smith*); With ITN Editor Deborah Turness, 2007 (*David Sandison/The Independent/REX/Shutterstock*); With Mary Nightingale in the *Evening News* studio, 2009 (*ITV News*); Hurricane Sandy in America, 2012 (*ITV News*); In the *News at Ten* studio with Julie Etchingham, 2016 (*ITV News*); In the crowds on The Mall for the Diamond Jubilee, 2012 (© *Ben Williams*); Meeting the Queen at a journalists' charity reception, 2014 (*Mark Large/Associated Newspapers/REX/ Shutterstock*); In Rwanda with Immaculate Mukanyaraya (*ITV News*); Reconciliation Village, Rwanda (*ITV News*); Cricket match (*WENN Ltd/Alamy Stock Photo*); Playing drums at the O2 in London (*Danny Martindale/ITN/Contributor/Getty Images*); Royal Television Society Presenter of the Year, 2015 (*ITV News*); 'Ant and Dec's Saturday Night Takeaway', 2015 (*REX/Shutterstock*); With Maddy (*Dave J. Hogan/ Getty Images*); Reporting live for Sky News from the roof of the Washington bureau, 2018 (*Courtesy of the author*)

INDEX

338